Researching Language Teacher Cognition and Practice

NEW PERSPECTIVES ON LANGUAGE AND EDUCATION

Series Editor: Professor Viv Edwards, *University of Reading, Reading, Great Britain*

Series Advisor: Professor Allan Luke, *Queensland University of Technology, Brisbane, Australia*

Two decades of research and development in language and literacy education have yielded a broad, multidisciplinary focus. Yet education systems face constant economic and technological change, with attendant issues of identity and power, community and culture. This series will feature critical and interpretive, disciplinary and multidisciplinary perspectives on teaching and learning, language and literacy in new times.

Full details of all the books in this series and of all our other publications can be found on http://www.multilingual-matters.com, or by writing to Multilingual Matters, St Nicholas House, 31–34 High Street, Bristol, BS1 2AW, UK.

Researching Language Teacher Cognition and Practice

International Case Studies

Edited by

Roger Barnard and Anne Burns

MULTILINGUAL MATTERS
Bristol • Buffalo • Toronto

Library of Congress Cataloging in Publication Data
A catalog record for this book is available from the Library of Congress.
Researching Language Teacher Cognition and Practice: International Case Studies/
Edited by Roger Barnard and Anne Burns.
New Perspectives on Language and Education: 27
Includes bibliographical references and index.
1. Language and languages – Study and teaching – Psychological aspects.
2. Language teachers – Training of--Cross-cultural studies. 3. Language and
education – Cross-cultural studies. 4. Interaction analysis in education – Cross-cultural
studies. 5. Cognition. 6. Psycholinguistics. I. Barnard, Roger- II. Burns, Anne
P53.7.R47 2012
418.0071–dc23 2012022105

10 0814761 1

British Library Cataloguing in Publication Data
A catalogue entry for this book is available from the British Library.

ISBN-13: 978-1-84769-790-5 (hbk)
ISBN-13: 978-1-84769-789-9 (pbk)

Multilingual Matters
UK: St Nicholas House, 31-34 High Street, Bristol BS1 2AW, UK.
USA: UTP, 2250 Military Road, Tonawanda, NY 14150, USA.
Canada: UTP, 5201 Dufferin Street, North York, Ontario M3H 5T8, Canada.

The policy of Multilingual Matters/Channel View Publications is to use papers that
are natural, renewable and recyclable products, made from wood grown in sustainable
forests. In the manufacturing process of our books, and to further support our policy,
preference is given to printers that have FSC and PEFC Chain of Custody certification.
The FSC and/or PEFC logos will appear on those books where full certification has been
granted to the printer concerned.

Typeset by R. J. Footring Ltd, Derby
Printed and bound in Great Britain by Short Run Press Ltd

Contents

Contributors

Roger Barnard is a senior lecturer in applied linguistics at the University of Waikato. Before taking up his present post in New Zealand in 1995, he worked in England, mainland Europe and the Middle East as a teacher, teacher educator, manager and advisor to ministries of education. He has recently accepted visiting professorships in Japan, Korea and Vietnam, where he has taught undergraduate and postgraduate courses and undertaken joint research projects.

Simon Borg is Professor of TESOL at the School of Education, University of Leeds. His key areas of research in the field of language education are teacher cognition, teacher education and teacher research and he has published widely in these areas. Full details of his work are available at http://www.education.leeds.ac.uk/modx/people/staff/academic/borg.

James Dean ('JD') Brown is Professor in the Department of Second Language Studies at the University of Hawaii at Manoa. He has spoken and taught courses in places ranging from Brazil to the former Yugoslavia, and has published numerous articles and books on language testing, curriculum design, programme evaluation, research methods and connected speech.

Anne Burns holds joint positions as Professor of Language Education, Aston University, Birmingham, and Professor of TESOL, University of New South Wales, Sydney. Her research interests include action research, teacher education, the teaching and learning of speaking and teacher cognition. Her most recent book is *Teaching Speaking: A Holistic Approach* (co-authored with Christine Goh, 2012, Cambridge University Press). She is a Member-at-Large of the International Association of Applied Linguistics (AILA) and from 2011 she was appointed Academic Advisor to the Oxford University Press Applied Linguistics Series.

Jill Burton is Adjunct Associate Research Professor at the University of South Australia, Adelaide, covering applied linguistics and TESOL education. She has supervised doctoral students for some years and edited journals and many books. Her current research interests are academic writing practices and qualitative research methodologies.

Martin Bygate is Professor of Applied Linguistics and Language Education at the University of Lancaster. His main interests are task-based language learning, the teaching and learning of L2 speaking and pedagogical grammar, especially the connections between tasks, language, the teacher and learning. His most recent publication is *Tasks in Second Language Learning* (co-authored with Virginia Samuda, 2008, Palgrave). He co-edited the journal *Applied Linguistics* from 1998 to 2004 and was President of the International Association of Applied Linguistics (AILA) from 2008 to 2011.

Thomas S.C. Farrell is Professor of Applied Linguistics at Brock University, Canada. His professional interests include reflective practice and language teacher education and development. His recent books include *Essentials in Language Teaching* (co-authored with George Jacobs, 2010, Continuum Press) and *Teaching Practice: A Reflective Approach* (co-authored with Jack Richards, 2011, Cambridge University Press).

Jenny Field has taught ESOL in New Zealand for 13 years and presently manages a community-based organisation – English Language Partners Waikato – which works with migrants and refugees. She is interested in language acquisition for those from oral traditions as well as language teacher cognition and has a particular interest in Timor-Leste. She recently completed her MPhil at the University of Waikato.

Donald Freeman is a Professor at the School of Education, University of Michigan. He was a former graduate faculty member at the School of International Training, where he chaired the Department of Language Teacher Education and founded and directed the Center for Teacher Education, Training, and Research, a unit that designed and implemented teacher education projects around the world. His research focuses on the role of programme design and implementation in teacher professional learning.

Susan Gass is University Distinguished Professor at Michigan State University, where she is Director of the English Language Center and the Second Language Studies PhD programme. She has served as President of the International Association of Applied Linguistics (AILA). She has published widely in the field of second-language acquisition.

Jerry Gebhard is Professor of English Language Teaching at Pusan National University and Professor Emeritus at Indiana University of Pennsylvania. He has leadership roles in a wide range of graduate programmes there, and in his previous professorial posts, and has advised many doctorate candidates from many parts of the world. He publishes frequently on issues relating to teaching English as a foreign or second language, most recently the book *What Do International Students Think and Feel? Adjustment to Life and Culture at US Colleges* (2010, University of Michigan Press).

Andrew Gladman has a PhD in applied linguistics from Macquarie University, Sydney, and has been teaching ESOL for 17 years. He coordinated the development of the Direct Entry English Programme for postgraduate and undergraduate students at Massey University, in Auckland, in 2009–10. He spent 10 years teaching in Japan as an English language and linguistics lecturer at Miyazaki International College and at a number of junior colleges and high schools in Miyazaki and Okayama prefectures. He has also taught English to adults in Bristol, England, and Mississippi in the United States. His research interests include collaborative teaching, computer-mediated communication and textbook discourse.

Simon Humphries has been teaching English in Japan for over 10 years. He has a PhD in linguistics from Macquarie University. His research interests include action research, curricular innovation, textbook analysis and professional development in English language teaching. He is currently an assistant professor at Doshisha University in Kyoto.

Le Van Canh (MA TESOL, Saint Michael's College, USA; PhD Applied Linguistics, University of Waikato) is a Senior Lecturer at the University of Languages and International Studies, Vietnam, where he teaches research methodology in applied linguistics and TESOL methodology courses to graduate students. He is a regular presenter at international conferences and has published in various international journals. His research interests include teacher cognition, teacher professional development and English as an international language.

Jinrui Li completed her PhD at the University of Waikato. Her PhD project explored contextual and emotional issues in tutor cognition of assessing writing by applying a synthesised sociocultural approach and multiple methods of data collection. Before conducting this project in 2008, she was a lecturer, teaching college English and translation in Hebei Polytechnic University in China. Her research interests include assessing academic writing, qualitative research methods, language education and educational psychology.

Alan Maley has been involved in English language teaching for 50 years. He has lived and worked in Yugoslavia, Ghana, Italy, France, China, India, Thailand, Malaysia, Singapore and the UK. He has published over 40 books and numerous articles in the field. He is currently Visiting Professor at Leeds Metropolitan University, as well as spending much of his time in writing and lecturing worldwide.

Judy Ng was a lecturer in a private university in Malaysia. She obtained her BA and MA from Universiti Kebangsaan Malaysia and is currently completing her PhD at the University of Waikato. Her research interests are teacher cognition, feedback in second-language writing, socio-linguistics and teaching English as a second or foreign language.

Nguyen Gia Viet has been a language teacher and teacher trainer for more than 10 years in Vietnam. He earned an MA degree in TESOL studies at the University of Queensland, Australia, in 2005. Viet is currently completing his PhD thesis at the University of Waikato. His research interests include task-based language teaching, second-language acquisition and teacher cognition.

Jonathon Ryan has been a language teacher nearly all his adult life and currently teaches English at Wintec in Hamilton, New Zealand. He has previously taught at schools in Ireland and Mexico, and managed a private language school in New Zealand. His PhD from the University of Waikato was entitled 'Acts of reference and the miscommunication of referents by first- and second-language speakers of English'.

Introduction

Roger Barnard and Anne Burns

This book emerged from our combined interest in, and experiences of, conducting or supervising research on language teacher cognition. We planned the contributions in such a way that we hope will be helpful to emergent researchers, particularly Masters and PhD students – and, perhaps, their supervisors – in understanding some of the practical implications of collecting qualitative data, with a focus on this particular field of research.

The book aims to fill the gap between conventional research methodology books and published reports of research such as are found in academic journals. While volumes on methodology may explain how and why a particular approach to data collection should be used, they tend not to give specific and detailed examples of the 'messiness' of research – what may go wrong and how to overcome the obstacles that invariably get in the way of a smooth research journey. The constraints of writing up a report of a research project for a journal in, usually, 5000 or 6000 words mean that all too often accounts of how data are collected are cursory and 'rough patches' may be smoothed over. It is an all too common experience of qualitative researchers that their best-laid plans and schedules, as Robert Burns said, 'gang aft aglay' and they have to improvise on the spot in order to make the best of what may sometimes be a bad lot. But sometimes, too, these ad hoc decisions lead to surprisingly interesting outcomes and may even turn the project into a much better one than was originally conceived.

It is worth starting this introduction by explaining why this collection of case studies focuses on language teacher cognition, a field of research that has expanded rapidly over the last two decades. As Simon Borg makes clear in the following chapter, it is evident that what teachers do in the conduct of their professional activities is shaped, though not entirely determined, by what they believe and know. Interestingly, while this phenomenon has been well understood in mainstream educational circles since at least the 1970s, it is only relatively recently that the language teaching profession has started to investigate the implications. This recognition is largely due to Borg's seminal work in his many publications, and especially in the overview of empirical studies and the methodological framework he developed for further research (Borg, 2006). Without such an impetus, none of the studies reported in this volume – and indeed the book itself – might have been possible.

All the contributors to this book believe, and we anticipate our readers will agree, that teaching is more than merely transmitting information. Indeed, the management, motivation and sustainability of learning can be understood only by exploring what teachers believe and do in their specific working contexts. After all, teachers are the executive decision-makers of the curriculum: it is they who put into practice the principles and procedures devised or mandated by others, such as course-book writers, methodological experts and officials of ministries of education. Failure by such people to take into account what teachers believe and know about language teaching will lead to failure to realise the intended curriculum.

However, the exploration of language teacher cognition is an extremely complicated matter. In the first place, the goals of language teaching have expanded over the past few decades – for example, from understanding linguistic structures at sentence level to communicative competence at discourse level to intercultural communicative pragmatic competence, in a world where acronyms reflect the changing awareness of the English language itself, ESL and EFL transmogrify into EIL and ELF. So, it is essential, but far from easy, to find out what teachers know and believe about fundamental issues such as: the place of grammar in the language learning curriculum and, indeed, what is understood by the word 'grammar'; the most appropriate ways to teach the language skills and sub-skills; the respective roles of teachers and learners in innovatory approaches to language teaching, such as task-based language learning; the appropriate classroom use of the learners' first language; how language learning could and should be assessed or evaluated – and many other matters.

What teachers believe and what they know about any of these issues is a complex nexus of interacting factors. One of the most important initial influences on teachers' cognition is their experience (good or bad) of their own language learning at school, college or university. To a greater or lesser extent, professional training or development programmes, whether pre-service or in-service, also affect teachers' knowledge and beliefs. Many teachers also increase their awareness of their role by reading books and articles by influential authorities, and perhaps by attending conferences and seminars. Teachers also learn from their own past and present professional experiences as teachers, and by interacting with their learners, their colleagues and other teachers in a wider community of practice. The influence of 'significant others' in their personal lives – spouses, partners, family, friends – cannot be discounted. Finally, the imposition of authority – whether by school principals, inspectors, examination boards or ministries of education – also shapes teachers' knowledge and beliefs.

Although teachers may have strongly held beliefs, they do not always put these into practice. The reasons need to be understood by exploring the specific contexts in which they work, each of which is itself a complex and dynamic system (Larsen-Freeman & Cameron, 2008) in which physical, temporal, cognitive, social and cultural factors interact to provide affordances for, or constraints on, the practical application of beliefs about teaching and learning, which in turn influence what teachers believe and know. Teaching and learning occur within certain physical and temporal boundaries, which will tend to affect the teacher's ability or willingness to act in accordance with his or her beliefs; for example, fixed seating arrangements may hinder effective group work, or the wish to introduce a new topic may be inappropriate at a specific time. Understanding teachers' practices should be tempered by awareness of the nature of the cognitive and affective styles and strategies among their learners; a belief in co-operative learning may be thwarted by a realisation that – at this stage at least – the specific group of learners are unaccustomed to such practices and would resist its adoption. Indeed, because teaching and learning are quintessentially social activities, unpeeling the complexities of the interaction of cognition and classroom action requires deep engagement with the conditions operating in the environment.

Borg (2006, and in his methodological analysis in the subsequent chapter of this volume) points out that among researchers there is a wealth of, and perhaps some confusion about, terminology, and it may be worth indicating how some key terms are understood by the authors of the eight case studies in this book. *Assumptions* may be regarded as axioms which enable us to make pre-judgements about the world around us; for example, a teacher facing a new class of learners will assume that, in a number of respects, they will be similar to classes she or he has previously taught. After working for some time with these new learners, the teacher will *perceive* that there are similarities with, and differences between, this class and previous ones, and new, somewhat tentative *attitudes* will emerge. With further experience, these attitudes will tend to be refined, rejected or reformulated and then incorporated into a set of firmer and more stable *beliefs*. What distinguishes a belief about something from a *knowledge* of something is that respected members of one's community accept it as a fact. Thus, in pre-Copernican times, ordinarily people did not believe that the sun revolved around the earth: they *knew* it. It is in this comprehensive sense that the authors regard cognition as being contextually situated and socially distributed.

The above discussion clearly points to the need for research into teacher cognition to be exploratory, in the sense made clear by Allwright (2006), who argues, among other things, that researchers should seek to describe and understand the complexity of classroom teaching, and to recognise that idiosyncrasy within a particular setting is a more important phenomenon than what is common across classrooms. Thus, classroom research should not be reductionist in the sense of looking for simplistic, generalisable findings that can apply beyond the specific context; rather, accounts of classroom research should be sufficiently transparent and honest to enable the reader to judge the trustworthiness of the reports and, where appropriate, relate the findings to his or her own context. Such research also needs be longitudinal, in order to account for the inevitably changing relationships over time between key issues, and participatory, so that meanings behind behaviour can be explained by the key actors. Finally, explorations of teachers' beliefs and classroom practices should adopt a judicious blend of methods of data collection in order that the information that emerges can be compared, contrasted and triangulated to provide thick descriptions of the context, which in turn can lead to rich interpretations (Geertz, 1973) of the extent of convergence and divergence between what teachers believe and what they actually do.

The authors of the case studies in Chapters 1–8 are themselves emergent researchers, in most cases having recently completed doctoral projects in various countries. All of them have employed multi-methods of data collection in their studies, but each has selected only one of these methods to report in this book. They recount 'tales from the field' (Van Maanen, 1988) by introducing the aims and context of their study, briefly reviewing relevant published studies on the topic and explaining the methodological issue they have decided to focus on. The next part of their account is more detailed information about their study and examples of the data they have collected. These descriptions are followed by a discussion of the methodological implications arising from their particular project, and their story is completed with a reflection on the lessons they have learned from the experience. The second author of each chapter is an internationally recognised researcher and scholar, with a particular interest in the methodological approach discussed in the case study. Each provides an insightful commentary on the tale from the field from the perspective of a well informed outsider.

The third part of each chapter throws the issues back to you, the reader, by providing discussion points and questions for you to consider, and if possible discuss with others, and activities to try out if you yourself are planning to collect qualitative data using the approach described in the chapter. An ideal way to use these questions would be to join with other researchers, possibly colleagues conducting research for graduate dissertations and theses, and use them as starting points for exploring one of these methodological approaches. Equally, the ideas for small-scale action could be tried out among a supportive group of research colleagues, to gain insights into the pros and cons of using different methods.

The focus of all these chapters is on exploring the beliefs and practices of (language) teachers about various issues related to their profession. But the lessons the authors have learned are relevant to other qualitative research topics, whether of teaching and learning situations or of wider social issues.

In Chapter 1, Judy Ng discusses her use of questionnaires with lecturers in a private university in Malaysia. The survey was intended to be a scoping study for her main project by obtaining key biodata from her respondents, eliciting their attitudes and reported practices of giving feedback on their students' written assignments and – importantly – recruiting volunteers to participate in the subsequent phases of the project. As Judy reports, she encountered a number of unanticipated difficulties, which led her to make several ad hoc decisions in the field. Ultimately her project veered away from its original purpose, but this shift actually led to a more valuable study than was originally conceived. Her story is commented on by J.D. Brown, who has long enjoyed an international reputation for his interest and expertise in quantitative research designs, but who has also recently published an extremely useful chapter (Brown, 2009) that discusses how to devise qualitative questionnaires. In his commentary on Judy's case, he suggests that the data-gathering phase of any study, but especially in interview/questionnaire research, is likely to be the most difficult. This is because the researcher may have to rely on the goodwill of people who have generally critical attitudes towards questionnaires as a result of past experience. It is necessary to overcome these difficulties in order to get a good response rate and credible data. But this does not mean that research should be rigid and inflexible; rather, like Judy, he has found that anomalies in his own research often lead in interesting and useful directions.

The second chapter focuses on the adoption by Nguyen Gia Viet of narrative frames (Barkhuizen & Wette, 2008) with Vietnamese teachers attempting to apply task-based language teaching (TBLT) in their high-school classes. Viet reports that this form of guided composition scaffolded the participants to reflect on their classroom experiences and to give expression to their beliefs in their first language. The frames also enabled him to gather data which could reasonably easily be compared and analysed. In his discussion of the methodological implications, Viet reports his experience of administering the frames, focusing especially on the novelty of this technique for both himself and his participants, and on linguistic, ethical and validity issues. His commentator, Martin Bygate, is at the forefront of TBLT methodology (e.g. Bygate, 1999; Van den Branden et al., 2009). Viet's study prompts Martin to pose and discuss three issues: the contextual background in which a particular data-collection procedure is used; the question or puzzle that the procedure is intended to illuminate; and, most importantly, the quality of the data which it generates. After fully addressing these points with regard to Viet's case study, he points out that narrative frames, like other self-report instruments, are likely to produce ambiguous data which need to be further investigated by the researcher.

Andrew Gladman's case study in Chapter 3 discusses his use of focus groups (Morgan, 1996; Morgan & Krueger, 1993) in a liberal arts college in Japan. This institution employs an unusual team-teaching practice in which a specialist in teaching English to speakers of other languages (TESOL) and a specialist in the academic subject of the class integrate their specialties to team-teach English language and the academic subject in parallel. His intention was to elicit the participants' key concerns about team-teaching and the development of effective partnerships. Andrew discusses the methodological implications of his study in terms of the small number of participants in each focus group, the fact that they were well known to each other and his researcher role as an institutional insider. The commentator on Andrew's case study is Donald Freeman, whose contributions to the field of research on teacher professional knowledge (e.g. Freeman, 1996, 2002) have been not only extensive but also highly influential. In his commentary, he points out that there are two views on the use of language in a focus group: one is that people use the session as an opportunity to talk about what is on their minds; and the other is that the language used in such a social situation actually creates thinking. After pointing out that Andrew's work illustrates the first of these positions, Donald suggests that the strength of the focus group as a research tool lies in *how* it recognises, acknowledges and capitalises on the specific social conventions of who says what to whom, when and how.

In the fourth chapter, Le Van Canh reports on the sociocultural and institutional factors that affected his use of semi-structured interviews with a group of Vietnamese high-school teachers. Despite being a very well established data-collection method, interviewing is far from being an easy or routine option, as it requires both linguistic and interpersonal skills, as well as context sensitivity (Roulston, 2010). Canh relates the difficulties he overcame to gather the teachers' knowledge and beliefs about grammar teaching, which he then compared with what they did in their classrooms.

Interestingly, he found a strong convergence between beliefs and practice and he explains why this should be so. Alan Maley's commentary is built on his long experience of working with many teachers in Africa, Europe, China, India and, more recently, Vietnam, as well as being a series editor for resource books for language teachers. His comments cover logistical, contextual and methodological issues, as well as the actual findings of Canh's study. With regard to the first three areas, he acknowledges both the problems that Canh encountered and his success in overcoming them. With regard to the final point, he suggests that while the findings of this case study are in themselves unremarkable – and indeed his own recent experience corroborates them – the strength of the empirical study lies in the meticulous ways that Canh collected his data, which thus established his status as a competent researcher.

In Chapter 5, Simon Humphries reports his experience of observing four Japanese teachers of English to explore and compare their use of traditional textbooks and more recent, communicative-based textbooks. As elsewhere (e.g. Richards, 1997), these teachers were nervous, even suspicious, of being observed and/or video-recorded. Despite their reservations, Simon obtained useful data to complement the information he obtained by interviewing his participants. Among the methodological implications he draws out are the effect of the 'observer's paradox' (Labov, 1972), especially when the researcher is an institutional insider. He also ponders the questions of what to do with unusable data, whether or not the observer should, even when invited, intervene in the lesson, and the difficulty of concentrating when observing lessons. Simon's commentator, Jerry Gebhard, has spent many years observing teachers in a wide range of countries, including Japan, and has long been interested in exploring teachers' beliefs (e.g. Gebhard & Oprandy, 1999). In his commentary on this case study, he points out that the issues Simon has faced are common in observational studies and he makes a number of practical suggestions about each of them, based on his own and other published studies. He concludes with the point that classroom observation is not just a way to collect data, but the unexpected issues that arise make such research 'an adventure in exploration and new discoveries that keeps the researcher (or teacher) fascinated, animated and renewed'.

In the sixth chapter, Jinrui Li reports the 'think aloud' (TA) procedures she used with her participants – university tutors in New Zealand – to explore their cognitive processing during their actual marking of written assignments submitted by their undergraduate students. Most previous studies applying TA have been undertaken in controlled (quasi-) experimental conditions, but Jinrui explains why she felt that it is more valid to capture 'cognition in flight' (Vygotsky, 1978) in natural settings with participants actually carrying out a real-world task, rather than a task specifically designed for research purposes. In her discussion of some of the methodological implications, she considers whether the researcher should be present or absent during TA sessions and the effect that such presence might have on the participants. She also addresses the extent to which TA can represent actual cognitive processing and the multiple roles which have to be played by the researcher. The commentary by Thomas Farrell, an extensively published researcher of classroom processes and teacher reflection (e.g. Farrell, 1999, 2007), begins by pointing out that knowing more about how markers assess undergraduates' written work is of great importance to those who teach in university settings and he commends the use of TA procedures to research this issue. He discusses three particular matters with regard to Jinrui's study: the researcher's presence or absence during a TA session (a matter about which he tends to disagree with Jinrui); the probable necessity of giving participants practice in TA procedures; and how best to analyse TA data.

Next, in Chapter 7, Jonathon Ryan discusses his use of stimulated recall (SR) following interactions between pairs of English-speaking teachers and non-native English-speaking undergraduate students (SL2) in a New Zealand university. The particular focus for his investigation was to understand how miscommunication might occur when a listener does not understand a speaker's reference to a person, place or object. His participants, paired as 'speakers' (some of whom were students) and 'hearers' (some of whom were teachers of English as a second language), watched extracts from a Charlie Chaplin film, *Modern Times*, and the hearer was briefly called away while the speaker continued watching. When the hearer returned, the speaker related what had happened in the film while the hearer was away. This interaction was video-recorded, after which Jonathon held an SR session with the hearer to identify what may or may not have caused strained communication or miscommunication. Susan Gass is an authority on the use of SR techniques (e.g. Gass & Mackey, 2000; Polio *et al.*, 2006) and thus her commentary provides a valuable perspective on both SR as a research tool in general and on Jonathon's study in particular. She regards his study as innovatory, in terms of its both topic – miscommunication – and the story-telling method which he adopted. She notes that Jonathon encountered many of the same practical difficulties that others have found in applying SR techniques. She also points out that in his report he acknowledges these problems frankly and took sensitive steps in his research to overcome them.

The final case study (Chapter 8) is of the use of oral reflective journals with a group of Timorese English-language lecturers at the National University of Timor-Leste. Jenny Field is a member of a wider curriculum renewal project involving, among other things, the introduction and normalisation (Bax, 2003) of computer-mediated language learning. She explains why she decided to ask the teachers to reflect on their initial perceptions of the software by completing a series of discussions with a colleague and thus jointly to produce an oral journal. She presents and briefly discusses examples of the transcribed speech, some of which was spoken in the national language, Tetum. Jill Burton has published frequently in the area of teacher reflection and journal writing (e.g. Burton, 2005; Burton & Carroll, 2001) and in her commentary on this case study she commends Jenny for having thought carefully about the merits of different methods of data collection and their effect on her participants. In doing so, however, she wonders whether Jenny had considered, as fully as she might have, her own requirements to obtain sufficient data to meet the aims of the project. This challenge is often the case where the researcher has to change roles, as Jenny did, from colleague to investigator – a common problem for new researchers.

We hope our readers will enjoy the discussions that follow, and find points of interest and practical value in the various suggestions made by the case study authors and their commentators. As we have said, we also hope that readers will continue the conversations by reflecting and acting on the questions and issues raised at the end of every chapter, preferably with others in their community of research practice.

References

Allwright, D. (2006) Six promising directions in applied linguistics. In S. Gieve and I. Miller (eds), *Understanding the Language Classroom* (pp. 1–10). Basingstoke: Palgrave Macmillan.

Barkhuizen, G. and Wette, R. (2008) Narrative frames for investigating the experiences of language teachers. *System*, 36(3), 372–387.

Bax, S. (2003) CALL – past, present and future. *System*, 31(1), 13–28.

Borg, S. (2006) *Teacher Cognition and Language Education: Research and Practice*. London: Continuum.

Brown, J.D. (2009) Open-response items in questionnaires. In J. Heigham and R.A. Croker (eds), *Qualitative Research in Applied Linguistics: A Practical Introduction* (pp. 202–219). Basingstoke: Palgrave Macmillan.

Burton, J. (2005) The importance of teachers writing on TESOL. *TESL-EJ (Electronic Journal for English as a Second Language)*, 9(2). Available at http://www.tesl-ej.org/ej34/a2.html.

Burton, J. and Carroll, M. (2001) *Journal Writing*. Alexandria, VA: TESOL Inc.

Bygate, M. (1999) Task as context for the framing, reframing and unframing of language. *System*, 27(1), 33–48.

Farrell, T.S.C. (1999) Reflective practice in an EFL teacher development group. *System*, 27(2), 157–172

Farrell, T.S.C. (2007) *Reflective Language Teaching: From Research to Practice*. London: Continuum.

Freeman, D. (1996) 'To take them at their word': Language data in the study of teachers' knowledge. *Harvard Educational Review*, 66(4), 732–761.

Freeman, D. (2002) The hidden side of the work: Teacher knowledge and learning to teach. A perspective from North American educational research on teacher education in English language teaching. *Language Teaching*, 35, 1–13.

Gass, S.M. and Mackey, A. (2000) *Stimulated Recall Methodology in Second Language Research*. Mahwah, NJ: Lawrence Erlbaum Associates.

Gebhard, J. and Oprandy, T. (1999) *Teaching Awareness: A Guide to Exploring Beliefs and Practices*. Cambridge: Cambridge University Press.

Geertz, C. (1973) Thick description: toward an interpretive theory of culture. In C. Geertz (ed.), *The Interpretation of Culture* (pp. 3–30). New York: Basic Books.

Labov, W. (1972) *Sociolinguistic Patterns*. Oxford: Blackwell.

Larsen-Freeman, D. and Cameron, L. (2008) *Complex Systems and Applied Linguistics*. Oxford: Oxford University Press.

Morgan, D.L. (1996) Focus groups. *Annual Review of Sociology*, 22, 129–152.

Morgan, D.L. and Krueger, R.A. (1993) When to use focus groups and why. In D.L. Morgan (ed.), *Successful Focus Groups: Advancing the State of the Art* (pp. 3–19). Newbury Park, CA: Sage.

Polio, C., Gass, S. and Chapin, L. (2006) Using stimulated recall to investigate native speaker perceptions in native–nonnative speaker interactions. *Studies in Second Language Acquisition*, 28(2), 237–267.

Richards, K. (1997) Teachers for specific purposes. In R. Howard and G. Brown (eds), *Teacher Education for LSP* (pp. 115–126). Clevedon: Multilingual Matters.

Roulston, K. (2010) *Reflective Interviewing: A Guide to Theory and Practice*. Thousand Oaks, CA: Sage.

Van den Branden, K., Bygate, M. and Norris, J.M. (eds) (2009) *Task-Based Language Teaching: A Reader*. Amsterdam: John Benjamins.

Van Maanen, J. (1988) *Tales from the Field: On Writing Ethnography*. Chicago, IL: University of Chicago Press.

Vygotsky, L.S. (1978) *Mind in Society*, translated by M. Cole. Cambridge, MA: Harvard University Press.

Current Approaches to Language Teacher Cognition Research: A Methodological Analysis

Simon Borg

Introduction

In *Teacher Cognition and Language Education* (Borg, 2006) I noted the rapid growth that had occurred since the mid-1990s in the study of language teacher cognition and that trend has continued in recent years. The purpose of this chapter is to provide an analysis of recent contributions to this body of work, with particular attention to their research methodology and the manner in which this has been reported. Through my analysis I will seek to uncover both contemporary trends in the study of language teacher cognition as well as to highlight, more critically, methodological issues which merit discussion.

Scope

My focus is on contemporary publications (mainly journal articles but also some book chapters) which report research on language teacher cognition. I define 'contemporary' as works published in 2011, and language teacher cognition includes what second- or foreign-language teachers think, know and believe (these are the three constructs most often cited in teacher cognition research and which also form the core of my definition of the term in Borg, 2006); however, in this chapter I also include as part of teacher cognition constructs such as attitudes, identities and emotions, in recognition of the fact that these are all aspects of the unobservable dimension of teaching. Identity, in particular, while not a salient theme in my 2006 analysis, has since emerged as a contemporary area of interest in language teacher education (e.g. Miller, 2009; Morton & Gray, 2010; Tsui, 2007) and should be recognised as an important strand of teacher cognition research. Emotion, on the other hand, has typically been viewed in opposition to cognition; however, it has never been my intention to exclude emotion from the study of language teacher cognition, given that our learning and actions as professionals are shaped by our emotional responses to our experiences. Beliefs, in particular, have an affective quality to them (Nespor, 1987), which by definition implies a role for emotion. Contemporary thinking in neuroscience does in fact argue against traditional divisions between the rational and emotional dimensions of decision-making. For example, Lehrer (2009: 26) argues that 'the process of thinking requires feeling, for feelings are what let us understand all the information that we can't directly comprehend. Reason without emotion is impotent.' The study of teacher cognition, given its concern for understanding the unobservable dimension of teachers' lives, in no way excludes attention to emotions.

Methodology

In identifying sources for this analysis I drew on my existing bibliography of language teacher cognition research (http://www.education.leeds.ac.uk/people/staff/academic/borg) and supplemented this with items identified electronically using Zetoc (http://zetoc.mimas.ac.uk), as well the search facilities provided on the websites of major publishers of language-teaching journals such as Elsevier and Sage. My searches used a range of keywords (e.g. beliefs, knowledge, thinking, decision-making, attitudes) and were limited to publications in English which were published in 2011.

A total of 25 sources were identified. After reading each source to confirm it was an empirical report (rather than, for example, a literature review) I analysed it with reference to the following issues:

- the focus of the study;
- context and participants;
- the research stance;
- data collection;
- data analysis.

I will now examine, against the above themes, these 25 examples of language teacher cognition research.

Focus of Studies

As Table 1 shows, the studies addressed a wide range of topics, with replication in this respect being unusual. Three studies examined teacher identity, three addressed teacher cognition in relation to learner autonomy (in one case, with specific reference to self-assessment), two focused on teacher roles

Table 1 Focus of studies

Source	Focus
Ahn (2011)	Implementation of CLT during the practicum
Borg (2011)	Impact of INSET on teachers' beliefs
Borg and Al-Busaidi (2011)	Teachers' beliefs about learner autonomy
Bullock (2011)	Teachers' beliefs about self-assessment
Cowie (2011)	Emotions of experienced EFL teachers
Farrell (2011)	Professional role identities
Gao *et al.* (2011)	Conceptions of research of primary-school English teachers in China
Griva and Chostelidou (2011)	EFL teachers' beliefs regarding multilingualism
Kanno and Stuart (2011)	L2 novice teachers' identity development
Khodabakhshzadeh and Shirvan (2011)	Teachers' personality traits and conceptions of effective teaching
Kim (2011)	Teachers' understandings of curriculum reform
Kuzborska (2011)	Links between teachers' beliefs and practices and research on reading
Li and Ni (2011)	Attitudes towards technology of primary English teachers
Li and Walsh (2011)	Teachers' stated beliefs and their interactions with students
Liu and Xu (2011)	Language teacher identity
Mak (2011)	Tensions between conflicting beliefs of an EFL teacher in teaching practice
Ong'Ondo and Borg (2011)	The influence of supervision on the practice of English-language student teachers
Pan and Block (2011)	Teachers' beliefs about English as a global language
Trent (2011)	Teacher identity construction a short-term international experience programme
Wan *et al.* (2011)	Students' and teachers' beliefs about EFL teachers' roles
Werbinska (2011)	The transition from student teacher to teacher
Woods and Cakir (2011)	Teachers' understandings of CLT
Wyatt and Borg (2011)	Development in teachers' practical knowledge
Yoshiyuki (2011)	Teachers' attitudes to learner autonomy
Young and Sachdev (2011)	Teachers' beliefs and practices regarding intercultural communicative competence

(though Farrell's study of professional role identities could also be classified as an 'identity' study), while two further studies examined teachers' understandings and implementations of curricular reform. The remaining 15 studies all addressed teacher cognition in relation to specific individual themes or from particular perspectives. One overall point to note is that, unsurprisingly given its broad remit, current language teacher cognition research is substantively diverse. The prominence of 'identity' studies is also worth noting.

Contexts and Participants

Table 2 summarises the contexts and participants involved in the 25 studies. In terms of geographical context, mainland China leads, with six studies, with a further two studies conducted in Hong Kong, followed, also with two studies apiece, by Japan, Korea and Oman. Overall, 16 countries are represented, covering Europe, North America, the Middle East, Asia and Africa. Only one study utilised data from more than one geographical context. In the majority of cases (18), the studies involved teachers for whom English was not their first language and who worked in state institutions (22). This profile contrasts with that emerging in Borg (2003), where a limited range of geographical contexts was represented and where studies tended to involve native-speaker teachers of English working in private institutions (by 2006, I had noted progress in both these issues). Additionally, the majority of the studies involved practising teachers. This, too, is a change in emphasis from my earlier analysis, where I was somewhat critical of the widespread use of captive audiences of pre-service teachers in language teacher cognition research.

In terms of the sample size, the studies range from 105 teachers down to one, with a mean sample of just over 25. Sixteen of the studies involved 10 or fewer teachers and there is a clear trend for smaller-scale studies. Methodologically, it is also interesting to consider the manner in which the choice of participants in these studies is explained. Firstly, in none of the studies is statistical logic cited as the basis for overall sampling decisions. Borg and Al-Busaidi (2011) did use stratified random sampling in selecting their sub-sample of interviewees from a larger group of questionnaire respondents, while Bullock (2011) explains her choice of a sub-sample of three interviewees by saying that 'three typical cases were selected to explore these responses further since even in a small-scale study, it is advisable to include a representative sample' (Bullock, 2011: 118). (We are not told, though, in what ways the interviewees chosen were typical.) Overall, then, non-probability samples dominate. Secondly, while descriptive information

Table 2 Contexts and participants

Source	Context	Participants	Career stage*
Ahn	Korea	1 student teacher during the practicum	P
Borg	UK	6 female in-service EFL teachers on a training course	I
Borg and Al-Busaidi	Oman	61 teachers (questionnaire) and 20 interviewees at a university language centre	I
Bullock	Ukraine	10 teachers of English to teenagers	I
Cowie	Japan	9 experienced EFL university teachers	I
Farrell	Canada	3 experienced native English-speaking ESL college teachers	I
Gao *et al.*	China	33 primary-school English teachers (questionnaire) on training course; 10 in focus groups	I
Griva and Chostelidou	Greece	86 state school EFL teachers	I
Kanno and Stuart	USA	2 MATESOL students	P
Khodabakhshzadeh and Shirvan	Iran	8 EFL teachers	I
Kim	Korea	1 practising middle-school teacher	I
Kuzborska	Lithuania	8 EAP teachers working at a university (no TESOL qualifications)	I
Li and Ni	China	72 primary EFL teachers	I
Li and Walsh	China	Two secondary state school teachers of English	I
Liu and Xu	China	One university teacher of English	I
Mak	Hong Kong	One student teacher on a PGDE programme	P
Ong'Ondo and Borg	Kenya	Six student teachers on a BA	P
Pan and Block	China	41 university English teachers and 637 students**	I
Trent	Hong Kong	8 teachers during overseas phase of PGDE	I/P
Wan *et al.*	China	33 EFL English teachers; 70 students	I
Werbinska	Poland	64 novice teachers of English	I
Woods and Cakir	Turkey	6 novice language teachers	I
Wyatt and Borg	Oman	3 teachers of English on an in-service programme	I
Yoshiyuki	Japan	74 high-school teachers of English; 4 additional teachers for focus group	I
Young and Sachdev	UK, USA, France	21 teachers of English	I

*For career stage, P=pre-service and I=in-service
**This study states that 'The questionnaires were distributed to 53 university teachers.... The return rate for teacher questionnaires was 77%' (p. 4), but the actual number of respondents was not stated and I have calculated this to be 41 (actually a 77.4% response rate)

about the sample is typically plentiful in these studies, the reasons for involving particular individuals are in most cases not articulated. In fact, 10 of the studies provide no explicit comment on the logic underpinning their choice of sample. For example, Griva and Chostelidou explain that:

> The participants involved in the study were 86 EFL teachers employed in state primary (52.3%) and secondary schools (47.7%) in Northern Greece; of them 75.6% are female and 24.4% male. Their teaching experience varied: the least experienced teachers have been working from one to five years (31.4%), a significant percentage (39.5%) had an experience ranging from six to fifteen years, while the most experienced teachers had been teaching foreign languages (FLs) for more than fifteen years (29.1%). It should be noted that a considerable percentage of the participants (38.4%) are highly qualified and hold a Master's degree. (Griva & Chostelidou, 2011: 1781)

Why these individuals were selected for this particular study is not stated. Even where non-probability samples are selected for a study, there needs to be some logic for the inclusion of particular teachers – even if it is simply convenience (i.e. teachers were available and willing to participate). Although the term 'convenience' does have connotations which are antithetical to the notion of rigorous enquiry, the reality of much research involving language teachers is that it does rely on convenience samples. Only one of the studies I am discussing here acknowledged an element of convenience in its sampling:

> The participants comprised a convenience sample since they had been asked to voluntarily fill out the questionnaire by their co-workers or colleagues who kindly cooperated in the research. In this, a 'snowball' sampling strategy (whereby several key informants were identified and then were asked to further introduce other potential participants, such as their colleagues or the members of their study groups) was implemented to reach as many teachers of English as possible, and most of the actual questionnaires were administered by mail or email or handed directly to the participants. (Yoshiyuki, 2011: 903)

There is also reference in this extract to snowball sampling, but given that this typically applies to situations where the researcher wants to recruit members of difficult-to-find groups (Gomm, 2009) and must rely on each successful contact to identify a subsequent participant, I am not convinced that it is appropriately used here to describe the recruitment of English-language teachers in completing a survey.

In five further cases, the authors utilised purposeful sampling (i.e. where participants are chosen because they meet predetermined criteria). Cowie, for example, explains that 'A purposeful sampling strategy ... was used to select nine experienced EFL teachers working in Japanese universities' (Cowie, 2011: 236) and states that his primary selection criteria were that teachers were experienced and committed to EFL as a career. Young and Sachdev also note that 'in seeking volunteers for the study as a whole, our approach to sampling was "purposeful" ... in that we sought the input of participants who have direct professional experience' (Young & Sachdev, 2011: 85). This example raises interesting questions about how specific the criteria for selecting a sample purposively should be – in this case what the authors seem to be saying is that they needed practising teachers, as opposed to those with no experience, but this is a very broad criterion, so broad, in fact, that it may come across as a retrospective attempt to add rigour to what was most likely convenience sampling.

Overall, there is scope in the body of work under discussion for a more candid, systematic and informed approach to discussions of sampling. Two other points to note here are the lack of studies which utilise probability samples and, more generally, of studies which are large in scale. The study by Garton *et al.* (2011), while not wholly about teacher cognition, does, though, provide insight into the perceptions that 4696 teachers of English to young learners from around the world have about their work, while Borg's (2013) study of teachers' conceptions of research involved 1730 English language teachers and managers.

Research Stance

In this section I consider the stance of the studies under review with reference to their methodological orientation (qualitative, quantitative or mixed methods) and the extent to which they were cross-sectional or longitudinal. Longitudinal here means that a study was concerned with changes in teacher cognition over a period of time. Of the 25 sources under discussion, one was wholly quantitative (Li & Ni, 2011), eight used mixed methods designs and 15 were qualitative. The remaining study (Griva & Chostelidou, 2011) collected qualitative data but reported these largely quantitatively. Nine of the studies were longitudinal, examining language teacher cognition over periods spanning from four weeks to three years. For example, Ahn (2011) studied the experiences of a student teacher during a four-week practicum, while Wyatt and Borg (2011) drew on data about the development, over three years, of teachers' practical knowledge in using communicative tasks.

Overall, this analysis suggests that contemporary research in language teacher cognition is strongly aligned with an interpretive research stance (see, for example, Ernest, 1994). Authors did not always explicitly discuss the rationale for such a methodological orientation but here are two examples where they did:

> A qualitative case study was chosen as the best approach to investigate teachers' beliefs and the interrelationships between pedagogical beliefs, classroom interaction and professional practices, which allows different methods to seek in-depth understanding of some social phenomenon, especially when such understanding encompassed important contextual conditions.... (Li & Walsh, 2011: 43)

> Representing an interpretive research paradigm, the study makes hardly any claim to be generalizable to other contexts. Instead, its value lies in attention to significant details as seen through the eyes of the subjects themselves, in highlighting and sensitizing to clues that might have been lost in numbers and statistics. (Werbinska, 2011: 184)

Such arguments emphasise the value of studying teacher cognition qualitatively because this orientation allows for in-depth, contextualised understandings of cognition which have strong local relevance; Werbinska above, for example, is explicit in denying any claims about the generalisability of her findings. Cowie similarly explains that:

> The context for this study is very specific in being confined to EFL teachers working in Tokyo universities. Such a perspective is in tune with the post-modern turn in which research is moving away from 'grand theories' towards more local understandings in which knowledge is specifically located. (Cowie, 2011: 237)

Such sentiments recur in a number of the papers in the present volume.

As noted above, only one study in this review was exclusively quantitative. This does not imply that quantitative analyses of language teacher cognition are lacking, as in seven of the eight mixed-methods studies (Mak, 2011, is the exception here) the primary data were based on questionnaires. Nonetheless, there would seem to be a recognition that quantitative analyses of language teacher cognition can be productively deepened through qualitative work, typically in the form of follow-up interviews with a sub-sample of questionnaire respondents (Yoshiyuki, 2011, is distinct in that his interviewees did not contribute to the prior questionnaire survey). Borg and Al-Busaidi (2011: 3), for example, explain simply that 'The purpose of the interviews was to explore in more detail issues addressed in the questionnaire' while Gao *et al.* (2011: 66) similarly note that in their focus group interviews 'the participants were asked to further elaborate on their answers to the questionnaire'. Young and Sachdev (2011) provided a variation on the typical approach to mixed-methods research by using a questionnaire during the second phase of their study after first generating insights into teacher cognition through a smaller-scale qualitative phase. Overall, though, the mixed-methods studies in this group typically involved quantitative data and qualitative data being collected sequentially.

Data Collection

Table 3 provides a quantitative summary of the data-collection strategies used in the 25 studies of language teacher cognition. One immediate point is that, like the case studies reported in the present volume, 21 studies were multi-method in nature. This is a positive feature, given the limitations inherent in studying language teacher cognition through one method. Interviews, by far the most common strategy, appeared in 24 of these studies (in most cases in a semi-structured format); second most common were questionnaires (11), followed in turn by observations (9) and documents (i.e. lesson plans, course assignments) (8). Journals were used in five cases; in three of these (Ahn, 2011; Borg, 2011; Kanno & Stuart, 2011) they were written as part of a teacher education programme rather than specifically for research purposes, while in one other case (Young & Sachdev, 2011) the authors note that they did not actually see (i.e. collect and analyse) the teachers' journals that are claimed to be part of their dataset. Their comment on this limitation is the rather obvious one that 'future investigations of teachers' beliefs and practices involving diary studies should aim to draw on actual diary content, rather than reports of the content' (Young & Sachdev, 2011: 96). Chapter 8 in this volume focuses on oral reflective journals.

The 'Other' category in Table 3 comprises four data-collection strategies that occurred only once: written narratives (Werbinska, 2011), reflective group discussions (Farrell, 2011), a sentence completion task (Woods & Cakir, 2011) and observing and reacting to the teaching of others (also Woods & Cakir, 2011). The sentence completion task (part of a study of teachers' understandings of communicative language teaching)

> took ten sets of words/phrases related to the common principles or
> themes taken from the descriptions and definitions in literature on

Table 3 Data-collection strategies

Source	Interviews	Questionnaires	Observation	Journals	Stimulated recall	Conferences	Documents	Other
Ahn	✓		✓	✓	✓	✓	✓	
Borg	✓	✓		✓			✓	
Borg and Al-Busaidi	✓	✓						
Bullock	✓	✓						
Cowie	✓							
Farrell	✓							✓
Gao et al.	✓	✓						
Griva and Chostelidou	✓							
Kanno and Stuart	✓		✓	✓	✓		✓	
Khodabakhshzadeh and Shirvan	✓		✓					
Kim	✓		✓		✓			
Kuzborska	✓		✓		✓		✓	
Li and Ni		✓						
Li and Walsh	✓		✓					
Liu and Xu	✓			✓				✓
Mak	✓	✓	✓			✓	✓	
Ong'Ondo and Borg	✓		✓				✓	
Pan and Block	✓	✓						
Trent	✓							
Wan et al.	✓	✓						
Werbinska	✓							✓
Woods and Cakir	✓	✓					✓	✓
Wyatt and Borg	✓		✓				✓	
Yoshiyuki	✓	✓						
Young and Sachdev	✓	✓		✓				
Total	24	11	9	5	4	2	8	4

communicative language teaching, and required the teachers to put them into sentences which articulated their own views. (Woods & Cakir, 2011: 7)

This is an interesting strategy which has the potential to contribute to methodological development in the study of language teacher cognition; the lack of more concrete detail will, though, frustrate readers who would like to experiment with the strategy in their own research. For example, a brief description of the words and phrases used and of the instructions that accompanied them would have been very useful.

The above quantitative analysis masks variations in the ways in which a single widely used data-collection strategy can be implemented. To take the most common strategy, an analysis of these 2011 papers highlights various ways in which interviews can be used (Chapter 4 here also focuses on interviews):

- background interviews in which teachers are encouraged to talk about their professional histories and teaching context (e.g. Cowie);
- post-lesson interviews in which teachers are invited to comment on their teaching and the thinking behind it (e.g. Li & Walsh);
- video stimulated recall (VSR) interviews in which teachers speak about their teaching as they watch a video-recording of their lesson (e.g. Kuzborska; see also Chapter 7 in this volume);
- focus group interviews, where small groups of teachers comment on the issues under study (e.g. Yoshiyuki, and Chapter 2 here);
- follow-up interviews which seek further detail about data previously provided by teachers, most typically questionnaire data (e.g. Borg & Al-Busaidi);
- stand-alone interviews which serve as the sole means through which teachers' perspectives on a particular issue are elicited (e.g. Griva & Chostelidou);
- member checking interviews through which teachers are asked to comment on the researcher's interpretation of the data (e.g. Wyatt & Borg).

Within these various options, further methodological divisions are possible. For example, two conceptualisations of the use of VSR are possible (Borg, 2006; Lyle, 2003). One is that showing teachers a video of their own teaching can retrospectively elicit and capture teachers' interactive thinking during a lesson. The second is that VSR facilitates discussion of the thinking behind teachers' work without assuming that their interactive thinking at specific points during the lesson can be recreated. Of the four studies here that use VSR, one (Ahn, 2011) makes no reference to its position in this respect, while Kim is explicit in stating that the purpose of VSR (or SRP – stimulated-recall protocols as she calls them) is 'to gain access to information about Hee-Won's [the teacher] classroom decision making and thoughts while teaching' (Kim, 2011: 228). Kanno and Stuart (2011) and Kuzborska (2011), in contrast, share the view that VSR stimulates discussion and commentary without presuming to access interactive thinking during lessons; the former, for example, note that 'In each stimulated recall session, the participant was asked to view the video and provide commentary on his or her lesson' (Kanno & Stuart, 2011: 241).

In describing the manner in which data were collected in these studies, researchers also varied in the level of detail provided. Werbinska (2011: 184) describes her data-collection strategy in 20 words – 'asking 64 first-year teachers to write a narrative about their first year of working as an English teacher at school' – while Griva and Chostelidou (2011: 1781) explain their procedures as follows (with an apparent omission of a section c):

> Semi-structured interviews were used as the basic research instrument, which comprised the following sections: a) conceptualization of multilingualism, b) multilingual competence of citizens, d) the role of English as a 'lingua franca', e) introduction of foreign languages in early stages of education, f) development of multilingual education.

Mak (2011) provides information about how data were collected without going into any detail of, for example, the nature of the questionnaire used, how many interviews were conducted, or what these were about. Even allowing for the fact that authors will be writing under length constraints, judgements about research rigour cannot be made if readers are not provided with adequate detail of how a study was conducted; some excellent examples of how this can be achieved are in evidence in the 2011 studies under review here (e.g. Kanno & Stuart, Kuzborksa, Yoshiyuki). Even in these more detailed accounts, though, limited space was allocated to the discussion of deeper methodological principles; for example, despite the widespread use of semi-structured interviews, comments on the interactive, co-constructed nature of such interviews are rare (a point made about interviews in applied linguistics research more generally by Mann, 2011). Cowie is an exception, noting that his interviews with teachers 'were carried out using a social-constructivist approach in which interaction between the researcher and participants results in a jointly constructed meaning making view of reality' (Cowie, 2011: 236).

Another dimension along which the 2011 studies differ very significantly, methodologically, is the volume of data they draw on. For example, although the study reported by Li and Walsh is based on a larger one, their paper focuses on one lesson and one interview for each of two teachers; in contrast, Kim's analysis is based on 34 observed lessons, four interviews and four VSR sessions. Kanno and Stuart draw on 49 observed lessons, 24 interviews and journals and documents. Of course, volume of data is not on its own a determiner of research quality; it is, though, interesting to note the substantial variations evident here.

Data Analysis

The final issue I will analyse is the manner in which these studies report the analysis of data. All the papers do so, though in some cases the analysis is not described for all the forms of data collected (e.g. no information is provided about the analysis of the focus group interviews in Yoshiyuki or the questionnaire results in Bullock). Quantitatively, the space allocated to a description of data analysis in these papers varies from 84 words (Griva & Chostelidou) to 582 (Borg), with an average of 241. In particular, some of the qualitative studies provide very brief accounts of how data were analysed; for example, both Ahn and Kim reduce to just over 90 words what were undoubtedly complex analytical procedures involving multiple data sources: both accounts refer to activity theory, grounded content analysis and the constant comparative method of analysis, yet a concrete sense of what the researchers actually did with their data remains elusive. Word constraints often contribute to such brevity, though there are cases in the studies under discussion where authors have managed to dedicate substantial space to data analysis (e.g. over 400 words in Borg, Cowie, Kuzborska and Liu & Xu). Overall, though, the reporting of qualitative data analysis does not provide sufficient insight into the procedures through which data were analysed. Common concepts in qualitative data analysis recur, such as content or thematic analysis, cyclical, recurrent, iterative or recursive analysis, coding, categorising and data reduction. But the lack of specifics generally means that the sections on qualitative data analysis have a generic feel to them. Consider this paragraph:

> The data were read thoroughly and analysed qualitatively using grounded content analysis. This involved selecting text, defining content categories, sorting material into categories, and drawing conclusions from the results. Thus, by assigning small chunks of data to emerging codes, we were able to identify broader themes through a recursive

process of data reduction, verification and further data analysis. To understand the meanings of the data, the procedures of the constant comparative method were also adopted. In order to encompass the multiple realities that are likely to be encountered and to fully describe the setting in which the teachers worked, an inductive approach to data analysis (based on indigenous concepts) was applied (though reference was also made, deductively, to sensitizing concepts from the literature). The concurrent and iterative nature of data collection and analysis provided opportunities to verify tentative interpretations, and to follow up new understandings and unanticipated themes in the data. The use of multiple sources facilitated triangulation, while verification was also achieved via member checking.

Prima facie this may come across (especially if it is enhanced with a few references to the research methodology literature) as a persuasive account of qualitative data analysis; it is actually, though, an artificial example I have created by piecing together extracts from the reports under discussion. Its illustrative and instructional value is minimal in that it fails to provide any insight into what exactly the researchers did as they transformed data into findings. There are thus interesting questions here about the precise purpose that sections on qualitative data analysis have in empirical research papers; my conclusion, based on the examples examined, is that they often have a formulaic quality through which they fulfil the requirement that something be said about analysis; however, they do not contribute to the development of readers' understandings of how to analyse data. Whether they should, of course, is a matter for debate (in quantitative studies, perhaps due to well established analytical procedures, there is less of a need for researchers to provide an instructional commentary on their procedures); my position is that, within the word limits all authors face, it is important for the methodological development of the field that sufficient concrete detail of how language teacher cognition data are analysed be provided.

One final comment on analysis relates to the manner in which authors argue for the quality of their work. While not all the reports make explicit reference to the strategies used to enhance the quality of the analysis, the two most common strategies cited are respondent validation (also called member checking – eight studies) and triangulation (explicitly mentioned in four studies). Cowie (2011: 238), for example, explains that:

> Member checking involves taking analysis and interpretation back to the participants at various stages of the research process in order to elicit their views and comments. This was carried out by sending examples

of data and interpretation to the teacher-participants and asking for comments which were then incorporated into the research process in a number of ways such as confirming or altering interpretations.

Regarding triangulation, Farrell (2011: 57), for example, explains that:

The technique of triangulation was also utilized to ensure the findings were credible. During data triangulation, a piece of evidence was compared and crosschecked with other kinds of evidence (such as comparing the researcher's log with interview notes, audio tape transcripts [with] group discussion transcripts).

Explicit reference to strategies for enhancing the quality of data analysis is a positive feature of many of the papers under discussion. More critically, though, what is often lacking is the acknowledgement that, particularly in qualitative research, strategies such as triangulation and respondent validation may enhance, but not ensure, validity or trustworthiness. Additionally, debates about such strategies in the research methods literature need to be more widely acknowledged. For example, Bloor (1997), among others, is critical of the use of both respondent validation and triangulation as strategies for validating research findings. It is important that, even within the limited space generally available for the discussion of such issues, accounts of data analysis demonstrate a critical awareness of broader debates in social research methodology and avoid what may come across as a facile acceptance of trendy terminology.

Conclusion

The analysis I have provided of 25 recent empirical papers on language teacher cognition illustrates the continuing growth of this domain of research. This substantively varied set of papers can be characterised, methodologically, as:

- international in scope;
- using non-probability samples;
- involving teachers of English as a foreign language who are not native-speakers of English and who work in state institutions;
- modest in scale (in terms of numbers of participating teachers);
- using mixed methods or qualitative methods, in either a cross-sectional or a longitudinal design;
- multi-method in nature, with interviews by far the most common

data-collection strategy, followed by questionnaires, observations and document analysis.

The case studies discussed in this book reflect many of these trends.

I have also highlighted various methodological aspects of language teacher cognition research which merit further attention:

- larger-scale studies, including those which allow for comparisons in the cognitions and practices of language teachers working in different countries;
- greater specificity and candour (e.g. in distinguishing between convenience and purposeful sampling) about the rationale underpinning the selection of participants;
- more concrete detail about how data were collected, including examples of the instruments used, particularly where these are innovative;
- greater practical illustration and criticality in accounts of how data are analysed, with a view to making these accounts instructional rather than generically formulaic;
- more critical commentary on the research methods adopted, including an acknowledgement of methodological debates in social science research more generally.

Additionally, there are four final observations I would like to make:

- The study of language teacher cognition involving teachers of foreign languages other than English does take place but does not currently have a high international profile; strategies are thus required for bringing this work to the attention of a broader global audience.
- Visual methods have not yet been widely adopted in the study of language teacher cognition and there is clear scope here for the use of strategies such as photo-based interviews (Hurworth, 2003) and elicitation techniques based on drawing (for a recent overview of the field of visual methods research, see Margolis & Pauwels, 2011).
- The 25 papers analysed do not illustrate the use of statistical techniques developed in the field of psychology (e.g. repertory grid and Q methodology) which can be used in studying language teacher cognition (see, for example, Sendan & Roberts, 1998). In the interests of methodological pluralism, it is important that an awareness of these options is maintained, particularly at a time when qualitative approaches in language teacher cognition research are predominant. An introduction to Q

methodology is available at http://facstaff.uww.edu/cottlec/QArchive/ Bps.htm.

- The papers I have analysed provide limited concrete insight into the challenges involved in studying language teacher cognition. There are at least two reasons for this: space constraints (word limits) and a tendency for researchers to provide neat and linear representations of their work. In this sense, the space that authors in the current volume have been afforded to discuss the challenges they have faced in studying language teacher cognition is very welcome. More transparent acknowledgement and discussion of the methodological challenges researchers face in studying language teacher cognition can only be beneficial for the continuing development of the field.

References

Ahn, K. (2011) Learning to teach under curricular reform. In K.E. Johnson and P.R. Golombek (eds), *Research on Second Language Teacher Education* (pp. 239–253). London: Routledge.

Bloor, M. (1997) Techniques of validation in qualitative research: A critical commentary. In D. Miller and R. Dingwall (eds), *Context and Method in Qualitative Research* (pp. 37–50). London: Sage.

Borg, S. (2003) Teacher cognition in language teaching: A review of research on what language teachers think, know, believe, and do. *Language Teaching*, 36(2), 81–109.

Borg, S. (2006) *Teacher Cognition and Language Education: Research and Practice*. London: Continuum.

Borg, S. (2011) The impact of in-service teacher education on language teachers' beliefs. *System*, 39(3), 370–380.

Borg, S. (2013) *Teacher Research in Language Teaching: A Critical Analysis*. Cambridge: Cambridge University Press.

Borg, S. and Al-Busaidi, S. (2011) Teachers' beliefs and practices regarding learner autonomy. *ELT Journal*, doi:10.1093/elt/ccr065.

Bullock, D. (2011) Learner self-assessment: An investigation into teachers' beliefs. *ELT Journal*, 62(2), 114–125.

Cowie, N. (2011) Emotions that experienced English as a foreign language (EFL) teachers feel about their students, their colleagues and their work. *Teaching and Teacher Education*, 27(1), 235–242.

Ernest, P. (1994) *An Introduction to Research Methodology and Paradigms*. Exeter: School of Education, University of Exeter.

Farrell, T.S.C. (2011) Exploring the professional role identities of experienced ESL teachers through reflective practice. *System*, 39(1), 54–62.

Gao, X., Barkhuizen, G. and Chow, A. (2011) 'Nowadays teachers are relatively obedient': Understanding primary school English teachers' conceptions of and drives for research in China. *Language Teaching Research*, 15(1), 61–81.

Garton, S., Copland, F. and Burns, A. (2011) *Investigating Global Practices in Teaching English to Young Learners*. London: British Council.

Gomm, R. (2009) *Key Concepts in Social Research Methods*. Basingstoke: Palgrave.

Griva, E. and Chostelidou, D. (2011) English language teachers' conceptions and attitudes to multilingual development in education. *Procedia – Social and Behavioral Sciences*, 15, 1780–1785.

Hurworth, R. (2003) Photo-interviewing for research. *Social Research Update*, issue 40. Available at http://sru.soc.surrey.ac.uk/SRU40.pdf (accessed 13 November 2011).

Kanno, Y. and Stuart, C. (2011) Learning to become a second language teacher: Identities-in-practice. *Modern Language Journal*, 95(2), 236–252.

Khodabakhshzadeh, H. and Shirvan, M.E. (2011) Discovering iranian EFL teachers' personality traits through their conceptions of effective teaching. *Canadian Social Science*, 7(4), 21–33.

Kim, E.J. (2011) An activity theory analysis of a teachers' experience. In K.E. Johnson and P.R. Golombek (eds), *Research on Second Language Teacher Education* (pp. 225–238). London: Routledge.

Kuzborska, I. (2011) Links between teachers' beliefs and practices and research on reading. *Reading in a Foreign Language*, 23(1), 102–128.

Lehrer, J. (2009) *How We Decide*. Boston, MA: Houghton Mifflin Harcourt.

Li, G. and Ni, X. (2011) Primary EFL teachers' technology use in China: Patterns and perceptions. *RELC Journal*, 42(1), 69–85.

Li, L. and Walsh, S. (2011) 'Seeing is believing': Looking at EFL teachers' beliefs through classroom interaction. *Classroom Discourse*, 2(1), 39–57.

Liu, Y. and Xu, Y. (2011) Inclusion or exclusion? A narrative inquiry of a language teacher's identity experience in the 'new work order' of competing pedagogies. *Teaching and Teacher Education*, 27(3), 589–597.

Lyle, J. (2003) Stimulated recall: A report on its use in naturalistic research. *British Educational Research Journal*, 29(6), 861–878.

Mak, S.H. (2011) Tensions between conflicting beliefs of an EFL teacher in teaching practice. *RELC Journal*, 42(1), 53–67.

Mann, S. (2011) A critical review of qualitative interviews in applied linguistics. *Applied Linguistics*, 32(1), 6–24.

Margolis, E. and Pauwels, L. (eds) (2011) *The SAGE Handbook of Visual Research Methods*. London: Sage.

Miller, J. (2009) Teacher identity. In A. Burns and J.C. Richards (eds), *The Cambridge Guide to Second Language Teacher Education* (pp. 172–181). Cambridge: Cambridge University Press.

Morton, T. and Gray, J. (2010) Personal practical knowledge and identity in lesson planning conferences on a pre-service TESOL course. *Language Teaching Research*, 14(3), 297–317.

Nespor, J. (1987) The role of beliefs in the practice of teaching. *Journal of Curriculum Studies*, 19(4), 317–328.

Ong'Ondo, C.O. and Borg, S. (2011) 'We teach plastic lessons to please them' – The influence of supervision on the practice of English language student teachers in Kenya. *Language Teaching Research*, 14(3), 509–528.

Pan, L. and Block, D. (2011) English as a global language in China: An investigation into learners' and teachers' language beliefs. *System*, 39(3), 391–402.

Sendan, F. and Roberts, J. (1998) Orhan: A case study in the development of a student teachers' personal theories. *Teachers and Teaching: Theory and Practice*, 4, 229–244.

Trent, J. (2011) Learning, teaching, and constructing identities: ESL pre-service teacher experiences during a short-term international experience programme. *Asia Pacific Journal of Education*, 31(2), 177–194.

Tsui, A.B.M. (2007) Complexities of identity formation: A narrative inquiry of an EFL teacher. *TESOL Quarterly*, 41(4), 657–680.

Wan, W., Low, G.D. and Li, M. (2011) From students' and teachers' perspectives: Metaphor analysis of beliefs about EFL teachers' roles. *System*, 39(3), 403–415.

Werbinska, D. (2011) The first year in the classroom: crossing the borderland from being a student to being a teacher. In M. Pawlak (ed.), *Extending the Boundaries of Research on Second Language Learning and Teaching* (pp. 181–196). New York: Springer.

Woods, D. and Cakir, H. (2011) Two dimensions of teacher knowledge: The case of communicative language teaching. *System*, 39(3), 381–390.

Wyatt, M. and Borg, S. (2011) Development in the practical knowledge of language teachers: A comparative study of three teachers designing and using communicative tasks on an in-service BA TESOL programme in the Middle East. *Innovation in Language Learning and Teaching*, 5(3), 233–252.

Yoshiyuki, N. (2011) Teachers' readiness for promoting learner autonomy: A study of Japanese EFL high school teachers. *Teaching and Teacher Education*, 27(5), 900–910.

Young, T.J. and Sachdev, I. (2011) Intercultural communicative competence: Exploring English language teachers' beliefs and practices. *Language Awareness*, 20, 81–98.

1 Questionnaires

Case Study: Judy Ng
Commentary: J.D. Brown

CASE STUDY

Introduction

This chapter reports on aspects of an in-depth study I conducted at a private university in Malaysia which sought to investigate lecturers' beliefs about the value of feedback on their students' written work and the extent to which the lecturers' practices converged with their self-reported beliefs. The study adopted various procedures for data collection – including interviews (see Chapter 4), think aloud (see Chapter 6), stimulated recall (see Chapter 7) and focus groups (see Chapter 3) – but the specific focus of the chapter is the design and administration of the questionnaires issued to the lecturers.

The value of teachers' feedback on students' writing has always been controversial, some researchers advocating various forms of feedback (e.g. Ferris, 1995, 2009), while others (e.g. Truscott, 1996, 2007) deny its usefulness. It has long been recognised that what teachers do in practice is largely influenced by their beliefs and values (Clarke & Peterson, 1986) and one of the most vital aspects of this issue is the study of the contextual factors that shape teachers' beliefs (Borg, 2006; Goldstein, 2005). While there have been wide-ranging surveys of aspects of teacher beliefs in some Asian educational contexts (Littlewood, 2007; Nunan, 2003), there is a lack of in-depth studies, and this is particularly true of tertiary education in Malaysia. In his comprehensive overview of studies of language teachers' beliefs, Borg (2006) pointed to the need for more studies in areas such as second-language writing. He also emphasised the need to examine the extent to which teachers' reported beliefs are actually put into practice.

Methodological Focus

Brown (2001: 6) defines questionnaires as 'any written instruments that present respondents with a series of questions or statements to which they are to react either by writing out their answers or selecting from among existing answers' and he points out that questionnaires can elicit individuals' reactions to, perceptions of and opinions of an issue or issues. Other functions of questionnaires include: obtaining demographic information about respondents (Creswell, 2005); scoping the respondents (Cohen *et al.*, 2007); and eliciting and measuring abstract, cognitive processes, individual preferences and values (Brown, 2001; Dörnyei & Taguchi, 2010; Wagner, 2010).

The issue of sampling is essential in a questionnaire study (Brown, 2001; Creswell, 2005; Dörnyei & Taguchi, 2010). The major difficulty with sampling is in the accurate representation of the target population (Dörnyei & Taguchi, 2010; Gillham, 2000). It is usually very difficult and expensive to obtain a probability sample (Dörnyei & Taguchi, 2010: 60) that reflects the actual population. However, individual researchers can get reliable results using various non-probability sampling strategies. Some of the procedures for choosing the samples include random sampling, stratified random sampling, convenience sampling, quota sampling and snowball sampling (in which the researcher identifies key respondents who meet the criteria for the research and with their help is able to contact and recruit other participants).

A questionnaire can be administered in a number of ways, such as via post, email or online (Creswell, 2005; Dörnyei & Taguchi, 2010). However, there is a risk of getting a low return rate (Brown, 2001). There are, though, two approaches that give high return rates: one is one-to-one administration, whereby the questionnaires are personally delivered to the respondents and collected either there and then or later; another way is through group administration, when all the respondents are gathered together in the same place.

Most questionnaires contain both closed- and open-ended items. The former require respondents to choose from predetermined responses to various (Likert-type) scales, to select multiple-choice items or to rank order various alternatives (Brown, 2009; Dörnyei & Taguchi, 2010; Gillham, 2000). Although the range of possible responses is restricted, such close-ended items enable a straightforward analysis of the data. Several authors (Brown, 2001, 2009; Cohen *et al.*, 2007; Dörnyei & Taguchi, 2010; Gillham, 2000) have suggested the use of more open-ended questions for smaller numbers of respondents and those who are doing qualitative research. Open-ended items typically include short-answer questions to elicit information which might otherwise have been overlooked; they can also serve to cross-check the validity of responses (Brown, 2009; Dörnyei & Taguchi, 2010).

It is necessary to pilot the questionnaire to ensure that the questions are not ambiguous and to check the feasibility of the procedures (Gillham, 2000; Wilson & McLean, 1994).

Once the questionnaires are completed and collected, the data need to be analysed. The type of analysis depends on the nature of the research and the number of respondents. If the number of respondents and/or items is large, Dörnyei and Taguchi (2010) recommend the use of a spreadsheet program such as Microsoft Excel or the Statistical Package for the Social Sciences (SPSS). Open-ended questions are more difficult to analyse due to the potential wide range of response types. In order to solve this problem, Brown (2001) suggests grouping similar responses together with the aid of a software program; for instance, recent versions of NVivo (Bazeley, 2007) can assist with the collation, management, coding and triangulation of data from multiple sources, including questionnaires.

Two recently published studies were particularly relevant to my research; Lee (2003, 2009) used questionnaires to examine whether teachers' beliefs converged with their reported practices. The relevance of these two studies lies less in their findings (which, will, however, be briefly discussed below) than in their use of questionnaires to provide baseline date for subsequent phases of data collection; Lee's (2009) study followed up an initial survey of 206 teachers by telephone interviews with a convenience sample of 19 participants. Lee (2009) went on to indicate 10 mismatches between teachers' beliefs and written feedback practice. In my view, such findings, although plausible, cannot be accurately inferred from the participants' responses. The following might be considered a typical example from the report:

> In the questionnaire survey, about 70 per cent of the teachers said they usually mark errors comprehensively. Such practice, however, does not seem to be in line with their beliefs, since the majority of the teachers practising comprehensive marking (12 out of 19) said in the interview that they prefer selective marking. (Lee, 2009: 15)

The point is that it is at least possible that the 12 interviewees were among the 30% who disagreed with the item about comprehensive marking, and if this were the case then there would not be a mismatch about this particular belief. The lesson I drew from this is the need to be very careful in extrapolating data from two sources and make generalisations based on them. It is more accurate, wherever possible, to analyse the findings from individual respondents, as will be shown below.

The Study

The overall aim of this research was to elicit lecturers' beliefs about the value of feedback and to compare them with their own observed practices at a private university in Malaysia. As a first step in the multi-method data-gathering strategy, I based many of my questionnaire items on Lee's (2003) study because her research was also conducted in Asia and, like Lee, I wanted to study the extent of mismatch between the English-language lecturers' beliefs and their actual practices of providing feedback. However, my questionnaire covered more ground than Lee's. In addition to background data, my questionnaire included:

(1) the types of assignments assessed;
(2) a five-point Likert-scale frequency check about the respondents' use of criteria;
(3) a similar check on features focused on when providing feedback;
(4) a four-point agreement scale relating to their purposes in giving feedback;
(5) a checklist to be completed regarding who makes the decisions about the types of feedback to be used;
(6) three open-ended questions.

The questionnaire was intended to serve three purposes: to obtain some background information on the lecturers; to elicit the lecturers' general attitudes towards feedback and their self-report of their practices of providing feedback (to inform my subsequent data collection); and to invite volunteers to participate in the subsequent phases of the research. As will be noted below, although I had to adjust my original plans for this questionnaire, the three aims were broadly achieved, especially in terms of obtaining participants and the general attitudes towards feedback. Even though some of the data gained from the self-reported beliefs contradict the findings from the other data-gathering methods, this shows that relying on a single data-gathering tool raises the issue of validity, which will be explained in detail below.

Questionnaire data samples

After a preliminary analysis of the data from a total of 35 participants, I decided to restrict the number of volunteers in the subsequent phases of data collection to 10: five English-language lecturers (coded E1–5), three (S1–3) from the engineering faculty and two (S4 and S5) from the applied science faculty. I made this decision either because the number of potential participants from the other departments was too small or because the type of courses taught were too varied to enable a coherent pattern of beliefs and practices to emerge. To enable a brief discussion of some of the findings, Tables 1.1 and 1.2 show the range of responses to two of the questionnaire items with a four-point agreement scale relating to their purposes in giving feedback.

Table 1.1 shows convergence of views among all 35 respondents: all but one agreed or strongly agreed that feedback ought to consider the overall structure of an assignment. More specifically, in their subsequent interviews, all five science lecturers (S1–5) considered content an important aspect in their feedback, and in their think aloud sessions (see Chapter 6) S4 and S5 checked the content by searching for correct use of scientific terminology. Although accurate referencing was not formally assessed, when they were actually marking the assignments, S3 and S4 noted students' use of citations. When asked in the stimulated recall sessions about their beliefs about this, both mentioned that citations and referencing are important because their students need to do research when completing their studies abroad. In their interviews, the three science lecturers who marked lab reports (S1, S3 and S5) said they placed considerable importance on the discussion section because they needed to evaluate the students' ability to critically discuss their findings. Also, S3 and S5 were extremely concerned that students followed the correct format in their lab reports. S5 mentioned that she allocated marks for each section because the format is a standard practice among all scientists. When S3 was asked in the stimulated recall session (see Chapter 7) why format was so important, he said that he liked everything to be standardised as it made it easier for him to read the report.

Some discrepancies emerged. For example, S4 mentioned in the interview that he did not really check or make any corrections to students' errors in language. However, during the think aloud session, he corrected some spelling and grammatical errors or wrong choice of words. During

Table 1.1 Responses to item 14f, 'It is important for teachers to provide feedback on the overall structure of a piece of writing'

	Strongly agree	Agree	Disagree	Strongly disagree
35 general responses	11	23	1	0
5 science/engineering (S1–5)		5		
5 English (E1–5)	1	4	0	0

the stimulated recall session, when this issue was raised, he said he needed to make the corrections because wrong grammar or misuse of words might change the intended meaning.

All five English lecturers focused in their think aloud and stimulated recall sessions on lower-order concerns of writing – such as sentence structure and choice of words – with a lesser emphasis on format, problem solving or critical and creative thinking. Two interesting observations were made when the English specialists were marking their students' assignments: four of them tended to use linguistic terms which students might not understand (e.g. 'fragment', 'run-on sentence', 'topic sentence'); and the same four used marking codes to indicate sentence-level errors (G for grammar errors and SP for spelling, etc.). These practices seem inconsistent with their concern, as reported in the questionnaire, for the overall structure of the assignment.

There was similarly overall convergence among the 35 responses to the second issue, regarding multiple drafts (Table 1.2). Within the subset of 10, S1 was the only lecturer who responded in the interview that multiple drafts did not help his students. By contrast, S4 not only strongly believed that multiple drafts helped students to produce the correct referencing system but actually marked students' drafts in the think aloud sessions. However, although S5 responded positively to the questionnaire item, in the interview she said that she felt that multiple drafts took too much of both the lecturers' and the students' time. She allowed students to submit drafts only of the research project paper. In the interviews, S2 was non-committal about the benefit of multiple drafts and S3 shifted from his questionnaire response, saying that he did not in practice accept multiple drafts.

In their interviews, three of the five English lecturers (E1, E3, E4) diverged from their questionnaire responses by saying that they did not believe that multiple drafts helped students to improve their writing skills. E3 made the following comment:

Table 1.2 Responses to Item 14h, 'Multiple drafts help students improve their writing'

	Strongly agree	Agree	Disagree	Strongly disagree
35 general responses	14	17	3	1
5 science/engineering (S1–5)	3	1	1	0
5 English (E1–5)	1	4	0	0

you make the corrections for them, of course the end product it will be very beautiful in the sense that all the grammar mistakes will disappear and you will have an easy time to mark it but I feel that that's not very good because the students are not learning from their mistakes.

Even though E5 responded positively in the questionnaire, she chose to be neutral in the interview. She did not make it clear in what way she thought multiple drafts were beneficial and did not mention her views in her think aloud session. E2 was more consistent than her colleagues; in her interview, she repeated that multiple drafts were useful, saying that 'practice makes perfect' and although she did not actually mark them in her think aloud session, she showed me samples of her students' drafts.

The most important thing I learned from this experience was to not to take data elicited in questionnaires and interviews at face value. There are many reasons why people might not answer questions reliably and this uncertainty points to the utmost need to triangulate self-reported data with data from other sources. This view justifies not only my own multi-method approach to exploring teachers' beliefs but is also in line with the perspectives offered in all the other chapters in this volume.

Methodological Implications

Six main issues about questionnaires are discussed in this section: item writing; piloting; gaining and maintaining access; administering the questionnaire; gaining further participation; and the role of the researcher as insider.

A variety of ways of *writing items* is essential in designing a questionnaire. According to Brown (2009), broad open-ended questions enable respondents to provide answers which are in line with their own perceptions, and are especially appropriate for small numbers of respondents (Cohen *et al.*, 2007; Dörnyei & Taguchi, 2010). However, I decided to include more closed-ended questions than open-ended questions because I was able to obtain and triangulate further information subsequently. Lee (2003, 2009) used a three-point Likert frequency scale, collapsing 'rarely' and 'never' into one category, but I felt that five points would produce finer-grained results. For the agree–disagree items, I decided that a four-point scale would make analysis of the data easier, by eliminating the possibility that some respondents might merely opt for a 'safe' middle ground. Another point of difference between my questionnaire and that developed by Lee (2003, 2009) is that while hers began with an open-ended question, I left mine to the end. I followed Dörnyei and Taguchi's (2010) advice, thinking that the extra psychological effort needed to formulate an initial response might lead respondents to give up answering the subsequent questions, or else answer them inaccurately simply to complete the questionnaire as quickly as possible. One of the major issues I needed to decide was which language to use. While it is usually more efficient – as well as courteous – to write the items in the respondents' mother tongue, this presents a number of problems in a multilingual society such as Malaysia; it would have been impractical to have written (and back-translated) versions in Bahasa Melayu, Tamil, Mandarin and Urdu – the first languages of my intended respondents. Therefore, because the respondents originally intended were a small number of English lecturers in three different departments, I used only English in the questionnaire.

Once the questionnaire was designed, it went through two phases of *piloting*, involving 30 volunteers, whom I asked to complete the responses and provide feedback on the clarity of the items. The first pilot was conducted with research students and others at the University of Waikato, New Zealand; a subsequently revised draft was piloted with Malaysians teaching English, but not at the research site. The final version included alterations to the wording of the instructions, the inclusion of more items relating to respondents' background, additional attitudinal items and some wording changes.

In any research project, it is important to ensure that *access to the setting and participants* can be initiated and sustained. I had little difficulty in obtaining formal permission to carry out my study because I was a former employee of the university in this study. Once the president of the university signed the consent form for me to conduct the research, he instructed his staff to cooperate with my project. The questionnaire and the information about the research were circulated as an email attachment among the deans and directors involved. They then sent emails to approximately 40 English lecturers to complete the questionnaire. I assumed that the president's instructions would be adhered to, but in fact found that official sanction does not necessarily mean willing participation.

Actually *administering the questionnaire* was not straightforward. Although I had obtained permission to place the questionnaire on the university's website, the director responsible for technological support had more urgent matters to deal with at the precise time when his help was needed. My fall-back plan was to distribute the questionnaire via email attachment, but this did not work. Despite the support given by the gatekeepers, and even after reminders were sent, the number of completed questionnaires was very disappointing. One solution was to send personal emails to some of my ex-colleagues, but only three responded.

Thus I had to change my strategy of *gaining further participation*. The response rate improved somewhat after I met the lecturers to explain in detail what their involvement in my study would entail. I feel that people respond well when the researcher is willing to spend time with them individually and to answer all their enquiries about the research face to face. Once the volunteers agreed to participate in the in-depth study, I administered the questionnaire to each respondent personally and by hand. Through this method, I was able to match questionnaire responses to individual interviews to gain more accurate data than would be obtained by generalising the overall results gathered from the questionnaire.

Another important factor was that such networking was facilitated by being a cultural *insider*. However, there were also some disadvantages to being an institutional insider. A number of lecturers admitted to me that some viewed me as a threat to their professional face: in the process of data collection, their limitations or weaknesses in providing feedback would be revealed to me. As noted above, eventually I recruited 10 lecturers to participate in the subsequent stages of the project. This considerable change from my intended participants eventually shaped my final decision to compare the beliefs and practices of English lecturers and science lecturers.

Reflection

In conclusion, the value of a multi-method data-gathering method approach was demonstrated in this project because, although the scope of the project changed, the questionnaire essentially achieved the three purposes for which it was intended. The questionnaire was not rigorously applied as is usually recommended in the literature review, but its administration had to be handled heuristically in light of the institutional and sociocultural constraints that I unexpectedly faced. When using questionnaires for preliminary purposes such as I had in mind, I would say that the researcher needs to be entirely flexible in making decisions in the field about which data to collect, and when, from which participants (of those who are willing and able to cooperate). The shortage of intended participants for the subsequent stages of the project – specialist English lecturers – initially created difficulties. However, I believe that my eventual decision to compare and contrast lecturers from two different disciplinary areas allowed a valuable exploration of the beliefs and practices of academic staff who provide feedback on their students' written work.

COMMENTARY

The reflective narrative about questionnaire research written by Judy Ng begins by defining questionnaires and discussing their purposes. It then covers sampling issues, addresses problems in administering questionnaires and defines the main types of items (closed- and open-ended), as well as the need for piloting items, and strategies for analysing the quantitative and qualitative data that result from closed- and open-ended items, respectively. She also provides a brief review of empirical studies on teachers' beliefs and then describes her own study on the topic. Along the way, she makes several useful points that all survey researchers should carefully consider: the importance of using multiple research methods and being flexible during the research process (especially during the data-gathering stage). To help keep me oriented (and the reader too), I will use her headings to organise my commentary.

Methodological Focus

Judy stresses the importance of sampling when she says that 'The issue of sampling is essential in a questionnaire study' and tells us that 'The major difficulty with sampling is in the accurate representation of the target population'. In my view, the primary sampling difficulties that survey researchers face are a bit broader, and include problems in defining the population we want to study as well as the difficulties involved in randomly selecting a sample and getting 100% return rates so that the sample represents the population. For example, imagine trying to define the population of all students taking English as a foreign language (EFL) in Malaysia. All such students would comprise a very long list indeed and, given the transient nature of student populations, the list would probably be inaccurate the moment it was finished. Imagine further trying to contact a randomly selected subset of such EFL students and getting them all to cooperate in a research study. Impossible, right? Two strategies come to mind for overcoming this problem: (1) define the population very narrowly (e.g. as all the students taking Japanese courses 101 to 202 at the University of Hawaii who were in class on a particular day) and then administer the questionnaires in class (as we did – see Iwai et al., 1999); or (2) use one of the non-probability sampling techniques listed by Judy: stratified random sampling, convenience sampling, quota sampling and snowball sampling. I prefer strategy (1), but that is not always possible.

In discussing the convenience sample in the Lee (2003, 2009) studies, Judy says that:

> The lesson I drew from this is the need to be very careful in extrapolating data from two sources and make generalisations based on them. It is more accurate, wherever possible, to analyse the findings from individual respondents....

Her wariness of Lee's findings makes sense to me, as does her solution of using multiple data sources. However, an additional lesson we can all learn from such experiences is the importance of the qualitative research notion of transferability, especially with small ($n = 19$ in the case she is referring to) non-probability convenience samples. This concept has less to do with the design of the original study than with the reporting of the study. *Transferability* (analogous to generalisability in quantitative research) is the idea that the participants and conditions of the study should be described *thickly* (i.e. in depth) so that readers can decide for themselves whether the results of the study apply to their own language learning/teaching context.

The Study

Judy tells us that the overall aim of her research 'was to elicit lecturers' beliefs about the value of feedback and to compare them with their own observed practices at a private university in Malaysia'. She goes on to clearly describe the structure of her questionnaire: 'In addition to background data, I sought information about: (1) the types of assignments assessed; (2) a five-point Likert-scale frequency check about the respondents' use of criteria; (3) a similar check on features focussed on when providing feedback; (4) a four-point agreement scale relating to their purposes in giving feedback; (5) a checklist to be completed regarding who makes the decisions about the types of feedback to be used; and (6) three open-ended questions' (for more on these item formats, see Brown, 2000, 2001). She also explains that 'The questionnaire was intended to serve three purposes: to obtain some background information about the lecturers; to elicit the lecturers' general attitudes towards feedback and their self-report of their practices of providing feedback to inform my subsequent data collection; and to invite volunteers to participate in the subsequent phrases of the research'. Though she describes the structure of her questionnaire effectively, I think I would have framed the three purposes as more traditional research questions (and thereby drawn the reader's attention explicitly to where the study was heading), as follows:

> To those ends, I posed the following research questions:
> (1) What are the characteristics of the lecturers?
> (2) What are the lecturers' general attitudes towards feedback?
> (3) What are their self-reported practices in providing feedback?
> Answers to these research questions will hopefully inform my subsequent data collection when I invite volunteers to participate in the subsequent phases of the research.

Questionnaire Data Samples

On a more technical point, Tables 1.1 and 1.2 treat the data as though they are *nominal*. I think I would have additionally treated these Likert-scale items as *interval scales* (i.e. scales with equally distant points on them, like test scores). Doing so would allow the reporting of means and standard deviations in addition to the *nominal scales* (i.e. naming scales like male/female, German/American/French, high proficiency/low proficiency, etc.) that Judy is currently reporting with her tallies. Interpreting the Likert-scale items as both interval and nominal would also have been useful for making comparisons across questions. Note that numerous articles in the general literature on Likert scales (see references in the two citations at the end of the next sentence) have argued that they are *ordinal scales* (i.e. scales that order things, as in first, second, third, etc.). However, I am convinced that those authors are wrong, due to a misunderstanding arising largely from confusing the ideas of Likert items and Likert scales (Brown, 2011b; Carifio & Perla, 2007).

In several places, Judy advocates the use of a 'multi-method' approach, as in the following: 'The most important thing I learned from this experience was to not to take data elicited in question-naires and interviews at face value.... This view justifies not only my own multi-method approach to exploring teachers' beliefs, but is also in line with the perspectives offered in all the other chapters in this volume.' I agree that multiple sources of information are typically more reliable than single sources, but I wonder if using a *multi-method approach* is enough? Is it sufficient to just use multiple data sources, or should researchers carefully triangulate two or three aspects of their research (e.g. data, times, locations, investigators, theories, methodologies, etc.; for more on these, see Brown, 2001)? As pointed out years ago by Fielding and Fielding (1986: 31), who were themselves qualitative researchers, if not applied judiciously, 'using several different methods can actually increase the chance of error. We should recognize that the multi-operational approach implies a good deal more than merely piling on of instruments.' Indeed, in the years since Fielding and Fielding wrote their book, a new research approach has surfaced called the *mixed-method approach*, wherein the researcher combines quantitative and qualitative techniques and data in such a way that they reinforce and cross-validate each other. The goal is to examine both similarities and differences in results from different sources to reveal what is happening in a particular research context. It may seem like I am quibbling over terminol-ogy by distinguishing between multi-method and mixed-method approaches. However, mixed-method research has established itself so firmly that some of my colleagues are using the terms *multiple method* or *multi-method* to refer to research that just throws many observational techniques together, mistakenly assuming that doing so will automatically make the research valid.

Methodological Implications

In this section, Judy outlines and discusses five important steps in using questionnaires: 'item writing; piloting; gaining and main-taining access; administering the questionnaire; gaining further participation'. Naturally, compiling, analysing and reporting ques-tionnaire results are also important steps. Judy's discussion here is useful because of the way she highlights her biggest problems: administration and participation. Novice researchers should pay

attention to her warnings that 'Actually administering the questionnaire was not straightforward' (they seldom realise this) and that
she had to change her strategy for 'gaining further participation'.

In my experience, the data-gathering phase of any research is
always the most difficult part of the project. This is particularly true
in interview/questionnaire research, perhaps because: (1) we must
rely on the goodwill of others, (2) everyone is a critical expert in a
sense (since most educated people have taken many surveys) and
(3) everyone perceives themselves as very busy. Overcoming such
difficulties is crucial because survey studies depend heavily on a high
response rate, not only for their success but also for their credibility.
In fact, I have seen studies live or die because of what happened at
this stage.

Fortunately, Judy instructively points to a solution for these
perpetual problems when she writes that 'The response rate
improved somewhat after I met the lecturers face to face to explain
in detail what involvement in my study would entail. I feel that
people respond well when the researcher is willing to spend time
with them individually and to answer all their enquiries about the
research.' This not only points to the importance of person-to-
person interactions in such research but also to the advantages of
being (or becoming) a non-threatening insider.

Reflection

In this section, Judy makes the point that her 'questionnaire was
not rigorously applied as is usually recommended in the literature
review'. She also points out that 'the researcher needs to be entirely
flexible in making decisions in the field about which data to collect,
and when, from which participants (of those who are willing and
able to cooperate)'. I agree 100% that second-language researchers
must be alert and flexible while gathering data. However, that does
not change the fundamental definition of our type of research,
which I take to be 'any systematic and principled inquiry in second
language studies' (Brown, 2011a: 190). The systematic principles of
research generally take the form of ensuring that the observations
and data analyses have qualities of *consistency, verifiability, fidelity*
and *meaningfulness*. This is accomplished in the quantitative research

tradition by addressing concepts like reliability, validity, replicability and generalisability, while in the qualitative research tradition researchers attend to analogous concepts like dependability, credibility, confirmability and transferability (Brown, 2001, 2004). Other approaches to these four basic concepts exist in mixed-methods research, conversational analysis, discourse analysis, ethnography and so on. When second-language researchers work within some set of systematic principles related to their research, reviewers and readers have a framework within which to place and judge the work other than its own documentation. In contrast, if that documentation can assume nothing from some established research approach, the study must provide a complete epistemology unto itself – a tall order indeed for any research report.

Judy concludes by saying that her 'eventual decision to compare and contrast lecturers from two different disciplinary areas allowed a valuable exploration of the beliefs and practices of academic staff who provide feedback on their students' written work'. That her research changed somewhat in purpose does not surprise me. Indeed, it is the anomalies in my own research over the years that I have found to be the most interesting and productive results – often leading to other research ideas that would never otherwise have occurred to me. I am not sure why some researchers believe that research is necessarily rigid and inflexible, when that need not be the case at all. As my colleague Kathy Davis once put it in a course that we were team-teaching on qualitative and quantitative research methods, 'If you don't find any surprises in your research, you're not doing it right'.

REFLECTIVE QUESTIONS

(1) What are some of the technical skills necessary to construct a good questionnaire?

(2) What sort of lessons can be learnt by piloting a questionnaire?

(3) Some researchers opt to use the four-point Likert-scale rather than a five-point scale, as some respondents might merely opt for a 'safe' middle ground. However, other researchers feel that respondents ought to be given a chance to choose the middle ground if their genuine feeling is neutral. What are your views regarding this issue?

(4) To what extent is the researcher's position as an insider/outsider important in using questionnaires to elicit data?

(5) There are several ways of distributing a questionnaire: conventionally posting it; using email; posting it on an internet website; administering it to a group; putting it in office 'pigeonholes'; handing it to individuals – and probably other ways. If you were to elicit information by means of a questionnaire in your study, which of these options would you choose, and why?

(6) What are the advantages and disadvantages of using questionnaires to recruit participants for further phases in a research project? Would you do this in your research? What other ways are there of recruiting participants?

(7) Construct a short set of questionnaire items in your first language. Then ask a native speaker of a second language to translate these into his or her language. Then ask someone else to back-translate the items into your first language. What differences do you notice?

References

Bazeley, P. (2007) *Qualitative Data Analysis with NVivo*. London: Sage.

Borg, S. (2006) *Teacher Cognition and Language Education: Research and Practice*. London: Continuum.

Brown, J.D. (2000) What issues affect Likert-scale questionnaire formats? *Shiken: JALT Testing & Evaluation SIG Newsletter*, 4(1), 27–30. Available at http://www.jalt.org/test/bro_7.htm.

Brown, J.D. (2001) *Using Surveys in Language Programs*. Cambridge: Cambridge University Press.

Brown, J.D. (2004) Research methods for applied linguistics: Scope, characteristics, and standards. In A. Davies and C. Elder (eds), *The Handbook of Applied Linguistics* (pp. 476–500). Oxford: Blackwell.

Brown, J.D. (2009) Open-response items in questionnaires. In J. Heigham and R.A. Croker (eds), *Qualitative Research in Applied Linguistics: A Practical Introduction* (pp. 200–219). New York: Palgrave Macmillan.

Brown, J.D. (2011a) Quantitative research in second language studies. In E. Hinkel (ed.), *Handbook of Research in Second Language Teaching and Learning, Volume 2* (pp. 190–206). New York: Routledge.

Brown, J.D. (2011b) Likert items and scales of measurement. *Shiken: JALT Testing & Evaluation SIG Newsletter*, 15(1), 10–14. Available at http://www.jalt.org/test/bro_34.htm.

Carifio, J. and Perla, R.J. (2007) Ten common misunderstandings, misconceptions, persistent myths and urban legends about Likert scales and Likert response formats and their antidotes. *Journal of Social Sciences*, 3(3), 106–116.

Clarke, C.M. and Peterson, P.L. (1986) Teachers' thought processes. In M.C. Wittrock (ed.), *Handbook of Research and Teaching* (pp. 255–296). New York: Macmillan.

Cohen, L., Manion, L. and Morrison, K. (2007) *Research Methods in Education* (6th edition). London: Routledge.

Creswell, J.W. (2005) *Educational Research: Planning, Conducting and Evaluating Quantitative and Qualitative Research* (2nd edition). Upper Saddle River, NJ: Pearson Education.

Dörnyei, Z. and Taguchi, T. (2010) *Questionnaires in Second Language Research Construction, Administration and Processing* (2nd edition). New York: Routledge.

Ferris, D.R. (1995) Student reactions to teacher response in multiple-draft composition classrooms. *TESOL Quarterly*, 29, 33–51.

Ferris, D. (2009) Theory, research, and practice in written corrective feedback: Bridging the gap, or crossing the chasm? *New Zealand Studies in Applied Linguistics*, 15(1), 1–12.

Fielding, N.G. and Fielding, J.L. (1986) *Linking Data*. Beverly Hills, CA: Sage.

Gillham, B. (2000) *Developing a Questionnaire*. London: Continuum.

Goldstein, L.M. (2005) *Teacher Written Commentary in Second Language Writing Classrooms*. Ann Arbor, MI: University of Michigan Press.

Iwai, T., Kondo, K., Lim, D.S.J., Ray, G., Shimizu, H. and Brown, J.D. (1999) *Japanese Language Needs Assessment 1998–1999* (NFLRC NetWork 13). Honolulu: University of Hawaii, Second Language Teaching and Curriculum Center. Available at http://www.lll.hawaii.edu/nflrc/NetWorks/NW13.

Lee, I. (2003) L2 writing teachers' perspectives, practices and problems regarding error feedback. *Assessing Writing*, 8(3), 216–237.

Lee, I. (2009) Ten mismatches between teachers' beliefs and written feedback practice. *ELT Journal*, 63(1), 13–22.

Littlewood, W. (2007) Communicative and task-based language teaching in East Asian classrooms. *Language Teaching*, 40, 243–249. Available at http://journals.cambridge.org, doi:10.1017/S0261444807004363.

Nunan, D. (2003) The impact of English as a global language on educational policies and practices in the Asia–Pacific region. *TESOL Quarterly*, 37(4), 589–613.

Truscott, J. (1996) The case against grammar correction in L2 writing classes. *Language Learning*, 46(2), 327–369.

Truscott, J. (2007) The effect of error correction on learners' ability to write accurately. *Journal of Second Language Writing*, 16(4), 255–272.

Wagner, E. (2010) Survey research. In B. Paltridge and A. Phakiti (eds), *Continuum Companion to Research Methods in Applied Linguistics* (pp. 22–38). London: Continuum.

Wilson, N. and McLean, S. (1994) *Questionnaire Design: A Practical Introduction*. Newtown Abbey: University of Ulster Press.

2 Narrative Frames

Case Study: Nguyen Gia Viet
Commentary: Martin Bygate

CASE STUDY

Introduction

This chapter reports part of a multi-method research project which investigated teachers' beliefs and practices regarding their readiness for task-based language teaching (TBLT) in the context of Vietnam. Specifically, it describes the use of 'narrative frames' (Barkhuizen & Wette, 2008), a form of guided composition, to elicit teachers' approaches to teaching and their experiences of recent lessons in relation to TBLT.

TBLT has received much interest from researchers and practitioners since the 1990s (e.g. Bygate, 1999; Littlewood, 2007; Nunan, 2004; Samuda & Bygate, 2008). This teaching approach, engaging learners in using the language meaningfully through tasks, has potential benefits for language development. Therefore, it has been adopted by language policy-makers in Asia as the leading methodology in English-language curricula, although in practice it has encountered challenges and barriers (Littlewood, 2007). In Vietnam, a recently launched curriculum based on a mandatory set of textbooks for English-language learning and teaching in high schools is claimed to be 'adopting a communicative approach, in which task-based language teaching serves as the principal methodology' (Hoang *et al.*, 2006: 12).

However, research has indicated that there is often a gap between the *intended* and *realised* versions of curricular innovations, because the perceptions of teachers – the key decision-makers – have not usually been taken into account (MacDonald, 1991; McGee, 1997). Language teacher cognition, therefore, has been increasingly researched over the past two decades (Borg, 2006). This area of research is important because 'what teachers say and do in the classroom is strongly governed by their tacitly held beliefs' (Farrell, 2007: 35). Given the situation in Vietnam, where teachers, who are still used to traditional methods of teaching (e.g. Canh & Barnard, 2009), are required to use task-based textbooks, what teachers know, think and believe about TBLT, as well as how they apply TBLT strategies in their classroom teaching, need to be investigated.

This chapter reports and discusses the use of narrative frames. First, it reviews narrative enquiry and the use of narrative frames. It then goes on to describe the wider study and particularly the procedures used to collect narrative frames. Samples of data are then presented. The following section discusses in detail the implications of using this tool, and this is followed by some reflection.

Methodological Focus

Researchers applying narrative forms of data collection have commented on the advantages this approach presents. For example, both Creswell (2005) and Murray (2009) point out that narrative accounts make personal experiences in actual school settings easily accessible, and allow participants' voices to be heard. Creswell also points to the possibility that researchers and participants establish mutual trust, which should help to reduce the perception that teaching and research are separate activities. Pavlenko (2007) regards narratives as not only accessible but also aesthetically interesting and – because of the reflection involved – empowering to the participants.

Although little research on teacher cognition has relied on narratives, I chose this approach for my study because I believed that teachers' beliefs can be captured through their stories. I felt that participant teachers would welcome the opportunity to reveal factors contributing to classroom dilemmas, their emotions, their beliefs and the consequences of their teaching practice (Johnson & Golombek, 2002). However simple their stories might be, they would remain a useful source of data, in that 'they are able to accommodate the complexity of ongoing stories being told' (France, 2010: 92).

Barkhuizen and Wette (2008) designed 'narrative frames' to scaffold research participants unaccustomed to writing such accounts, when they ran workshops on language teaching methodology for English-language teachers in China. This form of guided composition consisted of a number of 'frames', each of which focused on a particular topic, and comprised a number of sentence starters that prompted participants to express their ideas and experiences. According to Barkhuizen and Wette (2008: 375, italics in original):

The concept of *narrative frames* is based on a similar concept in the field of writing education. *Writing frames* are used to provide a 'skeleton to scaffold writing' (Warwick & Maloch, 2003: 59). They are comprised of a template of 'starters, connectives and sentence modifiers which give children a structure within which they can concentrate on communicating what they want to say whilst scaffolding them in the use of a particular generic form' (Wray & Lewis, 1997: 122).

Narrative frames, therefore, are facilitative, rather than constraining, and help participants to construct meaningful stories – the frames to a certain degree allow narrators to express what they want to say. As an adaptation of Barkhuizen and Wette's (2008) method, the frames reported here consisted of three parts. The first two parts were intended to elicit teachers' personal approaches to language teaching and learning; the third part, the actual narratives, elicited teachers' stories of recent experience in specific lessons. In this way, these frames prompted the participants to move in stages from reporting their beliefs to narrating their experiences, while gaining familiarity with the procedure through completing one part at a time.

The Study

The wider study used a multi-method approach to data collection: sets of narrative frames, audio-recorded lesson planning sessions, classroom observations (see Chapter 5), stimulated recall discussions (see Chapter 7) based on the observation, and focus groups (see Chapter 3). The narrative frames were collected from 23 teachers from three schools in a suburban area in central Vietnam. These teachers, ranging from 25 to 40 years in age, all held a BA degree in English-language teaching, and had between 2 and 13 years of teaching experience.

My experience with the teachers and their academic background showed that these practising teachers were not familiar with TBLT, although they had been using the mandated textbooks for several years. The teachers in this study had attended textbook training workshops once a year, each of which dealt with one textbook. In these workshops, they were taught how to teach lessons in the textbook and watched 'model lessons', each of which dealt with one skill or language focus. In these workshops, however, no reference was made to TBLT as an innovation. My initial experience with the teachers led me to assume that TBLT seemed to be a foreign concept to them and that it would be difficult to explicitly ask them about this methodology.

Data collection was carried out as follows. The project began with a series of workshops which covered the principles of TBLT, organised on three consecutive Sundays in December 2009. In an interactive format, the workshops provided the participants with understandings of tasks, task types and task applications.

The narrative frames were mainly distributed and collected during the workshop sessions. As noted above, the narrative frames were divided into three parts, on separate sheets of paper, each of which was to be completed after one of the workshops. The teachers were instructed to read through the page to get a general idea of what to write, and in what way. They were also encouraged to ask questions before taking the frames home for completion, and were reminded to bring the completed frames to the next workshop.

Narrative data samples

Although the focus of the chapter is on the use of narrative frames, I would like to present three samples of the data obtained to provide the reader with a deeper grasp of this tool. (The original frames were written in Vietnamese. Sentence starters are in *italics*.)

Teacher 6

Part 1
In my opinion, to learn English well, students need to be provided with frequent practice. *Therefore, teachers need to always* clearly identify the objectives of the lesson, frequently research and be creative, concretize and realize the objectives of the lesson so as to motivate students to engage in their learning.

The success of an English lesson is much subject to the presentation of the teacher, especially the presentation must be clear, *because* once students understand the rules and how to do exercises, they will participate enthusiastically and thus the lesson will be more effective.

Part 2
I think students need not *master grammar rules, because* they are not a deciding factor of communication. *Therefore, the most important thing in learning on the part of students is* that they must incorporate harmoniously all the skills.

Part 3
A lesson that I recently taught was a speaking *lesson. The topic of the lesson is* World Population. *The lesson required students to* speak about causes to over-population, the problems facing over-populated countries

and poor countries, as well as suggest solutions to the problems. *The most successful part of the lesson is* that students could produce a list of problems and solutions. *However, I noticed students had difficulty in* finding words and structures to express meaning, *because* they lack structures and vocabulary of this area, and they mainly read out answers from a piece of paper. *I solved the problem by* dividing students in groups, one group find problems, one group find solutions, then put them together to share information and report to the whole class. *The lesson could have been better if* I had prepared the task more carefully, given more detailed instructions, set a time limit for the task, and clearly assigned each group a distinctive task.

Teacher 10

Part 1
In my opinion, to learn English well, students need to be provided with a repertoire of vocabulary and grammar structures, and a learning/communicative environment in which students can practice frequently. *Therefore, teachers need to always* reinforce their knowledge, have a teaching methodology appropriate to their own students, and create motivating environments for students. At the end of each lesson, teachers should get students to relax by providing games or songs, such as asking students to listen and fill in missing words in the song.

The success of an English lesson is much subject to students' capacity of acquiring language and the teacher's methodology of transmitting knowledge, *because* if students play a key role in communication with the teacher's effective guidance, the lesson is likely to engage much language use.

Part 2
I think students need *to master grammar rules, because* students will speak and write correctly. *Therefore, the most important thing in learning on the part of students is* to have a diverse repertoire of vocabulary, a firm repertoire of grammar structures and also some aptitude of foreign language learning.

Part 3
A lesson that I recently taught was a reading *lesson. The topic of the lesson is* 'the story of my village'. *The lesson required students to* learn the changes in the country and relate to where they live. *The most successful part of the lesson is* that students were able to tell the changes in the country. *However, I noticed students had difficulty in* expressing meaning in sentences, *because*

they usually made mistakes in pronunciation, vocabulary and grammar structures. *I solved the problem by* providing some more words necessary for the lesson, correcting students' pronunciation mistakes, and giving them more structures. *The lesson could have been better if* students worked harder, had known well the grammar and vocabulary, as well as related the lesson with their real life.

Teacher 15

Part 1
In my opinion, to learn English well, students need to be provided with constant practice and the opportunities to use the language. *Therefore, teachers need to always* find different ways, including new methods of teaching, to create various opportunities in which students can practice the language. Teachers also need to be flexible in teaching.

The success of an English lesson is much subject to the teacher's ability to design a lesson, because if [the] teacher is flexible and creative in designing lessons that suit her own students, the lessons will be easier and thus effective.

Part 2
I think students need *to master grammar rules, because* this is very important for their future examinations. It is even more important for those students who would like to sit for category D exam [university entrance exam that tests foreign language knowledge]. *Therefore, the most important thing in learning on the part of students is* that they must determine what their focus is for the future. Students who will take part in category D exam must know the grammar well, while those who won't only need to focus on fluency.

Part 3
A lesson that I recently taught was a writing *lesson. The topic of the lesson is* the Sahara Desert. *The lesson required students to* use information in the textbook to write. *The most successful part of the lesson is* they could make use of the outline provided to write enthusiastically. *However, I noticed students had difficulty in* using structures and vocabulary, *because* they don't practice frequently. *I solved the problem by* providing them with structures and vocabulary closely related to the lesson topic. *The lesson could have been better if* I had given students situations specific and close to the lesson, and allowed them more time to practice.

In general, these teachers' personal approaches and attitudes towards grammar teaching and the stories they tell appear to be contradictory. There is a divergence between their personal approaches and their reported classroom practices. On the one hand, they wrote that communicative activities play an important role in motivating students to learn. For example, teacher 6 expressed the view that students need to incorporate skills, rather than master grammar forms. On the other hand, their attitudes and stories reveal their strong belief in the value of explicit form-focused instruction, where most of them emphasised the role of grammar in language use, and the need for their students to produce language correctly in terms of grammar, vocabulary and pronunciation. In this respect, their reports may be perceived as merely paying lip service to communicative language teaching (CLT) (Hu, 2002) and a divergence from TBLT principles (Ellis, 2003; Nunan, 2004; Willis, 1996) can be interpreted from their reported approaches and stories. In this respect, their views, like those expressed in other empirical studies (e.g. Canh & Barnard, 2009; Pham, 2007; Tomlinson & Dat, 2004), reflect their inability to *realise* an ambitious *intended* curriculum.

Methodological Implications

Here I discuss in detail implications arising from this study, specifically the issues of administration, tool familiarity, the choice of language, truth value, ethical issues and data analysis, as well as limitations.

In terms of *administration*, there are a number of important factors that needed to be considered. Firstly, to ensure a maximum rate of return, most frames were delivered and collected during the workshops, although there were occasions when I had to remind participants to complete and return the frames after the workshops. In this study, unlike that of Barkhuizen and Wette (2008), I had the opportunity to go back to individual participants for further clarification and completion of the frames. Secondly, it was decided to divide the frames into separate parts, each to be completed before starting the next one, thus reducing the task burden at any one time. Thirdly, the participants were encouraged to read through each part of the frame before writing a response; in this way, it was hoped that what the teachers eventually wrote within each frame would be coherent.

Tool familiarity is an important issue. As noted by Barkhuizen (1995), writing reflectively for the first time is not always easy and this was true for my participants. Compared with questionnaires and interviews, writing narratives was an unfamiliar procedure for these participants and it took some time for them to feel comfortable. Questions such as 'What do you want me to say?' or 'Can you give me a clue?' had to be treated very tactfully. Some of the teachers' first attempts were short, tentative and, frankly, somewhat unreflective, and some contained 'a list of uncon-nected ideas' (Bakhuizen & Wette, 2008: 382); however, as they gained both familiarity and confidence in the procedure, they wrote at more length and more easily, coherently and critically. In the second and third frames, some teachers began to feel constrained by having to write within a frame, which they sometimes felt might not allow them to express their ideas fully; they were encouraged to write beyond the set boundaries if they wished to.

The *choice of language* is another matter to be considered. Even though the participants were teachers of English, the decision to use Vietnamese in all these frames, and in the task instructions, was crucial. I considered that using their first language would enable the participants to express themselves more thoughtfully and clearly than in English. I also felt that it was less threatening and easier for them to do so – an important matter given the novelty of completing narrative frames.

The *truth value* of the data should also be taken into account. The information provided in these frames presents the same potential threats to reliability as any other self-report method, however rigorously and consistently the procedures of data collection and analysis are carried out, and however transparently and honestly the findings are reported. It may be that the participants are not consciously aware of aspects of their own activity, and consequently they may unwittingly provide misleading data, or simply fail to provide necessary information. Even when they are fully cognisant, they may not be willing to disclose their knowledge to others, despite voluntarily participating in a research project. Such unwillingness might arise for various reasons, among them the perceived threat to their personal or professional position. In my case, with such a small number of participants, it was possible for me to build trust through various shared professional and social activities. However, in narrative enquiry, and especially in the case of the Part 3 frame in this study, it is possible that participants sometimes fictionalised their stories. Bell (2002: 209), though, claims that it is relatively unimportant that the stories are true, because:

[narrative] inquiry goes beyond the specific stories to explore the assumptions inherent in the shaping of those stories. No matter how fictionalised, all stories rest on and illustrate the story structures a person holds. As such they provide a window into people's beliefs and experiences.

Ethical issues need to be carefully addressed. As Morrison (1998: 186) notes: 'despite assurances that the work is "academic" one is never quite sure that the explanation is accepted'. Therefore, in order to avoid any suspicion of 'hidden agendas', all questions or concerns on the part of the potential participants were encouraged and fully addressed. On the basis of this information, the teachers were then asked to consent to participate and they were made aware that they could withdraw their participation at any time, with no need to give any reason for so doing. It is also strictly required that the data provided by participants are treated in confidence and their privacy is safeguarded.

In the case of narrative frames, this may present a dilemma to the researchers. If participants can be assured that their privacy can be entirely guaranteed because each narrative will be completed anonymously, and thus no one will know who has written what, then they are likely to write more fully and freely and perhaps (self-)critically. On the other hand, anonymous reports would not enable the researchers to follow up specific points made in the individual narratives in subsequent phases of the project. In the present case, it was decided that the participants should be invited to write their names on each frame, after being assured that only the researcher would know the identity of the writer and would not in any circumstances divulge the actual sources of any information thus derived. In this sense, the privacy of the individuals was in fact revealed (to the researcher) but their confidentiality was ensured. This does not altogether resolve the issue of truth value, but there is sufficient internal evidence among the narratives to suggest that the writers were being as honest as possible. To the extent that this is so, as mentioned, it is due to the academic and professional trust that was built up during the workshop sessions and after.

Concerning *the analysis of the data*, as with other forms of qualitative research (e.g. interviews), the narrative frames were subjected to the constant comparative methods of grounded analysis (Charmaz, 2006) and use was made of the software program NVivo8 (Bazeley, 2007). A preliminary analysis of the narrative data was carried out based on themes derived from the sentence starters in the frames. Barkhuizen and Wette (2008) point out that the structured nature of the data makes for easier analysis than if the stories were entirely free-flowing. In this study, the next step was to read all the narratives to compare and contrast the points within them; this was done by coding the data with ideas or events that emerged and re-emerged across the frames. Following this step, connections between the codes were identified and these links were grouped into categories and themes, 'to uncover the commonalities that exist across the stories that make up a study's database' (Polkinghorne, 1995: 14). The categories and themes were then revisited by comparing and contrasting them to features of TBLT. It was at this stage that the teachers' beliefs in relation to TBLT were generated. These beliefs would be a useful platform for analysis in subsequent phases of the wider project.

There were, inevitably, some limitations of the narrative frames, both in general and in this particular study. Although the original authors (Barkhuizen & Wette, 2008) discuss limitations of their specific research, some of which were relevant in my study, there were several others that I think are important. Firstly, the limited number of participants meant that it was not possible to generalise beyond the actual case histories, or to make any more than a tentative composite picture of a particular community of practice. Secondly, as previously indicated, the issue inevitably arises of the truth value of what the participants wrote: although in the present case there were opportunities to triangulate the narratives with other sources of data, the ultimate subjectivity of both the narrators and those analysing the data needs to be acknowledged. Another issue was to do with the specific topic that this study investigated. When analysing data in relation to TBLT, I found that I should have designed the frames in such a way that they usefully elicited relevant data. For example, the first sentence starter in Part 3 said, '*A lesson that I recently taught was a* (reading/listening /speaking/ writing/grammar) *lesson*'. Although I was interested in how teachers carried out tasks in skills lessons, several teachers simply chose to report grammar lessons in their frames.

Reflection

Narrative frames were useful and relevant in this study. They allowed respondents to provide as much information as they wished to give because frames are more open-ended than questionnaires. Participants also had more freedom to divulge information than might have been the case in potentially face-threatening interviews. Barkhuizen and Wette (2008) list a number of strengths of narrative frames which make it easy for participants to write. The sentence starters and connectors 'enable the teachers to write narratively by scaffolding them through the specially designed narrative structure, and they encourage reflection because of the nature of what they are required to write' (Barkhuizen & Wette, 2008: 381). What is important about this study, and different from the many surveys which have been carried out into teachers' attitudes, is that the participants' voices can be clearly represented through these narrative frames.

I have discussed how narrative frames were used to elicit teachers' personal approaches and experiences in the context of Vietnamese high schools. This was the first time that this tool had been applied in this context and was for me – as well as the participants – a valuable learning experience.

In spite of the various constraints and limitations, I feel that I have obtained some useful data, and in the process learnt more about my participants and how better to elicit valuable data from them. I would recommend that other teacher-researchers make similar efforts to engage with the complex world of language teaching through some form of narrative enquiry.

Acknowledgement

An earlier version of this case study was published in *Language Education in Asia*, 1(1), 77–86. It is published here with kind permission from *Language Education in Asia*.

COMMENTARY

In understanding teachers' thinking, it is clearly essential to find ways of eliciting their thoughts. Narrative frames involve providing participants with unfinished sentences, which give the respondents a topic focus, and then having participants complete the sentences in writing as they wish. Nguyen Gia Viet uses the procedure to investigate teachers' perspectives on TBLT in Vietnam. Narrative frames could be used to elicit participants' perspectives on a range of different aspects of their teaching. In this study, the teachers summarise their understanding of key aspects of teaching and learning, and choose a lesson which they had recently taught to describe it and comment on it.

As Viet says, the procedure can make it easier for informants to select what they want to say and to choose how to say it, while reducing threats to their 'face'. This implies that the procedure is relatively high in trustworthiness (or validity – Edge & Richards, 1998). Viet correctly notes that 'trustworthiness' can still not be guaranteed, but that it can be cross-checked against other data sources. He points out that careful use of analytical procedures can enable researchers to identify similarities and differences across a number of individual narratives. One of the recurrent themes of the actual data Viet provides is the possibility that teachers accept that communicative language use is important, and at the same time that they seem to prioritise accuracy for attention. How far might the notion of 'communicative accuracy' make sense to these teachers? I briefly return to this point at the end of this commentary.

There are three distinct questions prompted by the use of this kind of procedure: What is the context for its use? What question or puzzle is it intended to illuminate? And what kinds of data does it generate?

Firstly, I look at the context in which the procedure is used. The focus on TBLT sets a particular type of challenge. TBLT is an innovation which is promoted both by the research community and by educational authorities and, as Bygate *et al.* (2009: 497–498) point out, possibly the single most important problem in exploring the potential of TBLT is that, to date, its implementation has been a subject of academic or ministerial dictat, rather than being handled as a potential classroom-based professional and institutional innovation. Teachers' perspectives have often been neglected and a focus on teachers' perceptions is now timely. With this in mind, it is important to note that in his study Viet was seeking teachers' narratives on an approach to teaching that is relatively new and unfamiliar. It is therefore relevant to ask what history the informants have of using TBLT and what they know about it from sources outside the classroom. This is because, although TBLT is an innovation for teachers, they may not know much about it. Hence it is important for the reader to understand the contextual background in which the methodology is being used if the purpose is to assess the research methodology.

This leads to the second point: what question or puzzle is the procedure intended to illuminate? This question is important. If we are interested in how successful the narrative frames are in providing the kinds of information that we are seeking, a measure of this is how well they do the job we want them to do. A fishing net is a useful piece of equipment if you go fishing, but we would use a different net for different-size fish. For some fish (such as tuna) we would be better not using a net at all. What we need, then, is to see the procedure doing its job. In this respect too, it matters how familiar the teachers are with TBLT. If they are very familiar with it (whether in theory or practice) they can be expected to write about it. If the teachers are not familiar at all with TBLT, then the focus might be usefully changed: instead of trying to explore their perspectives on TBLT (which the teachers may not be ready to say much about), the narrative frames might be better used to find out their perspectives on familiar practices pre-TBLT: what current practices they like and dislike, and their attitudes to change. This would be helpful in preparing for the introduction of TBLT. On the other hand, if the teachers have just recently started to become familiar with TBLT, they may need more guidance from the framing sentences. In that case the framing sentences might be used to investigate teachers' initial perspectives on TBLT, or on limited aspects of the approach, and perhaps to relate their ideas about TBLT to their more familiar practices.

The third – and perhaps the most important – question to ask is what kinds of data the procedure generates, and more particularly in this case, what kinds of 'narrative', which is what the study aims to gather. A fundamental aspect of self-report data is the extent to which they are influenced by the researcher. The data can be influenced for example by the researcher's choice of topics, the choice of issues that the researcher raises about the topics and even the language that the researcher chooses to use. Framing devices can be seen as a form of relatively unstructured interview (see Chapter 4): the researcher identifies a few topics and leaves teacher-informants to respond as they wish – a freedom which Viet rightly notes. However, whereas an interviewer could ask for a bit more information – such as clarification, or elaboration or exemplification – the use of the written medium means that the direction and amount of detail are entirely in the hands of the teacher-informant. This may result in something different from a narrative.

More generally, if narrative is what is wanted, then a key question is, what kinds of narrative, and why? In what ways does a person's narrative account (as opposed to other kinds of discourse) help to shed valuable light on teachers' thinking? One limitation in the examples provided is that the use of the short extracts from the various informants makes it hard to see how the individuals' accounts unfold discursively through the writing, how their written account of their own beliefs and actions develops. If the purpose is to elicit a coherent narrative, it might have been valuable to be shown one or two whole narratives, to be taken through a reading of each one, and then to be drawn to appreciate the particular value of eliciting extended writing through the use of limited prompts. This would help to show more clearly what advantages can be gained by using personal written narratives, rather than, say, semi-structured interviews. If I may, I would like to consider this point a bit more closely.

The frames are used to shape the narratives into three 'parts', as in Table 2.1.

Table 2.1 Sentence frames used in the research

Part 1 frames

In my opinion, to learn English well, students need to be provided with..................
Therefore, teachers need to always...
The success of an English lesson is much subject to..

Part 2 frames

I think students............to master grammar rules, because...............................
Therefore, the most important thing in learning on the part of students is.............

Part 3 frames

A lesson that I recently taught was a ....lesson.
The topic of the lesson is...
The lesson required students to..
The most successful part of the lesson is..
However, I noticed students had difficulty in ....because ....
I solved the problem by ....
The lesson could have been better if...

Part 1 seems to invite participants to identify one or more key principles of learning and teaching – a very general level of reflection. So the first frame asks respondents to identify one or more key provisions: the phrasing could be read to imply a focus on *one* key provision, although semantically the frame is in fact open to a whole list of things that might need to be provided. This could be seen as quite constraining. The second frame shifts the focus to what the teacher needs to do, but the word 'always' requires the respondent to identify a constant provision – possibly in terms of essential elements for all lessons – again, a potential constraint on the narrative. Note that this implies a high level of generality, since the response must apply to lessons at all levels of proficiency and across all skills. The final frame in Part 1 focuses on what makes a lesson successful. This could include things mentioned in the previous two frames, but could extend well beyond them to include motivation, relationships with the teacher and classmates, classroom facilities, or even family circumstances. So the focus of the frames in Part 1 seems fairly wide and there is some possibility of overlap between the frames provided.

The focus of Part 2 is also wide. It asks participants' views on students' mastery of grammar rules and requires them to identify the single most important element in learning. This could overlap with what the teacher reported in Part 1. It is worth noting that Part 2 explicitly requires participants to nominate *one* most important element: here respondents are not required, encouraged or even allowed to suggest more than one. One striking aspect of both Parts 1 *and* 2, then, is that they do not generate genuine 'narrative' discourse, in the sense of a report of a sequence of events, but rather aim to elicit basic beliefs. Maybe the purpose here is to provide an introductory background for the following narrative. Yet the layout may not make that potential connection clear – indeed, that connection may not be intended.

Part 3 shifts the focus to a specific lesson recently taught by the teacher. It is noticeable that the frames used for Part 3 are a bit closer to narrative, because two of the frames specifically report actions or events ('I noticed...' and 'I solved the problem by...'), three frames provide background to the events and two of the frames were evaluative in orientation ('The most successful part of the lesson is...' and 'The lesson could have been better if...'). None of the frames here (or in Parts 1 and 2) actually mentions the term 'task' or 'TBLT', so presumably the focus is on the teachers' thinking around a sample lesson. The informants are free to choose whichever lesson they wish to talk about – it could be a typical lesson, or it could be a highly unusual lesson. Note that the frames leave it open to the teachers to decide how they will describe the kind and topic of the lesson.

Similarly, in responding to the frame 'The lesson required students to...', teachers are presumably free to choose whatever things they wish to comment on, and as many or as few as they wish (notice that a single lesson can require students to do quite a number of different but related things). Including a frame such as this can presumably enable the researcher to find out what teachers spontaneously think of and how they talk about it. Notice that there is a similar choice in the next frame, 'The most successful part of the lesson is...', although here teachers are once again explicitly asked to nominate just one instance of success: it is possible that some lessons were successful in various ways, but this frame may have been designed on the assumption that teachers typically recall one main aspect of a lesson.

However, the reader might wonder how teachers' responses can be interpreted – whether as a reflection of the teachers' *values* (that is, what they think is most important), as a reflection of their *perceptions* (i.e. teachers will typically notice some things more readily than others), or simply as a reflection of the *actual lesson*. It is worth commenting also that Part 3 includes two frames which assume that the teacher spotted a difficulty that the learners were having during the lesson and that the teacher then improvised a solution. Here the reader might ask whether the frame is forcing the teachers to identify, and possibly imagine, problems retrospectively which were not necessarily salient at the time of the lesson.

One final point concerns the possibility of ambiguity in the focus of some of the frames. This can be seen in some of the responses. For example, the frame *'The most successful part of the lesson is'* elicited the following responses:

- Of a speaking lesson, Teacher 6 wrote: 'that students could produce a list of problems and solutions'.
- Teacher 10 reported of a reading lesson: 'that students were able to tell the changes in the country'.
- Teacher 15, reporting on a writing lesson, stated: 'they could make use of the outline provided to write enthusiastically'.

It is possible that all three teachers are reporting success in their students' use of some macro-skill. However, it is not clear that the teachers are actually reflecting on a *part* of the lesson, or that they are clear about what they mean by 'success'. Also, it is difficult to interpret from the answers how far the success in each case was an unexpected achievement, or whether the students were in fact already able to do these things, or indeed whether the success of the students of Teachers 6 and 10 reflected background knowledge that the students had prior to the lesson.

In summary, Parts 1 and 2 are not strictly 'narrative' in style, are fairly general and offer some potential for overlap. Part 3 is distinct in that it requires the teachers to comment on a particular lesson that they taught. In general, the frames allow the teachers freedom to identify and verbalise responses as they wish, but some frames constrain the teachers by stating or implying that they should mention only one key feature, and more particularly by requiring teachers to note a problem that arose and a solution that was found. The flow of thought on the part of the teachers is to some extent constrained by the fact that it is prompted at each step by a new sentence frame.

The questions that I am raising here do not mean that the data are not useful. But as an outside reader, there are ambiguities about written self-reports such as these. An interviewer working through a semi-structured interview schedule would have made a point of teasing out many of these points. Of course, Viet is quite right that face-to-face interviews can pose problems of openness: if not conducted carefully, interviews can be quite threatening. However, the big advantage interviews offer is the opportunity to ask for clarification at each step of the way. It would be good to home in more closely on the qualities of narrative frame methodology and to bring out more clearly what is distinctive about this methodology.

Finally, underlying many of my comments is a fairly constant theme, which is fundamental to discussion of any self-report data. This is that, whatever the nature of the study, and whatever the nature of the data, research involves someone seeking answers to questions or responses to puzzles. The agency of the 'someone' is important – important in deciding what questions or puzzles to explore. Someone in the end has to 'own' the puzzles or the questions – the puzzles or questions must correspond to someone's own beliefs, values and concerns. This is just as important as the agency and ownership of the teachers in providing the data. So in considering the use of narrative frames, the issue remains: whose puzzles or questions, and about what? Are we really using narrative accounts to focus on the teachers' thinking about tasks? Or is the focus that emerges rather different? Unless we can sharpen the definition of those puzzles or questions, it will remain hard to evaluate the procedure. However well constructed the fishing net, unless there are fish in the water, and unless we see whether they are caught in the net or go through the holes, or whether other kinds of fishing equipment might do the same job, it will be difficult to gauge the value of the procedure.

REFLECTIVE QUESTIONS

(1) What are the advantages and disadvantages of using narrative frames as compared with (a) questionnaires and (b) interviews?

(2) Do you think such frames can be validly used for non-narrative or other purposes?

(3) How much do you think it matters if participants do not tell the literal truth in these frames? How would this affect your research?

(4) In your context, which language would you ask your respondents to use in completing these frames? Why?

(5) How can data from (narrative) frames best be analysed?

(6) Compare Viet's use narrative frames with the oral reflective journals used by Jenny Field in her Timor-Leste project (see Chapter 8).

(7) Construct a frame (narrative or otherwise) to elicit useful data for a research project you have in mind. Try it out on a colleague or two.

References

Barkhuizen, G. (1995) Dialogue journals in teacher education revisited. *College ESL*, 5(1), 22–35.

Barkhuizen, G. and Wette, R. (2008) Narrative frames for investigating the experiences of language teachers. *System*, 36(3), 372–387.

Bazeley, P. (2007) *Qualitative Data Analysis with NVivo*. London: Sage.

Bell, J.S. (2002) Narrative inquiry: More than just telling stories. *TESOL Quarterly*, 36(2), 207–213.

Borg, S. (2006) *Teacher Cognition and Language Education: Research and Practice*. London: Continuum.

Bygate, M. (1999) Task as context for the framing, reframing and unframing of language. *System*, 27(1), 33–48.

Bygate, M., Norris, J. and Van den Branden, K. (2009) Understanding TBLT at the interface between research and pedagogy. In K. Van den Branden, M. Bygate and J.M. Norris (eds), *Task-Based Language Teaching: A Reader* (pp. 405–499). Amsterdam: John Benjamins.

Canh, L.V. and Barnard, R. (2009) Curricular innovation behind closed classroom doors: A Vietnamese case study. *Prospect*, 24(2), 20–33.

Charmaz, K. (2006) *Constructing Grounded Theory: A Practical Guide Through Qualitative Analysis*. London: Sage.

Creswell, J.W. (2005) *Educational Research: Planning, Conducting, and Evaluating Quantitative and Qualitative Research* (2nd edition). Upper Saddle River, NJ: Pearson Education.

Edge, J. and Richards, K. (1998) May I see your warrant, please? Justifying outcomes in qualitative research. *Applied Linguistics*, 19(3), 334–356.

Ellis, R. (2003) *Task-Based Language Learning and Teaching*. Oxford: Oxford University Press.

Farrell, T.S.C. (2007) *Reflective Language Teaching: From Research to Practice*. London: Continuum.

France, B. (2010) Narrative interrogation: Constructing parallel stories. In S. Rodrigues (ed.), *Using Analytical Frameworks for Classroom Research: Collecting Data and Analysing Narrative* (pp. 90–108). Oxford: Routledge.

Hoang, V., Hoang, H.X., Do, M.T., Nguyen, P.T. and Nguyen, T.Q. (2006) *Tieng Anh 10: Sach giao vien [English 10: Teachers' Book]*. Hanoi: Education Publishing House.

Hu, G. (2002) Potential cultural resistance to pedagogical imports: The case of communicative language teaching in China. *Language, Culture and Curriculum*, 15(2), 93–105.

Johnson, K. and Golombek, P.R. (eds) (2002) *Teachers' Narrative Inquiry as Professional Development*. Cambridge: Cambridge University Press.

Littlewood, W. (2007) Communicative and task-based language teaching in East Asian classrooms. *Language Teaching*, 40(3), 243–249.

MacDonald, B. (1991) Introduction. In J. Rudduck (ed.), *Innovation and Change* (pp. 1–7). Milton Keynes: Open University Press.

McGee, C. (1997) *Teachers and Curriculum Decision-Making*. Palmerston North: Dunmore Press.

Morrison, D.E. (1998) *The Search for a Method: Focus Groups and the Development of Mass Communication Research*. Luton: University of Luton Press.

Murray, G. (2009) Narrative inquiry. In J. Heigham and R.A. Croker (eds), *Qualitative Research in Applied Linguistics: A Practical Introduction* (pp. 45–65). Basingstoke: Palgrave Macmillan.

Nunan, D. (2004) *Task-Based Language Teaching*. Cambridge: Cambridge University Press.

Pavlenko, A. (2007) Autobiographic narratives as data in applied linguistics. *Applied Linguistics*, 28(2), 163–188.

Pham, H.H. (2007) Communicative language teaching: Unity within diversity. *ELT Journal*, 61(3), 193–201.

Polkinghorne, D.E. (1995) Narrative configuration in qualitative analysis. *Qualitative Studies in Education*, 8(1), 5–23.

Samuda, V. and Bygate, M. (2008) *Tasks in Second Language Learning*. Basingstoke: Palgrave Macmillan.

Tomlinson, B. and Dat, B. (2004) The contributions of Vietnamese learners of English to ELT methodology. *Language Teaching Research*, 8(2), 199.

Warwick, P. and Maloch, B. (2003) Scaffolding speech and writing in the primary classroom: A consideration of work with literature and science pupil groups in the USA and UK. *Reading*, 37(2), 54–63.

Willis, J. (1996) *A Framework for Task-Based Learning*. Harlow: Longman.

Wray, D. and Lewis, M. (1997) *Extending Literacy: Children Reading and Writing Non-fiction*. London: Routledge.

3 Focus Groups

Case Study: Andrew Gladman
Commentary: Donald Freeman

CASE STUDY

Introduction

The research described in this chapter constituted the first of three linked phases within a PhD project designed to investigate team-teaching at a Japanese institution of tertiary education (Gladman, 2009). This institution, Miyazaki International College (MIC), is a liberal arts college using English as its medium of instruction. Within nearly all of its first-year and second-year classes, MIC employs an unusual team-teaching practice, called collaborative interdisciplinary team-teaching (CITT). In each CITT class, a specialist in teaching English to speakers of other languages (TESOL) and a specialist in the academic subject of the class integrate their specialties to team-teach English language and the academic subject in parallel, as derived from content-based language instruction (CBLI) models (Brinton *et al.*, 1989). The team-teachers adopt a highly collaborative approach, teaching each course jointly as equal partners, being present together in the classroom at all lesson times and sharing responsibility for all aspects of their course, including lesson planning, materials development, assessment and evaluation.

At the time of the study, I was a TESOL specialist at MIC, and the only person conducting research into CITT. Although it was evident that research into team-teaching was not uncommon in the TESOL literature, particularly with reference to the JET programme in Japan (Miyazato, 2006), such research was largely focused on unidisciplinary language instruction (i.e. two language teachers working in collaboration). There was potential for further research to explore less prevalent interdisciplinary collaborations, and CITT was particularly inviting in the sense that it represented 'high-end' collaboration (i.e. the teaching partners were expected to collaborate at every stage) across multiple classes for indefinite periods. MIC was unique in being the first tertiary-education institution in Japan to implement inter-disciplinary team-teaching across its entire curriculum (Stewart, 1996).

Although some MIC faculty had published on the subject of CITT in the past (e.g. Sagliano & Greenfield, 1998; Sagliano *et al.*, 1998), their publications had tended to be reflective in nature, typically discussing their experiences as CITT practitioners. A notable exception was an interview-based study by Perry and Stewart (2005), which aimed to investigate team-teachers' perceptions of CITT and identify common categories of response. However, though useful for comparative purposes, their study had certain limitations (see next section) and had been conducted almost five years earlier than my study; and there had been substantial turnover in the faculty body since that time. It was therefore decided that my first research study should start afresh, in the sense of taking an exploratory approach towards its subject, allowing initial data to emerge that could be used to guide the direction of successive CITT studies.

As a whole, my mixed-method approach (see Chapter 1 for discussion) to data collection investigated how classroom participants defined what CITT was, identified its important elements and described what they believed constituted effective or ineffective team-teaching. The first phase, using focus groups, elicited data from two small groups of practising team-teachers at MIC. The second applied online questionnaires (see Chapter 1) to elicit follow-up data from a larger, more representative group of team-teachers at the college, in an attempt to delve more deeply into issues raised. The third used paper-based questionnaires to survey a sample of team-taught students at MIC, in order to allow a broader perspective of team-teaching to emerge from all classroom participants. A qualitative data-driven approach was employed overall, relying heavily on open-ended questions, and allowing CITT participants to define and describe the processes of CITT in their own terms. The findings of this series of studies were then used to develop a conceptual model of effective CITT for application by practising team-teachers (see Gladman, 2009).

In this chapter, I focus on the first phase and some of the methodological issues that emerged in the implementation of that study.

Methodological Focus

The focus group was selected as an appropriate tool for generating initial exploratory data (Dushku, 2000; Frey & Fontana, 1993). Ho (2006) observes that the focus group has become an increasingly common method of col-lecting qualitative data in the social sciences because of its effectiveness in eliciting a wide range of relevant ideas and observations with respect to a given research topic. Participants are interviewed in groups, rather than as individuals, on the principle that the synergistic effect of group interaction can prompt more relevant responses than might be elicited from comparable one-on-one interviews (Ho, 2006; Johnson, 1996; Kitzinger, 1994). Thus, the primary goal of this study was to use focus group methodology to elicit a rich variety of pertinent data concerning CITT directly from its practitioners, and to provide an effective baseline of directions for follow-up studies, not just within my own research series, but potentially for any future researcher to use.

For this study, I decided to interview TESOL specialists and content specialists separately, since each group takes responsibility for different aspects of CBLI in the shared classroom, as relevant to its own particular fields of academic specialisation (MIC Faculty Council, 2006). According to Krueger and Casey (2000), in order to generate useful data, focus groups are best composed of participants with homogeneous characteristics common to the group from which they are drawn, and so this principle was applied to the two distinct groups of CITT practitioners at MIC.

In addition to generating an initial baseline dataset for the research project, the purpose of the study was to yield data that might offer pertinent comparisons with previous findings from the professional team-teaching literature. In particular, it was hoped that this study would allow conclusions to be drawn which were of relevance to Perry and Stewart's (2005) CITT study, by adding to their findings and perhaps compensating for any limitations of their methodology. To this end, my study differed from theirs in two important ways.

First, while Perry and Stewart (2005) sought to obtain a representative sampling of the CITT practitioner population for generalising purposes, I considered representativeness to be less important than identifying a rich variety of views to guide the points of departure for my research. Focus group methodology aligns well with such a purpose. While the intention is to allow a diverse range of viewpoints to emerge, there is no implicit claim within focus group methodology that the range must be representative of the population, but rather that it is illuminating (Fowler, 1995). Therefore, there was no need to randomise the selection of eligible participants. Later, when the findings from the focus group study had determined the direction my research series would take, the second phase of the project was designed to survey a more representative sample of CITT practitioners with questions that had been derived from the initial set of focus group findings, on the principle that the two research designs applied sequentially were complementary (Wolff et al., 1993).

Second, one of the limitations of the Perry and Stewart (2005) study was that their interview questions tended to confine respondents to the specific aspects of CITT which the researchers considered important, instead of allowing the respondents to determine which aspects of team-teaching were of importance to them. The potential weakness of such an approach is that it is more difficult for unexpected findings to emerge, and there is a greater likelihood of respondents being constrained by the researchers' expectations. Exploratory focus group methodology reduces this potential by broadening the opportunity for different insider opinions to be heard. While researchers prepare interview questions in a logical sequence to collect data of relevance to the research topic, they typically design the questions to be as open-ended as possible, to minimise researcher imposition on the participants' perspectives, while staying within the parameters of the topic itself (Anderson, 1990; Ho, 2006; Krueger & Casey, 2000). Thus, Grotjahn's (1987) 'exploratory-interpretative' conditions are created, allowing an appropriate range of data to emerge that the researcher can analyse to develop theoretical propositions.

In these respects, focus group methodology was considered suitable to 'set the scene' for the investigative purposes of the CITT research studies that followed.

The Study

In July 2006, four TESOL specialists and four content specialists, drawn from a total population of approximately 30 active CITT practitioners in the MIC faculty body, participated in two focus group interviews. A dedicated meeting room was used as the venue for both interviews. All discussions were audio-taped for transcription and data analysis, using three tape-recorders and three external microphones placed evenly around the meeting table. I acted as group interviewer (or 'moderator', a more typical designation in focus group terminology) for both discussions, using the same set of interview questions in both cases, which were designed to prompt participants to discuss what CITT meant to them, and how it did or did not work. I used the following questions to guide the focus group discussions:

(1) What does the term 'team-teaching' mean to you?
(2) What are the requirements of team-teaching that are different from the requirements of traditional teaching?
(3) What are the strengths and benefits of team-teaching for participating teachers?

(4) What are the strengths and benefits of team-teaching for participating students?
(5) What makes a team-teaching partnership work effectively?
(6) What are the weaknesses and limitations of team-teaching for participating teachers?
(7) What are the weaknesses and limitations of team-teaching for participating students?
(8) What prevents a team-teaching partnership from working effectively?
(9) Of the things we have discussed so far, what would you say is the single most important point about effective team-teaching?

I content-analysed the data to categorise the types of response which were of common importance to the respondents (Knodel, 1993). Responses of lesser prominence were filtered out of the final results listings, but all major categories of response that emerged from the data were identified and tabulated, without exception. The criteria for defining a category of response as a major category were that it must have emerged independently in the responses in both of the focus group discussions and be identifiable in quotes from at least two different respondents (though virtually all of the categories in the final results table well exceeded the minimum terms of these criteria in the frequency of their emergence in the data).

During the categorisation process, I attempted to strengthen the reliability of the procedure by conducting an inter-coder agreement check. I asked a fellow university researcher, as a disinterested party with no past or present association with MIC, to independently categorise a large number of randomly ordered response items drawn from the focus group data according to the category definitions I provided, and to offer general feedback. Though we were in agreement with how we grouped the items in most instances, a small number of incongruities emerged. In those instances of inter-coder disagreement, I clarified and improved the mutual exclusivity of the category definitions to resolve the disagreements and thus provide a more robust justification for my analysis.

Focus group data samples

Table 3.1 shows the final results. It provides definitions and descriptions of each major category of response, together with example quotes from the respondents to demonstrate how each category was manifested in the responses. The categories have also been collocated into general types for purposes of comparison and ease of reference. The first three categories of response appearing in Table 3.1, all focusing on team-teacher attributes, were identified by participants as the most important points about team-teaching that had arisen in the discussions.

The findings of the focus group study fulfilled their purpose in providing me with a clear direction for further study, by identifying the respondents' key concern with team-teachers' attributes and interactions in the development of an effective partnership. I consequently limited the focus of my second study to investigate this aspect of CITT, using questionnaire items to flesh out more details of the teaching partners' interpersonal dynamic. The focus group findings also suggested the possibility that tensions could emerge between partners attempting to apply mutually conflicting sets of behaviour and this, too, became a useful point of departure for the subsequent phases of the project.

The focus group findings aligned well with previous findings from the team-teaching literature, and supported commonly held conclusions. For example, respondents advocated the importance of teaching partners reaching role agreement (e.g. Eisen, 2000; Murata, 2002) and recommended allowing more preparation time than for single-teacher instruction (e.g. Carless, 2006; Kachi & Choon-hwa, 2001); they also identified the extra professional development opportunities that teaching collaboration offers (e.g. Carless & Walker, 2006; Woo, 2003). Yet less predictable findings also emerged that were not commonly reported in the literature, such as the perceived potential of team-teaching to promote critical thinking by raising students' awareness of valid multiple perspectives on given issues (see category H, Table 3.1).

Another unexpected finding was a strongly held minority viewpoint from respondents regarding the priority of student needs (see category K), which contrasted sharply with the more common view among CITT practitioners and this, too, was singled out for more detailed investigation in later studies. Many of the focus group findings also aligned well with Perry and Stewart's (2005) findings and helped to support their conclusions, with the noteworthy exception that no evidence emerged to support their claim that the gaining of CITT experience over time helps to resolve such problems as power-sharing disputes between partners.

Methodological Implications

In order to discuss methodological issues arising from my study, it is necessary to highlight the atypical features of its design compared with more standard focus group arrangements. The unusually small population of potential respondents for my study (i.e. working CITT practitioners) and the fact that the population was not geographically diverse, but a

Table 3.1 Major categories of response from the focus group study, with descriptions and example quotes

Category type	Category of response	Description	Example quotes
Team-teacher attributes	A. Respect for partner	Team-teaching partners show respect for each other as teachers and colleagues, and for what each contributes to the shared course	'In the case where it [my team-teaching relationship] didn't work, I think I didn't get the respect, and that's why everything I had planned became undermined or ignored'
	B. Openness	Team-teaching partners show willingness to communicate openly with each other about their shared course	'When these small conflicts do come up, the willingness to – the feeling that you can talk about it with your, with your partner'
	C. Flexibility	Team-teaching partners show professional flexibility, adapting well to sudden changes and new ways of doing things	'I think coming planned is good but being flexible is as important' 'Yeah, being flexible in the classroom is good, too – having plan B or C or D or whatever is good'
Team-teaching partner inter-actions	D. Equal power sharing	Team-teaching partners share authority equally within their team-taught course without arrogating individual power over each other or the course itself	'The thing is, I think, not to assume ownership of the class'
	E. Role agreement	Team-teaching partners jointly determine their roles within their team-teaching relationship to both partners' satisfaction, even if they share power unequally	'If you have a partnership that's worked out where you've just agreed, okay, I'm going to take an assistant role, regardless of what I'm supposed to do because you've taught this forever and it's useless – letting me take an equal role. I mean that can be okay'

	F. Advance joint planning	Team-teaching partners meet outside the classroom to jointly plan their lessons in advance of implementation	'Giving a plan of what I'm going to teach or what I'm going to talk about and trying to discuss: What about you? Would you do this part? Or, do we include the quiz here or do we – an exercise? And what would you do here? And so, things like this, so in a way we plan the choreography before, and – plan the show'
	G. Coordinated student instruction	Team-teaching partners are coordinated in their instruction to students, giving them non-conflicting information	'For students, maybe confusion sometimes. If it happens that you have a, as we talked about, you may…' 'Get two versions of the same … [instructions]' 'Yeah' 'Two non-complementary versions … [inaudible] … he said, she said'
Team-teaching benefits	H. Awareness of multiple perspectives	By modelling acceptance of each other's divergent opinions and viewpoints, team-teachers promote student awareness of multiple perspectives	'The strength [of team-teaching] is that the students will begin to very quickly realise that the teacher is not always right, because there's another expert opinion'
	I. Professional development opportunities	Team-teaching offers partners opportunities for professional development by learning from each other	'You can also learn about different teaching techniques that maybe you hadn't been exposed to'
Administrative requirements	J. Preparation time	Team-teaching requires more preparation time to implement than single-teacher instruction	'[Team-teaching is] time-consuming. Takes time to meet up, talk, talk through the things when you could just simply write it up, write up your, your curriculum, your course, on your own, on your time. So yeah, it takes time to meet up with someone…'
Student influences	K. Student needs to take priority	A successful partnership is one that meets student needs, regardless of the relationship between the team-teaching partners	'The students are the consumers and you're there to deliver a product and whatever it takes to make that work, that's good team-teaching'

single, close-knit group of people, all working together in a small college environment, meant that I had to deviate to some degree from the usual recommendations for focus group design.

First, the number of respondents in each of my two groups was atypically low at four. Though an acceptable number to some (e.g. Morgan, 1996) it is more commonly recommended that groups of 6–12 participants be used (Fowler, 1995; Krueger & Casey, 2000; Stewart & Shamdasani, 1990). However, these numbers tend to presuppose that respondents are drawn from substantially larger populations. Given that I was expecting to gather data from a larger representative sample of CITT practitioners in the second phase of the project anyway, I made the decision to reduce the size of my focus groups to four participants in each case, to act as exploratory probes into the subject matter at hand. Krueger and Casey (2000: 10) observe that groups of such size (which they call 'mini-focus groups') offer distinct advantages to larger gatherings, including giving participants 'more opportunity to share ideas'. Such advantages aligned well with my intention of generating a good range of insightful responses through synergistic interaction.

Second, my groups comprised people who were all known to each other, in fact were working colleagues, which was at odds with the common recommendation that participants should not know each other well, if at all (Anderson, 1990; Krueger & Casey, 2000; Morgan & Krueger, 1993). However, since I was drawing from such a limited population, I had no choice but to use the respondents at hand and attempt to compensate for the limitations of their familiarity with each other using a variety of means.

To some degree, the familiarity of the respondents was lessened by the separation of content and language teachers, as has been noted. In addition to the benefits of homogeneity, this separation also ensured that respondents in a single group had no direct experience of each other as teaching partners, since CITT requires both language and content specialists to form a team. In other words, respondents in a single group were colleagues, but did not engage with each other in closely collaborative relationships. This aspect was particularly important in the context of team-teaching because the close relationship between teaching partners requires a degree of mutual trust that creates potential difficulties for them if they are then required to voice critical opinions about team-teaching in the presence of a group that includes their partners, particularly if they must continue to maintain working relationships with those same partners afterwards (Dudley-Evans, 2001; Perry & Stewart, 2005).

Another benefit of the composition of these groups was that it minimised the potential for in-group power relationships to influence the discourse. All respondents in each group were of equal standing in terms of their roles as team-teachers and also in terms of institutional status in the faculty hierarchy, despite their academic differences. Therefore, no single respondent could reasonably claim authority over another, except perhaps in terms of his or her duration of experience as a CITT practitioner. Though I observed that the more experienced team-teachers did tend to have more to say, the small size of each group and the ample time made available for discussions gave the opportunity for every respondent to make a compre-hensive contribution. All respondents indicated at the end of the interviews that they were satisfied they had had a chance to express their views fully.

Other ways in which I attempted to compensate for the familiarity of the respondents within groups was through use of a 'rule of engagement' in the discussions and applying my own judgement to the suitability of potential respondents when inviting faculty to participate in the study. The discussion rule, which was made explicit to all participants at the beginning of each meeting, was that they should respect the confidentiality of other faculty members by not disclosing the identity of specific individuals when drawing on their own experiences to contribute to the discussion. The par-ticipants adhered to this rule by discussing the behaviour of team-teachers in general, or occasionally by referring to specific individuals in non-specific terms to minimise the chance of identity disclosure. In addition, using my insider judgement to select participants, I exercised my responsibility as moderator to create what Stewart and Shamdasani (1990) call a 'non-threatening' environment, by taking into consideration the potential for the participants to become disputatious with each other, and I did not invite any faculty member to participate if I believed he or she might jeopardise other respondents' feelings of safety in voicing their opinions honestly over the course of the discussions (though I did not believe this to be a serious concern for most of the available faculty). Given that convenience sampling was acceptable for this type of methodology, where representativeness was not a goal, my use of selective judgement in finding participants raised no ethical concerns.

My status as an insider of the population under study (i.e. MIC faculty member and active CITT practitioner) acting as researcher and moderator for the focus group study raises certain questions regarding methodological implications. Clearly, there were practical benefits in terms of my ability to maintain sole control over the research process without having to rely on third parties to correctly interpret and exercise their roles within that process. Not only was I able to exercise informed judgement when assem-bling the focus groups but also, as moderator, I had control over the course of the discussions and was present to ensure that the discussion rule was not transgressed and that the conversation did not stray unduly from the parameters of the research topic. Furthermore, the small-scale composition of the groups and my insider status simplified the data transcription that followed the meetings. My collegial familiarity with the respondents allowed me to identify each speaker easily from the playbacks and code their responses appropriately, while my institutional familiarity, supplemented by my own memory of the discussions, allowed me to understand and transcribe responses accurately that may have been less comprehensible to outsiders.

Nevertheless, the inherent danger of this close involvement with the process was that I might intrude too closely into the discussions and (consciously or otherwise) guide the direction of the emerging responses to best suit my preconceptions. Since I had intended that my research design might compensate for the potential researcher imposition of Perry and Stewart's (2005) earlier study, this type of intrusion would have been particularly detrimental. I was keenly aware of this concern when acting as moderator of the discussions, so I made every effort to discharge my formal responsibilities as correctly as possible, by constraining myself to the interview questions and refraining from contributing to the discussions as a fellow team-teacher. I also applied the technique of repeating the respondents' own words back to them as much as possible when prompting for further responses, in order to minimise the imposition of my own voice and to allow the respondents' viewpoints to emerge unhindered (Stewart & Shamdasani, 1990). In short, I kept my insider identity under certain restraints while moderating and tried to conform strictly to methodological procedure. My intent may have been only too evident to the respondents, since I retain an impression of some of them reacting with initial surprise, and occasionally smiling, at what I presume was the unusually serious formality of my discourse and behaviour during the focus groups, in contrast with my more typically relaxed collegial interactions at other times.

Reflection

On reflection, I feel that the study performed satisfactorily in meeting the expectations of its design and launching my CITT research project into productive investigative territory. Any concern that my close involvement as researcher and moderator with insider status might have intruded unduly on the responses should be balanced against the emergence of unexpected opinions, including a strongly held minority viewpoint, in the major response categories.

However, given my inclination to restrain my insider identity while moderating, it might also have been an instructive choice to appoint a peer with no insider status to act as moderator instead, using my interview questions. On the one hand, such a decision would have presented new dangers. Respondents may have been less inclined to interact naturally with an 'outsider' with whom they had not already established a friendly relationship as a colleague, as suggested by Ho (2006). On the other hand, arguments could be made for the advantages of an unfamiliar moderator. Participants may have needed to think more objectively from first principles about team-teaching, as part of the process of having to explain their responses to an interviewer with no prior knowledge of the topic. Also, the potential danger of friendly colleagues wanting to 'help' the moderator (consciously or unconsciously) by saying what they think he or she wants to hear might have been lessened, thus improving the chances of more controversial, but equally useful, insights to emerge that might otherwise have been left unspoken.

Other alternatives might have been for the participants to have been left alone to discuss the interview questions without a moderator; or for one of the focus group participants to assume the moderator role. Though these alternatives have their strengths, and certainly would have lessened the danger of researcher intrusion, they are more likely to have heightened the potential for counterproductive power imbalances to have occurred, with one or more participants dominating the discourse with their own responses and limiting opportunities for quieter participants to make full contributions. Also, as with the case of appointing an 'outsider' moderator, certain benefits of having an 'insider' interviewer present to moderate the discussions without also being a respondent are reduced by these alternative procedures. Such a moderator is well positioned to focus on keeping the dialogic space as open as possible for all respondents to make a range of pertinent contributions without being distracted by the need to contribute his or her own responses to the interview questions, while also having insider knowledge to best guide the 'on the spot' elicitation of follow-up information from participants. In the case of my focus group discussions, my impression is that there were occasions when respondents expressed themselves in 'shorthand' institutional terminology or potentially ambiguous utterances that were understandable to me and the participants in context, but might not have been clear to others in transcription. On such occasions, as moderator, I was able to probe with immediate questions that encouraged the speakers to clarify their meanings or elaborate their points so that they were less contextually embedded. I believe that this procedure helped to improve the rigour and usefulness of the data overall.

Whichever option a focus group researcher might choose in implementing his or her design, there can be no avoidance of the need to compensate for the inevitable limitations and weaknesses that are inherent in any process of eliciting data from complex human respondents. Yet I would argue that the richness of data accessible through focus group methodology well justifies the effort for the exploratory researcher.

COMMENTARY

In responding to the case study, the major question I want to address is, what does talking together reveal about thinking?

Andrew Gladman has done a fine job of laying out the complexities of using focus groups as a way to study what people – here, teachers in a university content-based English programme – think about what they do. In these comments, I want to use Andrew's work as a starting point to elaborate what I see as some of the central issues in this approach to data gathering (or, perhaps better put, 'data generation'). As is the case in so much research methodology, the 'devil is in the detail'. With focus groups, the 'detail' centres on how language, or more specifically talk, among a selected group of people captures what they are thinking. This claim – that talk can capture people's ideas or 'mental lives' – is fundamental to qualitative research generally, and to studies of thinking or cognition more specifically. In the commentary that follows, I will try to bridge comments about focus group methodology in particular with broader issues of language as data or information about thinking. I do so because, in my view, and in my experience as a researcher, the two are inextricably interconnected, though they are seldom addressed in this common frame.

Language as Data of Thinking

As the American author Eudora Welty once remarked about how she used details in her writing, 'the general resides in the particular'. In research methods, nowhere is this statement more applicable than it is to the role of language as data in qualitative work. We can talk about generalities of meaning-making, interpreting, valuing, positioning and the various hermeneutic processes that undergird qualitative studies, but each of these research moves comes down to how language is used in particular circumstances to capture what lies outside it. Put another way: any qualitative research involves, implicitly or explicitly, a general theory of what language is and how it works, which is then played out through the research methodology. To use a computer analogy, this theory provides the operating system for what the researcher does and thinks.

This is probably most easy to see and accept in oral research interactions like interviews or focus groups. But it is equally the case in doing field observations or documentary analyses. Even though the issue of language data may seem less fraught in these instances because it can be easier to establish some amount of triangulation, through which researchers and participants can agree on some common understandings, issues of language data are still present. They usually come to the fore in the ways in which insiders versus outsiders view and understand the phenomenon. It is telling to the argument I am making here that the labels for this difference in viewpoints were originally derived from the study of language. These terms, 'emic/etic', come from the anthropological linguist Kenneth Pike, who used analytic tools from structural linguistics to distinguish sounds as being *phonemic* (a sound difference that is meaningful to users) versus *phonetic* (a difference that is perceptible but may not carry meaning). So language data – and indeed pretty much any data used in qualitative analyses – hinge on (meaning that they are gathered through and define) these roles or position as insider or outsider. Both 'role' and 'position' are circumscribed, and even defined, by context. I take 'role' to be the ways in which a person is allowed or supposed to act in the context of a situation (Halliday, 1989), while the 'position' is the meaning that is or potentially can be attributed to the person by those in the situation. In this sense, the distinction is akin to de Saussure's *langue* (position) and *parole* (role) in structural linguistics (de Saussure, 1986).

This relation of emic/etic, or inside/outside, is a key tool in assembling any qualitative data. It is particularly relevant when studying cognition, since there are opposing ways to parse language as data of thinking. One can argue that thinking is 'inside', that it belongs to the individual, and is then expressed 'outside' through words. In this case, cognition is foregrounded and language is the vehicle to express it. Individuals think; and they talk about what is on their minds. Alternatively, one can argue that words themselves always come about 'inside' of a particular group of users; what comes from 'outside' is the occasion or demand to use them. In this case, language is foregrounded, and thinking recedes into the background because it is the occasion of using language that makes for thinking and not the reverse. While these two positions are somewhat simplified, they capture the fundamental dilemma of how researchers use language as data of cognition. In essence, Andrew's work illustrates the first position; my critique comes from the second.

We can see these two points of view if we turn to Andrew's initial framing of the focus group methodology. Citing Ho (2006), he describes the general purpose of using focus groups as follows (italics added):

> the focus group has become an increasingly common method of collecting qualitative data in the social sciences *because of its effectiveness in eliciting a wide range of relevant ideas and observations with respect to a given research topic.*

The devil in the detail lies here in the verb 'eliciting'. As Andrew (and Ho) describe it, these 'ideas and observations' are 'elicited' through the interactions of group members: 'the principle [is] that the synergistic effect of group interaction can prompt more relevant responses than might be elicited from comparable one-on-one interviews'. This view that the interaction 'elicits' participants' 'ideas and observations' argues a theory of language in which it is the vehicle for thought; words express what the participants are thinking, in other words their cognition. Interaction among the group participants generates thinking that is expressed in language.

The alternative view is that the thinking comes about as the group uses language as they talk to each other about the topic. This view looks at interaction as the spaces among speakers; it holds that what participants say – or more importantly may not say – is influenced by the attributes of that particular group: who is in it, when and where it is happening, and so on. In other words, the roles participants play in the focus group are shaped by their positions, both in the group and in the larger setting from which the group is drawn and which the group may be supposed to capture or represent. Here the theory is that language is socially constituted and situated;

in the words of the Russian Formalist Mikhail Bahktin (1981: 274), 'language is overpopulated with the intentions of others'.

Elliot Mishler, who has studied interviewing primarily in medical settings, critiques the first view that language data 'neutrally' express thinking as being 'behavioral and anti-linguistic'. He argues:

> By adopting an approach [that] relies on the stimulus–response model, and decontextualizes the meaning of responses, researchers have attempted to avoid rather than confront directly the interrelated problems of context, discourse, and meaning. (Mishler, 1986: 27)

The heart of the counterview, that language used in social situations creates thinking, lies at this nexus of 'context, discourse, and meaning', which is the problem of audience, or who can/does say what to whom (Cazden, 2001). In the absence of careful and disciplined consideration of how the mutual audience in the focus group shapes what is said, it is troubling to assert that these data represent what is thought. In other writing (Freeman, 1996), I have referred to this problem as the 'representational' versus the 'presentational' dimensions of language data. Others who work within a discourse analysis approach describe this problem of audience in terms of face and politeness norms (e.g. Rex, 2001). Together these concerns cluster around the problem of audience.

Twin Contexts: Of Situation and of Mind

The methodological point here is that for focus group data to be fairly interpreted, the researcher needs to consider those data as language, and the *contexts* both *of situation* (Halliday, 1989) and *of mind* (Cazden, 2001) that are present in – or arguably have led to – their generation. Simply put, it is doubtful that people, especially those who know each other and work together, just sit down and talk, saying whatever is on their minds. Rather, these contexts of situation (the physical, interactional and interpersonal settings) and of mind (what people think about the topic in terms of each other) define the audience for and content of their remarks. And therefore I would argue the audience shapes – if not constrains – the data that are produced.

In a sense, this is what Andrew acknowledges when he writes about being both the facilitator of the focus group and an insider to the phenomenon of team-teaching at his university that he is studying:

> Not only was I able to exercise informed judgement when assembling the focus groups but also, as moderator, I had control over the course of the discussions and was present to ensure that the discussion rule was not transgressed and that the conversation did not stray unduly from the parameters of the research topic. Furthermore, the small-scale composition of the groups and my insider status simplified the data transcription that followed the meetings.

To my way of thinking, though, Andrew is mistaken when he takes these basic facts of his position, a staff member on the faculty, and his roles as researcher and focus group facilitator, simply as methodological strengths. Rather, the position and roles must shape the responses to his questions and prompts. The social fact of this shaping of responses, and whether it is included as an element of the analytic procedures, has to enter into this research process. As Mishler (1986: 23) observed of interviewing, 'Each answer is a fragment removed both from its setting in the organized discourse of the interview and from the life setting of the respondent'. How we account for these 'life settings' of the speakers must be a central question in the validity of the focus group methodology.

How Does Topic Matter?

Which brings us to the issue of what is talked about and how 'topic' fits in this discussion. To some extent, one can reasonably argue that focus groups are less fraught linguistically and socially when they are talking about things that are happening or have happened, what Marton (1981) calls 'first-order' phenomena. Using this term, he distinguishes between 'the first-order perspective [in which] we aim at describing various aspects of the world and ... the second-order perspective, [in which] we aim at describing people's experience of various aspects of the world' (Marton, 1981: 177). Focus groups that are asked to discuss first-order phenomena (e.g. describing their working conditions) are making what Marton calls 'statements-about-reality'. These would contrast with discussions about 'second-order phenomena' (e.g. what they think about working conditions), which he defines as 'statements-about-perceived-reality' (Marton, 1981: 188).

In the day-to-day exercise of research methods, however, it may be that Marton is drawing a distinction without a real difference. Actually, focus groups generate both first- and second-order data. But it is worth considering how the researcher's approach – what he or she does with participants in the focus group setting – will give *de facto* primacy to one perspective or the other. Which is essentially my argument: if one is studying cognition, which certainly meets Marton's definition of a second-order phenomenon, then one has to give primacy to contexts of mind and of situation in language data. As a researcher, I think it borders on the naïve to simply say that people are telling you what they think. More likely, they are telling you what they think you want to hear; or some admixture of the two. Participants are speaking to you in your position as researcher and in whatever roles you have in the social setting of the interview or the focus group.

Which raises validity questions. At a minimum, these interactions ought to trigger the question, 'Why are they telling *me* this, *here*, *now*?' This question then frames three key analytic categories:

- *me*. How do *my position and the role(s) I am taking* in this interaction shape what I am being told and what I am hearing? This is the context of mind.
- *here*. How do *the specifics of the setting* – who is present and where we are talking – shape what I am being told and what I am hearing? This is the context of situation in terms of place.
- *now*. How does *the timing* – when we are talking, both immediately (e.g. time of day) and chronologically (i.e. in personal and organisational history) – shape what I am being told and what I am hearing? This is the context of situation in terms of time.

Andrew's case study is an articulate presentation of focus group methodology. My comments here are less in response to the particulars of what he writes than to the larger issues of language as data and qualitative methodology that his contribution raises. The central questions, it seems to me, are: What is the talk in the focus group doing? What is it capturing or making happen? From a less exotic perspective, a focus group is just an organised group discussion in the context of a research topic or problem. Like any occasion for group interaction, from a conversation at the family dinner table, to a lesson discussion in the classroom, to chatting at a cocktail party, norms will guide who says what to whom, when and how (Cazden, 2001). The strength of the focus group as a research tool lies in *how* it recognises, acknowledges and capitalises on this human fact, which in my view is the researcher's decision. I have called this process using a theory of language in the work. When the topic involves the second-order phenomenon of cognition, all the researcher has in essence are these norms of language use. To try to interpret what is said (or not said) without them is to try to separate the dancer from the dance.

REFLECTIVE QUESTIONS

(1) Andrew Gladman used focus groups to elicit data in the early stages of his project. What purposes might focus groups serve if they occurred towards the end of the data-gathering phase of a project?

(2) If you were to use focus groups in your own research, would you prefer to be present or absent? Why?

(3) What are the advantages and disadvantages of using audio rather than video to record focus group discussions?

(4) If you were to use focus groups in your research, what criteria would you use to select the participants? How might your position, as Donald Freeman describes it, and relationships influence the data you are able to gather from these participants?

(5) How could you address the key question raised by Donald Freeman, 'What does talking together reveal about thinking?', in analysing data from focus groups? What approaches could be used to take into account both context of situation and context of mind? You can use Donald Freeman's question 'Why are the participants telling *me* this, *here*, *now*?' to guide your thinking.

(6) Think of a relevant topic and write down some questions, or focus points, relating to this topic. Ask some colleagues to form a focus group to discuss these.

(7) It is normal ethical procedure to write a letter of information to potential participants explaining, among other things, in what ways they could help you. Draft a paragraph to be included in such a letter explaining why and how you want them to take part in a focus group.

References

Anderson, G. (1990) *Fundamentals of Educational Research*. London: Falmer.

Bahktin, M. (1981) *The Dialogic Imagination. Four Essays by M.M. Bahktin*. Edited by M. Holquist, translated by C. Emerson and M. Holquist. Austin, TX: University of Texas Press.

Brinton, D.M., Snow, M.A. and Wesche, M.B. (1989) *Content-Based Second Language Instruction*. Boston, MA: Heinle and Heinle.

Carless, D. (2006) Good practices in team teaching in Japan, South Korea and Hong Kong. *System*, 34, 341–351.

Carless, D. and Walker, E. (2006) Effective team teaching between local and native-speaking English teachers. *Language and Education*, 20(6), 463–477.

Cazden, C. (2001) *Classroom Discourse: The Language of Teaching and Learning* (2nd edition). Portsmouth, NH: Heinemann.

de Saussure, F. (1986) *A Course in General Linguistics*. Chicago, IL: Open Court.

Dudley-Evans, T. (2001) Team-teaching in EAP: Changes and adaptations in the Birmingham approach. In J. Flowerdew and M. Peacock (eds), *Research Perspectives on English for Academic Purposes* (pp. 225–238). Cambridge: Cambridge University Press.

Dushku, S. (2000) Conducting individual and focus group interviews in research in Albania. *TESOL Quarterly*, 34(4), 763–768.

Eisen, M-J. (2000) The many faces of team teaching and learning: An overview. *New Directions for Adult and Continuing Education*, 87, 5–14.

Fowler, F.J., Jr (1995) *Improving Survey Questions: Design and Evaluation* (Applied Social Research Methods Series, Vol. 38). Thousand Oaks, CA: Sage.

Freeman, D. (1996) 'To take them at their word': Language data in the study of teachers' knowledge. *Harvard Educational Review*, 66(4), 732–761.

Frey, J.H. and Fontana, A. (1993) The group interview in social research. In D.L. Morgan (ed.), *Successful Focus Groups: Advancing the State of the Art* (pp. 20–34). Newbury Park, CA: Sage.

Gladman, A. (2009) Collaborative interdisciplinary team teaching in Japan: A study of practitioner and student perspectives. PhD thesis, Macquarie University.

Grotjahn, R. (1987) On the methodological basis of introspective methods. In C. Faerch and G. Kasper (eds), *Introspection in Second Language Research* (pp. 54–82). Clevedon: Multilingual Matters.

Halliday, M.A.K. (1989) Part A. In M.A.K. Halliday and R. Hasan, *Language, Context and Text: Aspects of Language in a Social Semiotic Perspective* (pp. 1–49). Oxford: Oxford Univesity Press.

Ho, D. (2006) The focus group interview: Rising to the challenge in qualitative research methodology. *Australian Review of Applied Linguistics*, 29(1), 05.01–05.19.

Johnson, A. (1996) It's good to talk: The focus group and the sociological imagination. *Sociological Review*, 44(3), 517–538.

Kachi, R. and Choon-hwa, L. (2001) A tandem of native and non-native teachers: Voices from Japanese and American teachers in the EFL classroom in Japan. Paper presented at the Annual International Conference on Language Teacher Education, Minneapolis, MN.

Kitzinger, J. (1994) The methodology of focus groups: The importance of interaction between research participants. *Sociology of Health and Illness*, 76, 103–121.

Knodel, J. (1993) The design and analysis of focus group studies. In D.L. Morgan (ed.), *Successful Focus Groups: Advancing the State of the Art* (pp. 35–50). Newbury Park, CA: Sage.

Krueger, R.A. and Casey, M.A. (2000) *Focus Groups: A Practical Guide for Applied Research* (3rd edition). Thousand Oaks, CA: Sage.

Marton, F. (1981) Phenomenography: describing concepts of the world around us. *Instructional Science*, 10, 177–200.

MIC Faculty Council (2006) *Faculty Handbook: Teaching Partnerships 4.12.1*. Available at http://sekai.miyazakimic.ac.jp/Faculty_Handbook/policies.html#partners (accessed 20 November 2007).

Mishler, E. (1986) *Research Interviewing: Context and Narrative*. Cambridge, MA: Harvard University Press.

Miyazato, K. (2006) *Role and Power Sharing Between Native and Non-Native EFL Teachers: Three Cases of Team Teaching in Japanese High Schools*. PhD dissertation, Temple University.

Morgan, D.L. (1996) Focus groups. *Annual Review of Sociology*, 22, 129–152.

Morgan, D.L. and Krueger, R.A. (1993) When to use focus groups and why. In D.L. Morgan (ed.), *Successful Focus Groups: Advancing the State of the Art* (pp. 3–19). Newbury Park, CA: Sage.

Murata, R. (2002) What does team teaching mean? A case study of interdisciplinary teaming. *Journal of Educational Research*, 96(2), 67–77.

Perry, B. and Stewart, T. (2005) Insights into effective partnership in interdisciplinary team teaching. *System*, 33(4), 563–573.

Rex, L. (2001) *Discourse of Opportunity: How Talk in Learning Situations Creates and Constrains*. Creswell, NJ: Hampton.

Sagliano, M. and Greenfield, K. (1998) A collaborative model of content-based EFL instruction in the liberal arts. *TESOL Journal*, 7(3), 23–28.

Sagliano, M., Stewart, T. and Sagliano, J. (1998) Professional training to develop content-based instruction in higher education. *TESL Canada Journal*, 16(1), 36–53.

Stewart, D.W. and Shamdasani, P.N. (1990) *Focus Groups: Theory and Practice*. Newbury Park, CA: Sage.

Stewart, T. (1996) Organizing and teaching course content in fully integrated language and content instruction. *Comparative Culture: The Journal of Miyazaki International College*, 2, 1–17.

Wolff, B., Knodel, J. and Sittitrai, W. (1993) Focus groups and surveys as complementary research methods: A case example. In D.L. Morgan (ed.), *Successful Focus Groups: Advancing the State of the Art* (pp. 118–136). Newbury Park, CA: Sage.

Woo, Y-H. (2003) Critical reflections of experienced Korean faculty regarding team teaching in Korean language and culture classes for adult English speakers. *Dissertation Abstracts International, A: The Humanities and Social Sciences*, 63(12).

4   Interviews

Case Study: Le Van Canh
Commentary: Alan Maley

CASE STUDY

Introduction

Although interviewing is increasingly used in present-day qualitative research (Denzin & Lincoln, 1998; Talmy, 2010) as an important part of triangulated data collection, along with observation (see Chapter 5), diaries and questionnaires (Block, 2000; see also Chapter 1), little has been reported on the sociocultural constraints in using this methodological tool for researching teachers in developing countries, such as Vietnam. This chapter reports part of a qualitative case study which set out to explore Vietnamese secondary-school teachers' beliefs and practices regarding grammar instruction. The study employed a combination of interviews, classroom observations and stimulated recall interviews (see Chapter 7) to collect the data.

However, this chapter limits itself to an analysis of the challenges in conducting interviews with Vietnamese teachers regarding grammar pedagogy in the context of a public upper secondary school where English is taught as a foreign language for three hours a week. It looks reflexively at my own interviewing practices as they developed during my project. The chapter focuses on sociocultural issues such as gaining accessibility, building personal relationships and trust, choice of language, flexibility in time arrangements and logistic difficulties. In writing this chapter I was motivated by Roulston's (2010) caution about the dangers of applying context-free advice on best practice to particular interviews.

The place of grammar instruction remains controversial in the field of second-language teaching, as consensus has not yet been reached regarding whether grammar instruction helps learners gain proficiency in a second language. Perspectives on this question can be placed along a continuum, with extremes at either end (Gascoigne, 2002). At one end are highly explicit approaches to grammar teaching and at the other end lie implicit approaches that eschew mention of form. Contemporary research on the merits of both the implicit and explicit approaches has led to the consensus that an exclusive emphasis on either extreme impedes learners' acquisition of English as a second language (ESL). In fact, both the inadequacies of a traditional focus on language structure alone and the drawbacks of a strictly communicative approach have well been documented (e.g. Green & Hecht, 1992; Long, 1991; Norris & Ortega, 2000; Skehan, 1996). Inside the classroom, studies on the practices and attitudes of teachers (Borg, 2003; Borg & Burns, 2008; Farrell & Lim, 2005) and students (Polat, 2009) suggest that both groups are favourably disposed to some element of explicit grammar instruction in the classroom. Findings of studies on teachers' beliefs about grammar instruction show that teaching is a complex issue, which calls for greater attention to this emerging research avenue so as to gain better understanding of teachers' beliefs about grammar and their grammar practices in different contexts, especially where non-native teachers are teaching ESL in a state school (Borg, 2006).

Methodological Focus

One of the challenges of researching teachers' beliefs lies in the fact that beliefs are tacit (Kagan, 1992) and unobservable, and teachers may have difficulties articulating them (see also the Commentary in Chapter 3). This requires researchers to use appropriate methods to attempt to make those beliefs more explicit. One of those methods is interviewing, which can be either unstructured or semi-structured. However, there are challenges in using this method to conduct research on teachers, and the seriousness of those challenges varies from context to context.

Dushku reports how interviewing teachers in Albanian contexts was complicated by economic, political and social constraints, and concludes that 'a thorough knowledge of research contexts and cultures' is indispensable for the successful completion of interview research (Dushku, 2000: 767). Hobbs and Kubanyiova (2008) conducted doctoral research projects aimed at exploring the impact of two different types of training courses on language teachers' beliefs and practices in two markedly different contexts: pre-service native-speaking ESL teachers in England; and in-service non-native-speaking ESL teachers in Slovakia. They reported the great challenges that were encountered during their data collection at the selected research sites. Those challenges included teachers' withdrawal for personal reasons, the incompatibility between the researcher's agenda and the researched teachers' agenda, interrupted on-site interviews and power relationships. They suggest that success in interviewing teachers requires extraordinary creativity, flexibility and insight on the part of the researcher.

Another issue in using interviews as a means of access to what interviewees think or believe is 'the potentially important asymmetries that may be less directly observable but equally relevant' (Talmy, 2010: 137). These asymmetries include institutional status, age, language expertise and more. They require the interviewer to attend to power imbalances so that the 'complex pragmatics of interview practices' (Biggs, 2007: 555) are taken into account. Talmy (2010) also suggests that applied linguistics researchers reflect on the interview methods they use in their studies in order to contribute to the theorisation of interview methods not only as research instruments but also as social practices. This perspective is the purpose of this chapter.

The Study

My qualitative case study, part of which is reported in this chapter, set out to explore the beliefs of eight teachers and their practices regarding grammar instruction. Gaining access to a research site proved to be the first challenge. It took me some months before I was able to find a school which would allow me to conduct the fieldwork. I had approached several schools but all of them were unwilling to participate, especially when I explained the procedure for data collection and how they were expected to assist. In one school, even though the principal and teachers had signed the letter of consent, they changed their minds just at the time I was to visit the school because they did not like the idea of having their lessons videoed and lengthy 'conversations' recorded. Finally, through personal contacts, I managed to find a specialised (elite) upper secondary school located in a northern province of Vietnam.

Eight teachers agreed to participate in this study (see Table 4.1 for their profiles). I had known four of them well since they were university undergraduates. These four teachers, and especially the team leader of the English language group, helped me to invite four other teachers in the school to participate, through 'snowball' sampling (see Chapter 1). Data collection lasted 12 months, from December 2007 through to November 2008.

Originally, I planned to conduct preliminary interviews in English with all eight teachers, then to make an initial analysis of the data before observing teachers in the classroom. I decided to observe them in the morning, then conduct the stimulated recall interview in the afternoon so that I could have time to review the video-recorded lesson to identify

Table 4.1 Participants' profiles

Teacher (pseudonyms)	Sex	Age	Year of graduation	Number of years of teaching experience
Hoa	F	46	1985	23
Mai	F	44	1987	23
Hong	M	44	1987	21
Nhai	F	43	1987	22
Lan	F	32	1999	10
Xuan	F	31	2000	9
Cuc	F	26	2005	4
Dao	F	26	2006	2

meaningful episodes. However, after the first week I found that this plan did not work, for many practical reasons. Firstly, when asked about their language preferences, all teachers indicated they preferred Vietnamese as the working language. Secondly, I was unable to conduct preliminary interviews with all of them before observations started because it was impossible to invite them to an interview outside school hours. Instead, each week I was able to interview two teachers before I observed them; some weeks later I conducted follow-up interviews with these two teachers before observing them the second time. The third time I met them I interviewed them again if I found it necessary to clarify or add information before I observed them for a third time. I did the same with the other teachers. This process helped me to achieve time triangulation and, despite the limited time the teachers had for the interviews, I was able to obtain sufficient data. I found it necessary to do the stimulated recall sessions immediately after the observed teacher had finished the lesson; usually the teachers had one hour free after the first two lessons before they had to teach others. This circumstance obliged me to rely on my memory of lesson episodes that I thought might be significant, so that I could pause at those episodes while fast-forwarding the video. All the preliminary interviews were semi-structured; the interviewees had the freedom to talk in an open-ended manner in a supportive and non-evaluative environment (Borg, 2006), while I was able to probe issues in depth by following up on comments made by the interviewee.

Altogether I observed 24 lessons (three with each teacher) and conducted two or three interviews with every teacher. The preliminary interview lasted around 45 minutes, while the follow-up interviews took less time. Interview transcripts were then analysed through active ana-lytical processes throughout all phases of the research, using the constant comparative analysis approach (Strauss & Corbin, 1998). In the following section, extracts from some of the interviews are presented.

Interview data samples

Teachers' beliefs about the role of grammar

All teachers in this study used much the same language when talking about the role of grammar in learning English as a foreign language. It is evident that they spoke with the voices of their community (Lemke, 1995). For example, Mai, the head of the English language department, gave the following response:

> **Interviewer:** There has been a strong debate about the role of grammar in foreign language learning. Some say grammar teaching is necessary, others disagree. Could you tell me your opinion of this issue?
>
> **Mai:** In my opinion, grammar is as important as language skills. It is impossible to teach language skills without teaching grammar. If so, students would speak pidginised English like the English the postcard vendors on the streets speak. Grammar is one of the three pillars of language, the other two being pronunciation and vocabulary.

Sharing this view, Xuan strongly supported a traditional perspective, that students should be taught grammatical structures explicitly first, and then they should be given the opportunities to manipulate the instructed forms through drills or decontextualised production practice:

> **Interviewer:** There has been a strong debate about the role of grammar in foreign language learning. Some say students should be taught grammar, others believe grammar is best learned through using the language for communication. Could you tell me your opinion of this issue?
>
> **Xuan:** My view is conservative but the students first need to have a good knowledge of grammar so that they can apply that knowledge to speaking, listening, reading and writing. This is because supposing you want to make an utterance that you went to Hanoi yesterday, you cannot get the message across if you just know individual words such as 'go', 'yesterday', 'Hanoi', without knowing what the past tense is.

Hoa, the most experienced teacher in the group, believed that grammatical knowledge made language learning successful:

Interviewer: Some people believe that students don't need to be taught grammar. They learn grammar through exposure to the target language. Could you tell me whether you believe in the same way?

Hoa: No, I don't. Because [if so] students might be able to understand and speak [English] but it is not as effective as when they are taught grammar.

Interviewer: Tell me what you mean by 'effective'.

Hoa: For example, when students imitate mechanically but are unconscious of grammar, they cannot achieve accuracy, especially in writing.

Another teacher, Lan, believed that formal instruction was critical to students' communicative competence within the context of Vietnam, where meaningful opportunities to use English outside the classroom are rare:

Interviewer: Between communicative competence in English and grammatical knowledge, which do you think is more important to your students?

Lan: Communicative competence is important but it must be built on linguistic knowledge, including grammar, vocabulary and pronunciation. Therefore, grammatical knowledge is the foundation. It is unacceptable to say that this is the way I speak, I don't care about grammar. Without good grammatical knowledge you cannot become a fluent and accurate user of English.

Interviewer: But don't you think that grammar can be learned through communicative tasks?

Lan: I think in Vietnam the pupils do not have adequate conditions for language learning. They just learn the language inside the classroom; therefore they need to learn grammar. If you just let them use the language for communication without knowing grammar, who do they communicate with? If, for example, they are in the environment where they hear people speaking English frequently, they can imitate them, but here such an opportunity is almost non-existent.

Teachers' beliefs about students' expectations of grammar

Another reason for the importance of grammar teaching referred to by all the teachers was the students' expectations. Again, their responses in the interviews reflect their identity as members of a 'socially meaningful group' (Gee, 1996: 131). Nhai stated in her first interview that her students favoured grammar for the examination. In the second interview she said she emphasised grammar teaching because it was what her students preferred:

Interviewer: You think grammar is important, but teachers and students may have different opinions. Do you think the students think in the same way?

Nhai: I think the pupils prefer learning grammar. They are unwilling to learn to speak. In my afternoon lessons, I try to teach them language skills, but they insist that I should teach them grammar. They value it [grammar] more.

Since this was my second interview with her, she was becoming more relaxed and was quite open that her intuition told her that the students preferred grammar:

Interviewer: There must be some reason for the students' preference for grammar. Do you have any idea about this?

Nhai: Probably, they feel confused. I don't know whether they are not sure of their grammatical knowledge or they like learning grammar. When I tried teaching them communicative skills, they complained. It seemed that they disliked it [learning communicative skills].

Hong, the only male teacher, also stated frankly that he thought the students expected to be taught grammar:

Interviewer: Many scholars advise teachers to teach grammar by asking students to perform communicative tasks. What, in your opinion, are the opportunities and constraints of teaching grammar through communicative tasks to your students?

Hong: Developing students' communicative ability in English is limited because I observed that the students were unwilling to communicate in English for fear that their English was grammatically wrong.

For Mai, the students were more satisfied when they were taught grammar explicitly. She stated:

After each grammar lesson, the pupils seem more satisfied because they have gained something visible while their gains in the skills lessons are more abstract. On the surface, the skills lessons may be exciting, but pupils are just attentive to noting down [grammar] rules in their notebooks, viewing them as their own assets.

Convergence of beliefs and practices

One of the objectives of the research was to identify the extent of convergence between teachers' stated beliefs and their practices. The data obtained by interviews and observations indicated a high level of convergence. These teachers showed a strong inclination towards an explicit approach to grammar, which they believed would be more appropriate to their teaching context. Such a belief clearly translated into their observed instructional behaviours. This convergence could be explained by the fact that, working in an under-resourced environment where access to explicit theories was quite limited, the teachers' beliefs were rooted in their personal and collective experiences. Their teaching practices were regulated by normative ways of teaching and learning which were historically embedded in their local context (Canagarajah, 2005) and into which they were socialised. This situation implies that for teachers to change their beliefs (and accordingly their practices), conditions for successful experiences with the intended innovation should be created for them.

Methodological Implications

In much qualitative research, finding a convenient site, gaining gate-keepers' permission and persuading people to participate are not easy. In my study, I found it necessary to make my research agenda compatible with those of teachers who were already overburdened with heavy workloads as well as their own personal and professional concerns. As previously mentioned, I had to change my original plan because one school abruptly declined to cooperate and I began to wonder whether I would have to change the entire research design. However, I persisted and through personal contacts was able to locate my eventual setting, which was two hours from my home and workplace – not convenient, but manageable.

Although it is important to have a pre-determined interview schedule, researchers need to be flexible in order to respond to the opportunities and constraints within the sociocultural and institutional context in which the project is carried out. In Vietnam, as elsewhere, teachers earn very low salaries. An average secondary-school teacher is mandated to teach 16–18 hours a week and is paid approximately US$150 a month. Therefore, most of them have to teach elsewhere for additional income and are available at the school only according to the school timetable, which is always for half a day every weekday. Immediately after they have finished teaching they leave to do household work and/or to give extra classes. This situation makes it impossible to meet them for interviews at their school once they have done their daily teaching. On-site interviews can often be interrupted by mobile phone calls; teachers have to deal with their own priorities, even during their time off. Thus, it may be necessary, as it was in my study, to interview participants two or three times instead of just once (as originally intended). In fact, these constraints proved to be valuable because they helped me to achieve time triangulation. All interviewers are confronted with how to judge the honesty or truth value of what the interviewee says. By interviewing each teacher more than once, I was able to include some key questions that I had asked in a previous interview, but using slightly different wording so that the interviewee did not recognise that I was checking my understanding of what he or she had told me previously.

Understanding the culture of the interviewees offers a considerable advantage. If the researcher shares the same culture, this is likely to make participants feel more comfortable and relaxed, which is a key factor in the success of semi-structured interviews with teachers like those involved in this study, who did not have much experience of being interviewed and having their voices recorded. In a Confucian-influenced society like Vietnam, there are also other ways of ensuring participants feel at ease. First, even the way a researcher is dressed sends an important message; he or she needs to fit in with the way teachers dress at school rather than adopting formal clothing, such as a suit and tie, which would create an unhelpful power distance. Secondly, even when time is limited, researchers working with Vietnamese teachers are recommended to make small talk and ask tactful personal questions before each interview. Thirdly, the choice of language for interviews should be considered with care. Proficiency in English is always a sensitive issue for many teachers in ESL contexts like Vietnam because of their limited opportunity to communicate in English. Therefore, there is a strong case for using the shared first language wherever possible, on the grounds of empathy, shared cultural values and norms, shared professional understanding and experience, and membership of the same community of practice. In this study, I initially intended to use English so that time and energy would be saved in translating the interview transcripts and also to avoid the inadequacies of translation. However, before the interviews the teachers all responded that they would prefer using Vietnamese to articulate more exactly what they meant to say. To show respect for their choice, I used our shared language in all my contacts with the participants. If interviews had continued in English, the teachers would have felt less able to express themselves fully and accurately, and data quality could have suffered.

Power relationships are another issue to be addressed. In a hierarchical society like Vietnam, the researcher may be seen as an 'evaluator' or 'examiner', and teachers often feel that observation of their teaching and interviews inevitably involves some sort of assessment. Consequently, they may not be prepared to have their opinions, perceptions and teaching scrutinised by an outsider. Initially, the teachers in this study felt intimidated and nervous when asked to have their lessons and interviews audio- or video-recorded, and at first only four agreed to participate. This meant that I had to make efforts to equalise the power relationship so that the perceived power hierarchy would not lead to teacher–researcher relationship problems. By establishing a mutual trustful rapport with the first volunteers, a snowball effect occurred and four other teachers subsequently agreed to participate.

Teachers may tend to view a researcher, especially one who is a university lecturer, as an 'expert' in the field. I noticed that after each interview teachers often asked for my opinions of their responses. It is likely that they saw me as a source of information but also viewed themselves as being under surveillance. In such circumstances, my response was frequently along the lines of the following:

> There is no right or wrong about what I've asked you. They are controversial issues and different people have different opinions about them. What you have said is really important to me, but if you do want to know my opinions, I'll tell you after I've finished my fieldtrips.

Also, teachers' responses may be influenced by their view that the interviewer is more knowledgeable. If, for instance, they are asked, 'How important do you think grammar is in learning English?', they are likely to say 'Very important'. Aware of this possibility, I tried to neutralise my questioning, asking, for example, 'In learning English, some people think that grammar is important, others say that students don't need to learn grammar. Could you tell me your opinion of this?' When asked in this way, the teachers were not aware of my personal views and therefore were less likely to be influenced by presuppositions about my expectations. In addition, as a cultural insider, I was aware that the teachers' theoretical knowledge might be limited. During the interviews, I tried to avoid using terms which are common in the disciplinary discourse community, such as 'explicit', 'inductive', 'consciousness-raising' and so on. Instead, to avoid teachers' misconceptualisation, I used non-technical language that paraphrased technical terms. The final point to note, as mentioned earlier, is that teachers may have problems verbalising beliefs that are tacit. Therefore, I frequently asked them to exemplify what they had stated. For instance, when one teacher said that she always presented grammar in context, I asked 'Could you give me one example of how you present [the present perfect] in context?' This helped me to gain more accurate information about their 'wisdom of practice' (Shulman, 1987: 11).

The point also needs to be made that personal relationships may be a determinant of success in interviewing. While conducting this study, my personal relationships allowed me to gain, relatively easily, permission for entry to the research site in order to conduct my fieldwork over an extended period of time. The school principal even allocated me accommodation at the school's modest guest-house, which also provided a convenient and comfortable location to hold face-to-face interviews with each individual teacher. For this study, my personal relationship with teacher participants was established both previously and as a result of the research and led to the 'snowball effect' of gaining access to further participants. My personal relationship with all the participants grew throughout the research project and extended to social contacts (occasionally we had lunch or dinner together during my visits to the research site). This contact helped the teachers become more willing to be open. For example, when talking about the medium of instruction, Nhai, a retrained Russian teacher, said:

On many occasions when I spoke English they [the students] did understand. They enjoyed listening to my speaking English. But there are things which I find really difficult to explain in English. Then I have to resort to Vietnamese.

Similarly, Mai, the head of the department, stated quite honestly that the goal of teaching English in her school was to prepare the students for the standardised examinations, which were largely grammar-based. Speaking frankly, she said:

We have our own goal. We focused on formal knowledge to prepare the students for the examinations. I sound quite down on earth, but it is true. In the examinations, they test the students' grammar, reading comprehension and writing. Therefore, grammar is more important and we tend to teach it separately.

Such data might not be provided to researchers who do not develop strong personal relationships with the participants.

For novice researchers who are cultural outsiders in Vietnam and who wish to conduct interview research with Vietnamese high-school teachers, it would, in my view, be advisable to have a local research assistant. This person could serve such functions as: (1) sharing contextualised/situated sociocultural knowledge with the researcher; (2) facilitating access and assisting the development of rapport; (3) acting as interpreter during interviews when necessary; and (4) subsequently assisting as a translator. Finding a research assistant, who may also be a university lecturer and thus understand the purpose of research, is not necessarily a major problem when the researcher has local contacts, because personal relationships are always valued in Vietnamese culture. Alternatively, email interviews, which are asynchronous, may be feasible, although researchers need to take account of the fact that there may be substantial delays in gaining responses from teachers.

Reflection

Conducting this qualitative case study through interviews was a significant learning experience for me. I realised that although a qualitative interview is regarded as a 'conversation with a purpose' (Burgess, 1984: 102) or a 'professional conversation' (Kvale, 1996: 5), it is much more than simply a conversation. A conversation is primarily sociable, based on established rapport and mutual interests and shared purposes, whether personal or professional. On the other hand, an interview is inevitably to some extent structured because the topics and direction of the discussion are generated by the researcher's agenda. Importantly, an atmosphere of mutual trust needs to be created between the interviewer and the interviewee so that openness of exchange is achievable. A conversation typically takes place among acquaintances while an interviewer is, initially at least, a stranger to the interviewee. Thus, the interviewing researcher has, among other things, to establish good dialogic partnerships by understanding the research context and culture and developing network-building skills.

In Vietnam, each educational establishment is an enclosed territory in which strangers are not always welcomed. Both teachers and school managers dislike the idea of revealing their work to outsiders, for fear of criticism. Moreover, the formalities and bureaucracy of authorising field research always involve high-level official permission. Thereafter, personal relationship and mutual trust are keys to successful field research, especially – but not exclusively – in Vietnam. The teachers I worked with were often under stress from their busy professional and personal schedules. Initially they were uncomfortable spending precious free time answering interview questions, which they believed might turn out to be evaluations of their knowledge and skills. The personal relationships I sought to nurture with the school principal and the head of the English department enabled my project to begin and then to continue over a period of time. I am indebted to them and to the other teachers who participated, without whose coopera-tion and goodwill my study could not have been completed.

COMMENTARY

My comments on Le Van Canh's study will fall under four main headings: the logistical issues, the contextual issues, the methodological issues and issues arising from the research and the findings. Such divisions are of course to some degree arbitrary and there will be overlap between the categories. These comments will be followed by more general closing remarks relating to the significance of the study.

Logistical Issues

Being able to gain access to schools and to the teachers within them is clearly a major hurdle for researchers wishing to undertake research of this kind. In a hierarchically organised society like Vietnam, would-be researchers face daunting odds. On the one hand, they need to secure the necessary documentary approval from the authorities, which can be, and usually is, a time-consuming and frustrating business. On the other hand, they face the suspicion and even hostility of school principals, who regard research of this kind as a disruptive and potentially threatening intrusion into their domain. In addition, the teachers themselves are often suspicious of the motives of researchers. In any case, their packed programme of classes (often over 30 hours per week) and the extra jobs they undertake to supplement their meagre salaries leave little time for the luxury of extended interviews and observations, as Canh explains at length in the case study.

Contextual Issues

English is a foreign language in the Vietnamese educational context. Many students, especially outside major urban centres, cannot see any purpose in learning English. It is simply another subject on the timetable, in competition with many other subjects, and their aim is to pass the examination with as little effort as possible. Their teachers are often trained in only the most basic way. They are unsure of their own command of English, so they tend to fall back on the comforting support of the textbook, which is usually heavily biased towards grammar activities. In any case, with only three hours per week for English, taught in large classes, students have no chance of reaching even a threshold of competence in the language by the end of high school. The flourishing business enjoyed by private language schools and institutes in Vietnam (and many other countries like it) bears eloquent witness to the belated realisation among students that they have been ill-served by the public system.

The fact that the whole of secondary education (and to a large degree the university system as well) is driven by the final examination results (arrived at by dedicated adhesion to the syllabus and the textbook) makes it almost impossible for teachers to do anything except go through the prescribed motions. The educational context is heavily weighted in favour of a so-called Confucian model, where deference to authority serves a methodology dominated by rote learning and respect for declarative rather than procedural knowledge.

Deference to authority is also part of the problem faced by the researcher, who is *ipso facto* regarded as a potential 'inspector', with the power to inflict negative sanctions – or at the very least to make face-threatening judgements on teachers' performance. The context thus tends to encourage teachers to try to second-guess the researcher's motivations and to offer responses which they calculate will please, rather than to give genuine answers.

There is also the material context to consider. The researcher may have to travel long distances to obtain the data. The schools may be poorly equipped and unable to offer even basic facilities like a room for the interviews, or a reliable electricity supply.

Methodological Issues

Clearly, the methodology employed had to take account of the logistical and contextual factors outlined above. Canh had to find ways of circumventing the natural suspicion surrounding the research study and to establish an atmosphere of trust and relaxation in which the teachers would unwind and begin to offer genuine answers to the questions asked of them. He had also to find ways of double-checking the kinds of answers he was given in the interviews to ensure that they were genuine expressions of the teachers' beliefs and not simply an attempt to please the researcher. And he needed to be willing to be flexible if circumstances turned out to be different from those he had planned for.

Issues Arising from the Research and the Findings

In the research project described here, Canh was able in large measure to find a way through the thicket of logistical, contextual and methodological problems which faced him at the outset. He was able to use his position as a lecturer in a prestigious national university to obtain the necessary written authorisations. He was then in the happy position of being able to activate his network of contacts to find a school willing to allow him access, and to involve four of his ex-students who could be persuaded to cooperate in the research, and who subsequently persuaded four others to join them.

He showed his willingness to be flexible by slightly changing his initial plan so that the interviews did not impinge so much on the teachers' schedules. A friendly and non-threatening atmosphere was established, partly by holding interviews in the guest-house rather than in the school itself and by agreeing to use Vietnamese rather than English. The format of semi-structured interviews also allowed for flexibility and for the exploration of unforeseen opportunities as the interviews unfolded.

It is important to note how critical it was for the success of the project that Canh was an 'insider' – part of the same educational system (albeit at a higher level than the teachers) and who therefore knew it from the inside; also he was a native-speaker of the teachers' language and a person who shared their culture and society. It is difficult to imagine how any 'outsider' figure, say from London or Harvard, could have even started research of this kind, let alone brought it to a successful conclusion.

He was able to triangulate his results by using observations to verify the findings from the interviews, and to cross-check his interview data by rephrasing questions at different times to ensure consistency. Although his sample was too small for reliable generalisations to be made, the fact that he was able to observe each teacher three times (24 classes in total) and to conduct two or three interviews with each of the eight teachers involved ensured that he collected substantial data for analysis.

The findings themselves are unsurprising and very much what one might have predicted on the basis of intuition. But the fact is that they were not reached on that basis but on the basis of close observation and detailed interviewing, thus enhancing their credibility. By chance, I was able to corroborate these findings. In an assignment set for my MA students at the Open University in Ho Chi Minh City in the summer of 2010, I offered a choice of four topics. Well over 50% of the students (24 out of 44) chose one directly relevant to this study:

> The communicative approach to English-language teaching is now widely accepted. However, theoretical and practical objections have been raised in the context of Asian teaching situations. What are your views on this issue, based on your own teaching context and experience?

It is significant in itself that so many students (most of them teachers in schools) chose this topic rather than one of the other three on offer. Clearly, the issue was something very much at the forefront of their minds. All but one of the reflective essays adopted a highly negative stance to the feasibility of implementing a communicative approach in Vietnam. They cited precisely the kinds of factors reviewed above: teacher overload and lack of training, few hours of instruction and large classes, institutional and parental pressure to achieve success in exams, textbooks with a focus on form rather than communication, lack of motivation, culturally ingrained beliefs about learning, hierarchical power relationships and so on. Their conclusions were that, given these kinds of constraints, only a grammar-centred approach delivered by a top-down, teacher-led methodology had any chance of success.

Closing Remarks

I would like to close by commenting on two things: the fact of carrying out the research and the significance of the findings for the future of language teaching in Vietnam.

As noted above, the results of the research are unremarkable, in the sense that they tend to confirm what might have been expected on the basis of intuition. For the researcher, however, the project was a highly significant learning experience. Through it, Canh came to appreciate better the kinds of problems experienced on a daily basis by classroom teachers. Clearly, he also was able to refine his views on the role of grammar-led instruction and learned a lot about himself in the process. It is arguable that the teachers who participated in the study also learned a great deal, and through the interviewing process and the observations came to a better appreciation of their own personal theories of learning and of their own practice. The value of this research therefore extends well beyond its defined objectives. It became, in fact, an in-depth form of teacher development.

My second remark relates to the future of English teaching in Vietnam. As I mentioned above, 23 of the 24 students who opted to write about the appropriateness of the communicative approach in Vietnam adopted an overwhelmingly negative and fatalistic stance. For them, the difficulties – human, logistical, bureaucratic and cultural – were simply too constraining. Short of a complete shake-up of the educational system, it would never be possible to do anything different from what traditionally had been done. There was, however, one student who took a different line. 'As a Vietnamese teacher of English, I have had great success when using CLT [communicative language teaching] to teach English.... In general, Vietnamese students are not quiet and passive as some teachers complained....' She went on to list the kinds of activities she used to engage the students. She then referred specifically to the role of grammar: 'We should not teach grammar separately or deliver monotonous and boring grammar lessons. We should link grammatical knowledge to genuine communication and use grammar as a "supportive force" for communication.'

The experience of this teacher is supported by Littlewood's (2000) article, 'Do Asian students really want to listen and obey?', based on his experiences in Hong Kong. He suggests that 'problems' with teaching English for communication may be the result of teacher attitudes and past educational experience (we teach the way we were taught!) rather than of an immutable set of problems, real though they may be. Effecting change in teacher attitudes is clearly one of the major pressure points for future development.

REFLECTIVE QUESTIONS

(1) Le Van Canh interviewed his participants several times. What do you think are the advantages of doing this?

(2) What logistical issues/constraints would you face in interviewing participants in your research context? How would you plan to deal with the foreseen constraints?

(3) How important is it for the researcher to respect the participant interviewee's language preference? Why?

(4) Le Van Canh recommends that researchers who are unused to a particular culture seek a local research assistant. In your opinion, what would be the disadvantages of having such an assistant?

(5) Alan Maley, in his commentary, makes the point that being part of the same educational system is critical to the success of research on teachers. How far do you agree with him?

(6) Ethical issues arise in interviewing, as in any other form of data collection. Draft a (hypothetical) consent form which you would wish your potential interviewees to complete.

(7) Ask a colleague if you could interview them about a topic in which they are interested. Then, at a mutually convenient time and place, carry out the interview and record it. Afterwards, listen to the recording and evaluate the extent to which your interviewing strategy was effective. Consider both the content of what you said and the manner in which you spoke. (If you video-record the interview, you could consider the positive and negative effects of your body language.)

References

Biggs, C. (2007) Anthropology, interviewing, and communicability in contemporary society. *Current Anthropology*, 48(4), 551–567.

Block, D. (2000) Problematising interview data: voices in the mind's machine? *TESOL Quarterly*, 34(4), 757–763.

Borg, S. (2003) Teacher cognition in grammar teaching: A literature review. *Language Awareness*, 12(2), 96–108.

Borg, S. (2006) *Teacher Cognition and Language Education: Research and Practice*. London: Continuum.

Borg, S. and Burns, A. (2008) Integrating grammar in adult TESOL classrooms. *Applied Linguistics*, 29(3), 456–482.

Burgess, R.G. (1984) *In the Field*. London: Allen and Unwin.

Canagarajah, S. (ed.) (2005) *Reclaiming the Local in Language Policy and Practice*. Mahwah, NJ: Lawrence Erlbaum.

Denzin, K.N. and Lincoln, Y.S. (eds) (1998) *Collecting and Interpreting Qualitative Materials*. London: Sage.

Dushku, S. (2000) Conducting individual and focus group interviews in research in Albania. *TESOL Quarterly*, 34(4), 763–768.

Farrell, T.S.C. and Lim, P.C.P. (2005) Conceptions of grammar teaching: A case study of teachers' beliefs and classroom practices. *TESL–EJ*, 9(2), 1–13.

Gascoigne, C. (2002) *The Debate on Grammar in Second Language Acquisition: Past, Present, and Future*. New York: Edwin Mellen Press.

Gee, J. (1996) *Social Linguistics and Literacies: Ideology in Discourses* (2nd edition). London: Falmer Press.

Green, P.S. and Hecht, K.H. (1992) Implicit and explicit grammar: An empirical study. *Applied Linguistics*, 13(2), 168–184.

Hobbs, V. and Kubanyiova, M. (2008) The challenges of researching language teachers: What research manuals don't tell us. *Language Teaching Research*, 12(4), 495–513.

Kagan, D. (1992) Implications of research on teacher beliefs. *Educational Psychologist*, 27(1), 65–90.

Kvale, S. (1996) *Interviews: An Introduction to Qualitative Research Interviewing*. Thousand Oaks, CA: Sage.

Lemke, J. (1995) *Textual Politics: Discourse and Social Dynamics*. London: Taylor and Francis.

Littlewood, W. (2000) Do Asian students really want to listen and obey? *ELT Journal*, 54(1), 31–36.

Long, M. (1991) Focus on form: A design feature in language teaching methodology. In K. de Bot, D. Coste, R. Ginsberg and C. Kramsch (eds), *Foreign Language Research in Cross-cultural Perspective* (pp. 39–52). Amsterdam: John Benjamins.

Norris, J.M. and Ortega, L. (2000) Effectiveness of L2 instruction: A research synthesis and quantitative meta-analysis. *Language Learning*, 50(3), 417–528.

Polat, N. (2009) Matches in beliefs between teachers and students, and success in L2 attainment: The Georgian example. *Foreign Language Annals*, 42(2), 229–249.

Roulston, K. (2010) *Reflective Interviewing: A Guide to Theory and Practice*. Thousand Oaks, CA: Sage.

Shulman, L.S. (1987) Knowledge and teaching: Foundations of the new reform. *Harvard Educational Review*, 57(1), 1–22.

Skehan, P. (1996) A framework for the implementation of task-based instruction. *Applied Linguistics*, 17(1), 38–62.

Strauss, A. and Corbin, J. (1998) *Basics of Qualitative Research: Grounded Theory Procedures and Techniques*. Thousand Oaks, CA: Sage.

Talmy, S. (2010) Qualitative interviews in applied linguistics: From research instrument to social practice. *Annual Review of Applied Linguistics*, 30, 128–148.

5 Observation

Case Study: Simon Humphries
Commentary: Jerry Gebhard

CASE STUDY

Introduction

This chapter focuses on the classroom observation of teachers' use of traditional and new English language textbooks in a Japanese engineering college (*Kosen*). In these colleges, students (aged 16–20) study a mixture of engineering and general education subjects for five years. The *Kosen* where I worked replaced traditional ministry-approved English textbooks with materials from a British publisher for the compulsory English credits in grades 2–4.

The new textbooks sought to change the focus from teacher-fronted grammar translation and reading comprehension to learner-centred communicative activities emphasising listening comprehension and meaning-oriented conversation practice. However, policy change does not automatically equal shared ownership and adoption by practitioners (Fullan, 2007). Therefore, in order to explore the nature of the acceptance and implementation of the new textbooks by four Japanese teachers of English (JTEs) in the *Kosen*, I used a combination of interviews (see Chapter 4) and observations. Although the interviews formed an integral part of the data collection and analysis, this chapter focuses on the observations.

Although the Japanese government has introduced policies to encourage communicative learning in Japanese schools (MEXT, 2002, 2003), studies have shown that JTEs have tended to continue to use the traditional *yakudoku* (grammar translation) style of education (Kikuchi & Browne, 2009; O'Donnell, 2005; Sato & Kleinsasser, 2004). Despite some desire from JTEs to implement communicative approaches (Browne & Wada, 1998; Sakui, 2004), it seems they feel compelled to employ *yakudoku* to prepare students for prestigious university entrance tests (Gorsuch, 2001; Sakui, 2004; Watanabe, 2004).

Kosens differ from ordinary high schools. Firstly, they can implement their own curricula and materials; and secondly, students can study in-house for two additional tertiary-level years before transferring into the third year of a university course without an English entrance test (Humphries, 2011). This lack of an external test burden, combined with the introduction of a different type of textbook, could increase opportunities for different teaching approaches. This unique case (Duff, 2008; Miles & Huberman, 1994) prompted me to observe the effects of the change for the teachers.

Methodological Focus

Methods of data collection should match what the researcher wants to discover (Burns, 2010). This study aimed to examine the influence of the textbooks on the teachers' attitudes and practices. Interviews can lead to insights into attitudes and into how teachers *believe* they teach. However, 'it is not unusual for persons to say they are doing one thing, but in reality they are doing something else' (Corbin & Strauss, 2008: 29). Moreover, 'ultimately … we are interested in understanding teachers' professional actions, not what or how they think in isolation of what they do' (Borg, 2003: 105). Therefore, in combination with interviews, this study employed observations.

Naturalistic observations make an interesting topic for this book, because, when observing real people in real situations, many unexpected problems can arise. The main issue is the *observer's paradox*: 'the act of observation will change the perceived person's behaviour' (Cowie, 2009: 177). Three main factors can influence this phenomenon: level of participation, level of disclosure and the recording equipment.

Although naturalistic researchers may try not to participate, the students or teachers may request their involvement. For instance, in one study, two non-native-speaking teachers of the instructed language asked the native-speaker researcher for advice during the observations (Sato & Kleinsasser, 1999). In another example, the researcher was requested to lead an activity (Borg, 2006). In both cases, the researchers agreed to the requests, but acknowledged that the data could not represent typical instruction.

Full disclosure of the aims of an investigation can cause the observed person to concentrate on certain areas in an unnatural way (Cowie, 2009); however, concealing information can lead to suspicion (Borg, 2006). Six months after Richards (1997) began his study of the teaching culture in a language school, the instructors admitted to him that they no longer treated him as a spy. Until that point, they had presented the 'front' of success and 'hid any negative aspects or criticisms of higher management' (Richards, 2003: 127). The distortions in behaviour can increase if participants believe that they are being evaluated (see also the discussion in Chapter 4 in relation to interviews). For example, student teachers in a practicum in Kenya 'played the game' to pass the teaching licence. They focused on areas that they believed would please their assessors, such as the correct dress code, rather than taking risks to improve their teaching practice (Borg, 2010).

Equipment is an important consideration for recording data: 'it's pretty well impossible to record verbal exchanges accurately through notes alone' (Burns, 2010: 70). However, the intrusiveness of video-cameras can generate reactivity among the observed (Borg, 2006) and recording devices 'have become so associated with public scandals and/or media intrusion that people are perhaps even more suspicious of them than they used to be' (Richards, 2003: 177). However, as Barnard warns, any form of recording can be unintentionally threatening, 'although perhaps not as menacing as the observer who sits with arms folded and a fixed smile on his or her face' (Barnard, 1998: 52). In a study where teachers watched video playbacks of their classes to discuss their methodology, they admitted that they had become self-conscious and restrained in front of the camera (Woods, 1996). In an investigation by Duff (2002), although she received consent initially, the teacher asked her to stop video-taping, because a group of teenaged girls 'seemed to be too distracted by it, directing off-task comments and gossip at the camera microphone from time to time' (Duff, 2008: 140).

The Study

This study operated within the constructivist qualitative paradigm: it attempted to understand the socially constructed reality from the multiple perspectives of the teachers participating in the study (Richards, 2003). This entailed a multi-method, interpretive, naturalistic approach (Denzin & Lincoln, 1994). Therefore, for the observations, I analysed the salient patterns that occurred naturally in the classrooms, without imposing my own pre-set categories or beliefs. Concepts emerged through the constant comparison (Corbin & Strauss, 2008; Glaser & Strauss, 1967) of the teachers' observed actions and interview data. Therefore, the analysis took place during, as well as after, the data collection.

The English department contained six JTEs, two full time and four part time. Four male JTEs, who taught the first and second grades, volunteered to participate. A part-time female instructor also taught the first and second grades, but she declined to participate. Observing the participating teachers

Table 5.1 Summary of participants' characteristics

	Akira	*Bonda*	*Chikara*	*Daiki*
Age	55	43	55	41
Position	Part-time lecturer	Full-time professor	Full-time professor	Part-time lecturer
Years at this Kosen	1	16	6	5
Class proficiency	Lower-middle	Lowest	Highest	Lower-middle

enabled a comparison between the use of the traditional *Vivid* textbook (Minamimura *et al.*, 2006) in the first grade and the degree of implementation of *On the Go* (Gershon *et al.*, 2004), the new textbook used in the second-grade classes.

Table 5.1 outlines, at the time of the study, the participants' ages, contractual conditions, length of service at this *Kosen* and their class proficiency levels. The classes are labelled A, B, C and D, which correspond to the initial letters of the teachers' pseudonyms: Akira, Bonda, Chikara and Daiki.

The observations took place during a six-week period from 12 May to 30 June 2008. This period was chosen because it allowed the teachers and students to settle into classes after the beginning of the academic year, in April. In total, I observed 32 periods of 45 minutes, four periods for each teacher per grade, as shown in Table 5.2.

In addition to memos noted in a field journal (see Methodological Implications section), each observation was video-recorded, transcribed and translated into English by an independent translator. I recorded the classes from a central position at the back of the classroom to capture all the information from the blackboard and to enable off-camera observation of the students' behaviour. By using a digital video-camera, I could review the data and take screen shots of the blackboard and the positioning of the

Table 5.2 Number of observations

	Akira	*Bonda*	*Chikara*	*Daiki*	*Total*
Grade 1	4	4	4	4	16
Grade 2	4	4	4	4	16
Total	8	8	8	8	32

teacher, which facilitated the insertion of visual data to support the written thick description (Geertz, 1973) of the classes. This method avoided the potentially disruptive movement of a camera or photographer during the observation.

I focused on each teacher in turn (with some overlap), observing both his first- and second-grade classes during the same time frame. This strategy enabled comparisons of the patterns of use *between textbooks* for each teacher. The comparisons *between teachers*, while not neglected, were secondary, to avoid forcing generalisations (Stake, 2003).

Methodological Implications

Many issues arose during the observations, but the following discussion focuses on five areas: unusable data; the observer's paradox; error correction; concentration; and insider politics.

Before describing the *unusable data*, I must admit that this qualitative open-coding approach to observing generated more findings than I could fit into my thesis. Therefore, some areas of unusable data caused some relief, because they enabled a natural narrowing of the focus. The remaining areas could then be analysed and described in greater depth. Three areas of unusable data appeared, which are described below.

Firstly, within and between observations, Daiki changed his teaching approaches frequently. Moreover, during the interviews, he seemed to change his attitudes to various aspects of language pedagogy. When asked how he decided upon his different techniques, he responded that it was based on his 'feeling'. His uncertainty emerged, because he asked me how he should teach and indicated that he lacked confidence in his teaching ability and English proficiency. Daiki's frequently changing teaching approaches, combined with uncertain and contradictory interview responses, made it difficult to discern a principled pattern in his methodology.

Secondly, Bonda had his own worksheets, developed in advance for the whole year, which replaced the textbooks. He explained in the interviews that the worksheets guided the lowest-proficiency students to take notes effectively in English. Unlike Daiki, his classes followed a rigid pattern that matched his beliefs regarding classroom management and the students' English production. Data from Daiki and Bonda's observations could form the bases of two separate case studies, each with their own intrinsic value (Stake, 2003), but they lie outside the case boundary (Miles & Huberman, 1994) for understanding patterns in the application of the textbooks.

Thirdly, many students from all the classes gave inaudible answers. Therefore, I could record the teachers' interactions only with the confident minority. However, the quietness of the students' responses, combined with frequent pauses and silence, formed evidence of the class cultures and difficulties faced by the teachers as they tried to implement communicative approaches.

As explained above, the *observer's paradox* exists when people behave differently due to their awareness of the presence of an observer. Chikara's actions and the behaviour of Daiki's students provided the most vivid examples.

Chikara openly changed his behaviour. He admitted to the alterations in follow-up interviews and even announced the potential for changes to his students at the beginning of the first observation:

> **Chikara:** *Kameraga arunode kochiramo sukoshiyarikata kaerutokiga aru-kamoshiremasen* (a video-camera is here, so I might change things a bit).

Before this first observation began, I arrived a minute early, during the lunch break, to discover Chikara already in the classroom, handing back notebooks to all the students. In the follow-up interview, he admitted: 'This is because you said that you want to take the video, so, but, I also wanted to return the {pause} workbook to students and the {pause} answers to them so I went to the room earlier than usual'.

Although the observer effect usually occurs most strongly during the initial observations (Duff, 2008), Chikara's next change occurred during the third observation of his grade 2 class. This incident transpired when he initiated a role-play from the textbook. Following some pair-work practice, the teacher nominated two individuals (denoted here S1 and S2) to speak in front of the class.

> **Chikara:** *S1-kun sorekara S2-kun*. Stand up. *Haichotto kyouwane, anoshita no tango mite ittemoraouka. Soremiteano hai* Simon *no houmiteitte kudasai* (S1 and S2 'stand up'. OK, today, say the words while looking at Simon)
> **S1:** Eh! {Groans, stands up and briefly covers his face}
> **Observer:** <<to S1 and S2>> I'm sorry
> **Chikara:** *Hai, ookikoede hajime* (Okay, use a loud voice, start)

In the follow-up interview, Chikara explained that it was a minor change.

> **Chikara:** I asked some pairs to speak aloud instead of their classmates.

Interviewer: Oh yeah, was that the first time to do that?

Chikara: To look at you was the first time {laughing}. I usually ask two pairs or three pairs to make the conversations.

Despite the minor change, I felt concerned by the ethical problem of forcing the students to perform to the camera. Moreover, although I wanted to video naturally occurring data, on this occasion Chikara seemed to prefer to present a model performance.

In the first observation of Daiki's grade 2 class, the discomfort occurred in the opposite direction. One of the students seemed to take advantage of the presence of the video-camera to tease the teacher. He interrupted Daiki frequently to shout out various comments. For example:

Sensei, itsumo bokurani jyugyou yarasunoni kyouwa senseiga yattekurerunsuka? (Sir, you always leave us on our own, but are you going to teach us today?)

Hatsuon suruno mendokusaikara ittsumo rajikaseyan (You usually use the audio-player, because you can't be bothered to pronounce the words)

Kyouwa bideototterukara? Kiirokushitatte? (Are you using yellow chalk because you're being videoed?)

In addition to these comments, students also seemed to deride the teacher's pronunciation and some individuals began singing during his explanations. Three times during the observation, I reflected in my research diary whether my presence with the video-camera caused too much disruption. However, during the class, Daiki laughed at many of the students' interjections. He seemed to have developed a rapport with them that permitted some banter and he had taught the most rebellious student the previous year. Despite my reservations, Daiki indicated in the follow-up interview that he wanted the study to continue. Moreover, the students probably overcame their initial excitement, because, during later observations, despite the occasional comments, they tended to sit quietly.

Considering *error correction*, I felt concerned about whether to intervene when the JTEs made linguistic mistakes. The most problematic case occurred during the fourth observation of Akira's grade 2 class. Although the textbook contained an open-ended pair-work activity, where the students could ask for information about facilities on a fictional university campus, Akira developed his own questions on the blackboard and supplied the Japanese translations. He wrote:

1. Is there 設備 (facility)? はありますか? → Yes it is.
2. Are they open all the time? ずっと開いてますか? When is it open?
   開館時間は?
   開館 (opening time)
3. Where is it? それはどこにありますか?
   場所 (place)

Akira then directed the students to read questions in turn and assisted them to answer, as illustrated in the following interaction with students denoted S15–17:

Akira: S15, *tsugi nanika chigaumononi tsuite* is there *to kiitekudasai* (S15, next, please ask about something else using 'is there')
S15: Is there…
Akira: *nandemo ii* (anything is OK)
S15: tennis *so* court
Akira: Is there a tennis court? *Hai e~ S16, douzo.* No *ka* Yes *ka* {pause} Yes, it is *desune* (OK {pause} S16 go on, 'yes' or 'no' {pause} 'yes it is' isn't it)
S16: xxx
Akira: S17, *soshitara tsugino shitsumon desune. Tennisukoutono kaikanjikan* (S17, then it's the next question. The tennis court opening times)
S17: *dokokiki …* (where do I ask [from the blackboard])
Akira: *haikikeba ii dake. Kotaerun janakutte* (Okay, you only need to ask the question. You don't need to answer) When is it open? *ne.*
S17: When is it open?

Apart from replacing the flexible pair-work with a teacher-directed recitation exercise, the main problem arose from the grammatically incorrect pattern: 'Is there a ____?' – 'Yes it is'. There were 24 students present in the class, all of whom had to say one of the six lines; therefore, four different students were told to utter this grammatically incorrect reply. I felt uncomfortable each time he made a student repeat this phrase and considered whether I ought to correct this error. On this, and other occasions, I decided to avoid giving feedback. Firstly, if I intervened during the class, it could undermine the teachers' authority. I was a guest there to observe rather than instruct. Secondly, if I corrected the language after the class, it could damage the teacher's confidence to instruct in front of me and increase the observer effect. These errors would occur naturally if I were not present. However, despite this goal of non-interference, I responded to teachers' in-class enquiries regarding English culture and so on. The letter of consent had explained that I would help if necessary, because to refuse help in order to remain in a non-participant role 'would have been wrong' (Borg, 2006: 235). I kept my responses as brief as possible to avoid disrupting the natural flow of the lesson.

The next issue is *concentration* during observations, which refers to two related areas: finding a focus and maintaining attentiveness. It becomes more difficult when the study is open coded, because the observer needs to achieve two contradictory tasks. He or she needs to note recurrences of certain foci, but also keep an open mind to avoid missing new developments. In order to maintain concentration, the note-taking was critical.

During the observations, I took notes in my research diary on pages divided into two vertical columns. The left column contained notes from a tricolour pen. Black ink was used for factual data, descriptions of off-camera behaviour and descriptions of interactions between the teacher and students. For example, a black entry during observation 1 for Chikara, teaching grade 1 on 17 June 2008, partly reads:

13:33 – checking stds [students] awake.

Blue ink indicated *reflective remarks* (Miles & Huberman, 1994), such as emerging concepts, interpretations and episodes that needed highlighting. For example, a blue entry during observation 4 for Chikara, teaching grade 2 on 27 June 2008, partly reads:

09:29 – [the teacher] explains 'on weekends' about the [usage of] 's' – this would be an interesting episode to transcribe.

Red ink represented questions for follow-up interviews, which could collect the participants' explanations for their classroom practice and explore how they claimed they taught in non-observed classes. For example, a red entry during observation 3 for Chikara, teaching grade 1 on 30 June 2008, partly reads:

Do you ever use the wds [words], phrases, [and] questions at [the] bottom of [the] page?

The right-hand column remained blank during the observations. This column was saved for later reflections, which were entered following subsequent data collection. Dividing the page and the colours provided a visual way to delineate data collected and continually analyse them through the constant comparison approach.

One potential problem turned into an advantage. Due to my low Japanese proficiency, I could not fully understand the teachers' explanations, but this caused a strategy where I developed layers of comprehension. Short term, in the class, I used my research diary to note non-verbal cues, such as blackboard use, positioning of the teacher, pitch of the teacher's voice, the attitude of the students, routines and types of interaction (such as only the teacher talking, the teacher nominating students or asking for volunteers, and use of pair-work). In the medium term, I cleared gaps in my understanding by asking questions in the follow-up interviews. Longer term, I watched the videos of the classes with transcripts containing full English translations. This combination of note-taking and interviewing kept my brain active, noting emerging concepts, searching for patterns and asking questions. Watching the video later helped me to catch missing data and confirm or reject earlier suppositions.

Regarding the *insider politics*, as a member of staff in the college, I faced different challenges to researchers who enter unknown locations (see also the discussion in Chapter 3). I had to clearly define my research role to avoid misconceptions and maintain the trust that I had developed. In discussions with the management, I explained the value of the study in relation to the innovative nature of the *Kosen*'s changes and the feedback that I could give to colleagues upon completion of the study. However, I did not offer to publish the results in the in-house journal, in order to avoid the potential conflicts of interest that might arise if the directors used the findings for evaluative purposes (Barnard, 1998).

Before the study began, the four teachers signed letters of consent containing the title of the project, purpose, research procedures and a guarantee of confidentiality. However, one colleague admitted later that this process made him nervous. He explained that it was normal for parents and colleagues to observe classes and added that signing a consent form made him feel like he was about to 'donate a kidney'. This incident highlights cultural differences between ethical procedures and expectations in my Australian university and cultural norms at this college in Japan.

Reflection

This study took place in a natural context, where many unexpected problems arose. However, it also afforded benefits. This type of unstructured observation offers 'the advantage of serendipity: significant discoveries that were unanticipated' (Whyte, 1984: 27). An observer who is also a teacher can learn to see teaching differently (Gebhard, 1999; Gebhard & Ueda-Motonaga, 1992). Therefore, from a personal perspective, the most rewarding aspect was the development of increased sensitivity to the problems faced by Japanese colleagues and students. Moreover, such observations facilitate an increased awareness of one's own practice – 'seeing one's own teaching differently' (Fanselow, 1988: 115). Before the observations, my beliefs centred on my own teaching experiences. My communicative learner-centred classes probably worked effectively because my students tended to expect to speak English to me. Alternatively, in my colleagues' classes, the atmosphere seemed to be different. The students appeared reluctant to speak English: they often gave inaudible responses or stayed silent when nominated, chatted off-topic or slept. Faced with such passive resistance, it was easier for the teachers to revert to a 'chalk and talk' teaching style. I could empathise with the difficulty that the teachers might face if they tried to implement less controlled activities; however, while seated at the back of the classroom, listening to a foreign language (in my case Japanese), I could also share some of the students' possible boredom and incomprehension.

COMMENTARY

Simon Humphries employed observation (coupled with interviews) to understand classroom teachers' use of traditional and new English language textbooks in a five-year engineering college (*Kosen*) in Japan. His goal was to see whether the new textbooks changed the focus of teaching from 'a teacher-fronted grammar translation and reading comprehension' approach to a more 'learner-centred … meaning-oriented' approach that emphasises listening comprehension and conversation practice. Given the classroom context, goals of his project and a six-week time constraint on collecting data, his use of non-participant observation (and interviewing) within a constructivist qualitative paradigm are a fitting choice. However, as Simon learned through his research experience, classroom observation is not without issues.

Issues in Data Collection

One concern Simon discusses is that of *unusable data*. As he explains, Bonda used his own worksheets instead of the textbooks and Daiki changed his teaching attitudes and patterns frequently, rendering both teachers' classroom data unusable. Further, Simon could not use some data because of inaudible language from students, and I imagine it was not easy for him to discard data he spent time collecting because it did not fit within the boundaries of the case study or was inaudible. However, his decision not to use the data was appropriate and commendable.

Simon's problem with inaudible recordings has troubled many other observers. However, there are ways that observers can make easy-to-hear recordings, even when some students, like those in the classes Simon observed, have very soft voices. For example, to avoid the same kind of problem in her classroom observations in a Korean middle school, Nam (2011a) used a stationary video-camera angled at the teacher and class, but also strategically placed small audio-recorders with sensitive microphones among the students.

A second and related issue Simon faced is that of the *observer's paradox*. As he points out, the observer's paradox exists 'when people behave differently due to their awareness of the presence of the observer'. For example, it became evident to Simon that Daiki was aware of his presence in the classroom, even asking him during an interview about how he should teach. Chikara was also affected by his presence, admitting this to him during a follow-up interview, as well as announcing to the students that the lesson will change because the observer is in the class.

So, how can the observer make the teacher and students feel comfortable enough to go about their class in a natural way with an observer in the room and while being recorded? I have tried a variety of ways to make my presence less intrusive during observations, and I have come to a tentative conclusion that it really depends on who the students and teacher are and whether I can understand their reactions to my presence. I rely on my experience to predict how they might react, but I also am willing to try out different ways to collect descriptions of interactions while observing how the teacher and students react to these different ways. In one class they might find it less obtrusive if I sit very quietly and take notes while using stationary cameras. In another, they might find this disconcerting, and find it less conspicuous if I openly engage myself in recording, even using a handheld camcorder and moving around the classroom.

To add another level of complexity, the observer also needs to coordinate recording with the goals of the observation (Burns, 2010; Fanselow, 1987). For example, if the goal of the study is to understand the students' reactions to the teacher's instructions, then the observer can benefit from focusing the camera on the students. If the goal is record blackboard information and the positioning of the teacher, then the observer can benefit from positioning the camera at the back of the classroom, as Simon did.

Something that has made classroom observation, at least for me, a lot easier, enjoyable and functional in regard to the issues discussed in this chapter is a genuine attitude I take with me into the classroom research setting. I sincerely take a 'one down' position (Agar, 1996). This means that I genuinely feel privileged to be invited to observe classroom interaction and honestly express my appreciation for the opportunity to learn from the teacher and students I am observing.

Further, I also believe it is important to begin to gain the teacher's and students' accepting attitudes right from the start, by accounting for who I am and why I am there. What Berreman said many years ago is still true: we 'are faced immediately with accounting for [ourselves] before the people [we] propose to learn to know. Only when this has been accomplished, [can we] proceed to the task of seeking to understand the way of life of those people' (Berreman, 1962: 5).

However, while working to gain trust and acceptance, there is the issue of how much information about our research intentions we should disclose. Simon points out that too much disclosure about the goals of the research can cause observed people to behave in unnatural ways; conversely, giving too little information may lead to suspicion or mistrust. Agreeing with this thinking, I suggest each classroom observer carefully consider what and how much to disclose to the teacher and students, while at the same time trying sincerely to build trust and acceptance as an observer within the classroom culture.

Another matter Simon raises is *insider politics*. The particular issue he faced was related to doing his study within the same school where he taught. He had to clearly define his research role to avoid any misconceptions, while maintaining trust with school managers and teachers. Regarding this issue, Simon is correct to ask management and the teachers for permission to observe the classes. (I also wonder if he got permission from the students, something that students often appreciate.) However, as Simon points out, sometimes gaining permission can have unexpected consequences. The teacher in this study who felt like he was about to 'donate a kidney' after signing a consent form is an example. Another example comes from Kim (2011). As a part of her MA research, Kim asked the high-school principal where she taught if she could observe and interview teachers about what it means to be a newly appointed English teacher. The principal agreed, but he also told her he was interested in reading her thesis. Although Kim used pseudonyms to protect the identities of the teachers and students in her study, she was constantly concerned about whether or not she should include observations (and interview data) that might later create problems for the teachers.

An issue related to observation (and analysis) that Simon does not directly address is *bias*. As Adler and Adler (1994) and Agar (1996) point out, observers depend on their own perceptions about what is important and not important while collecting data, and all observers have preconceived notions about what might be important. As Agar (1996: 91–92) puts this: 'The problem is not whether the [observer] is biased; the problem is what kinds of bias exist'.

However, there are things observers can do to reduce bias. Simon interviewed the teachers to confirm or disconfirm his observations. He also used a variety of techniques, such as viewing video-recordings with and without English translation, raising questions about his perceptions, noting emerging concepts and viewing the video many times 'to catch missing data and confirm or reject earlier suppositions'. This is partly in line with what Erickson (1992, 1996) and McDermott *et al.* (1978) did through their use of ethnographic microanalysis. They viewed taped interaction repeatedly while trying to gain an unbiased descriptive understanding of how people in social contexts interact. Another way to reduce bias is to use multiple observers, who can collaborate on what is going on (Adler & Adler, 1994). Through such joint efforts, a variety of perceptions and opinions can be shared as the observers view and discuss recorded interactions.

Issues with Data Analysis

In his study, Simon used multiple sources of data, including observation field notes, recorded interviews and transcripts of classroom interaction from video-files. One value of having several ways to study the data is that he could cross-check the trustworthiness of his observation claims or findings. As findings emerged from his collected qualitative data, having an array of sources also helped Simon to address the goals of the research query he posed at the start of his study (to discern whether the new textbooks changed the focus of teaching from 'a teacher-fronted grammar translation and reading comprehension' approach to a more 'learner-centred meaning-oriented' approach).

However, in order to see emerging categories or themes in his data, Simon had to also make decisions about how to organise his data, and he made some of these decisions before (or early into) collecting data. For example, he decided to colour code his observation field notes. He used black ink to write notes about factual data, off-camera behaviour and descriptions of interactions between the teacher and students, blue ink for reflective remarks about concepts and interpretations, and red ink for questions he planned to ask during follow-up interviews.

Simon perceptibly understood that he also needed to look at his data methodically and repeatedly, and to help him do this he transcribed the classroom interactions. Again, his transcriptions of observed interactions are in line with how Erickson (1992, 1996), McDermott and Gospodinoff (1981) and McDermott et al. (1978) processed their observations using microanalysis of interaction. They did not just analyse what a person, such as the teacher, was doing, but also what was going on verbally, non-verbally and proxemically around the teacher and between the teacher and students, as well as between students.

It is worth pointing out that some researchers code transcripts with an observation system. For example, it is possible to use Fanselow's (1977, 1987) FOCUS, a low-inference category system that captures descriptions of communication between people. This is what Thamraksa (1997) did to understand classroom questioning behaviours within a Thai university English classroom. Likewise, Nam (2011a, 2011b) used FOCUS and her own transcription analysis categories to understand patterns of classroom interaction in a Korean middle-school class. Her goal was to interpret these patterns in relation to how interaction helped or impeded students from learning to communicate in English.

Further analysis leads to interpretations about what descriptive observation data mean in relation to the goal of the study, and I suggest that observers be careful about their interpretations of what the data mean. In this regard, I suggest observers read Fanselow (1997), who wants to see what he observes differently by giving multiple, even outlandish, interpretations about what his observations might mean. As Fanselow makes clear, for any one interpretation of observed data, there are many other possible interpretations. Such an approach can provide classroom observers with a way to expand awareness of their collected data.

Observation and Unexpected Awareness

Simon reveals that his use of observation to learn about how teachers use old and new textbooks not only brought about unexpected issues, but also (quoting Whyte) 'significant discoveries that were unanticipated'. One of these discoveries was his increased sensitivity to the 'problems faced by Japanese colleagues and students'. He gained more awareness of the challenges Japanese English teachers have, such as students' passive resistance and the teachers' use of 'chalk and talk'. I see value in Simon's discussion because such unexpected awareness about teaching makes observation not just a way to collect data, but an adventure in exploration and new discoveries that keeps the researcher (or teacher) fascinated, animated and renewed.

Concluding Remarks

Simon has very thoughtfully critiqued issues he personally had while using observation to understand whether new textbooks changed the type of interaction that went on in classrooms. His careful attention to the issues exemplifies what Wolcott (1994) refers to as *self as instrument* (discovered in Richards, 2003). He understands that 'observation is more than a mechanical process to be gone through; it is a commitment to apply the full range of our perceptual and analytic skills as intensely and extensively as we are able, in pursuit of understanding' (Richards, 2003: 106).

REFLECTIVE QUESTIONS

(1) To what extent do you agree that observers inevitably have preconceived notions or bias which will influence what they observe?

(2) If you agree with the notion in question 1, based on Jerry Gebhard's commentary and your own ideas, how can observers reduce bias?

(3) How can you reduce the inevitable gap between the researcher's agenda, beliefs and values, and the perceptions of the observed teachers and learners? Consider this question in the light of your own research or teaching context.

(4) In your own research context, how would you most effectively collect observation data?

(5) Simon Humphries explained that the data from Bonda and Daiki's classes were unusable for his focus on patterns of textbook use, but that they could be used for separate case studies. How might he use the data for different studies?

(6) Ways of obtaining permission to observe classrooms depend on the sociocultural context. With regard to your own setting, write down several different ways you can ask (a) school principals, (b) teachers and (c) students for their consent for you to observe their school/classroom.

References

Adler, P.A. and Adler, P. (1994) Observational techniques. In N.K. Denzin and Y.S. Lincoln (eds), *Handbook of Qualitative Research* (pp. 377–392). Thousand Oaks, CA: Sage.

Agar, M.A. (1996) *The Professional Stranger: An Informal Introduction to Ethnography* (2nd edition). New York: Academic Press.

Barnard, R. (1998) Classroom observation: Some ethical implications. *Modern English Teacher*, 7(4), 49–55.

Berreman, G.D. (1962) *Behind Many Masks: Ethnographic and Impression Management in a Himalayan Village*. Monograph No. 4. Oklahoma City, OK: Society for Applied Anthropology.

Borg, S. (2003) Teacher cognition in language teaching: A review of research on what language teachers think, know, believe, and do. *Language Teaching*, 36(2), 81–109.

Borg, S. (2006) *Teacher Cognition and Language Education: Research and Practice*. London: Continuum.

Borg, S. (2010) Qualitative research in studying language teacher cognition. Paper presented at the 44th Annual TESOL Convention and Exhibit, Boston, MA.

Browne, C.M. and Wada, M. (1998) Current issues in high school English teaching in Japan: An exploratory survey. *Language Culture and Curriculum*, 11(1), 97–112.

Burns, A. (2010) *Doing Action Research in English Language Teaching: A Guide for Practitioners*. New York: Routledge.

Corbin, J. and Strauss, A. (2008) *Basics of Qualitative Research* (3rd edition). London: Sage.

Cowie, N. (2009) Observation. In J. Heigham and R.A. Croker (eds), *Qualitative Research in Applied Linguistics: A Practical Introduction* (pp. 165–181). New York: Palgrave Macmillan.

Denzin, N.K. and Lincoln, Y.S. (1994) Entering the field of qualitative research. In N.K. Denzin and Y.S. Lincoln (eds), *Handbook of Qualitative Research* (pp. 1–17). Thousand Oaks, CA: Sage.

Duff, P. (2002) The discursive co-construction of knowledge, identity, and difference: An ethnography of communication in the high school mainstream. *Applied Linguistics*, 23(3), 289–322.

Duff, P. (2008) *Case Study Research in Applied Linguistics*. New York: Routledge.

Erickson, F. (1992) Ethnographic microanalysis of interaction. In M.D. LeCompte, W. Millroy and J. Preissle (eds), *The Handbook of Qualitative Research in Education* (pp. 201–225). New York: Academic Press.

Erickson, F. (1996) Ethnographic microanalysis. In S.L. McKay and N.H. Hornberger (eds), *Sociolinguistics and Language Teaching* (pp. 283–306). New York: Cambridge University Press.

Fanselow, J.F. (1977) Beyond Rashomon: Conceptualizing and observing the teaching act. *TESOL Quarterly*, 11(1), 17–41.

Fanselow, J.F. (1987) *Breaking Rules: Generating and Exploring Alternatives in Language Teaching*. White Plains, NY: Longman.

Fanselow, J.F. (1988) 'Let's see': Contrasting conversations about teaching. *TESOL Quarterly*, 22(1), 113–30.

Fanselow, J.F. (1997) Postcard realities. In C.P. Casanave and S.R. Schecter (eds), *On Becoming a Language Educator* (pp. 157–172). Mahwah, NJ: Lawrence Erlbaum.

Fullan, M. (2007) *The New Meaning of Educational Change* (4th edition). New York: Teachers College Press.

Gebhard, J.G. (1999) Seeing teaching differently through observation. In J.G. Gebhard and R. Oprandy (eds), *Language Teaching Awareness: A Guide to Exploring Beliefs and Practices* (pp. 35–58). Cambridge: Cambridge University Press.

Gebhard, J.G. and Ueda-Motonaga, A. (1992) The power of observation: 'Make a wish, make a dream, imagine all the possibilities!' In D. Nunan (ed.), *Collaborative Language Learning and Teaching* (pp. 179–191). Cambridge: Cambridge University Press.

Geertz, C. (1973) Thick description: Toward an interpretive theory of culture. In C. Geertz (ed.), *The Interpretation of Cultures* (pp. 3–30). New York: Basic Books.

Gershon, S., Mares, C. and Walker, R. (2004) *On the Go: English Skills for Global Communication*. Hong Kong: Pearson Education Asia.

Glaser, B.G. and Strauss, A. (1967) *The Discovery of Grounded Theory: Strategies for Qualitative Research*. London: Aldine Transaction.

Gorsuch, G. (2001) Japanese EFL teachers' perceptions of communicative, audiolingual and yakudoku activities: The plan versus the reality. *Educational Policy Analysis Archives*, 9. Available at http://epaa.asu.edu/epaa/v9n10.html (accessed 22 August 2007).

Humphries, S. (2011) The challenges of communicative pedagogy in *Kosens. Council of College English Teachers*, 30, 93–102.

Kikuchi, K. and Browne, C. (2009) English educational policy for high schools in Japan: Ideals vs. reality. *RELC Journal*, 40(2), 172–191.

Kim, J. (2011) What does it mean to be a newly appointed teacher at a synthesized Korean high school? MA thesis, Pusan National University.

McDermott, R.L. and Gospodinoff, K. (1981) Social contexts for ethnic borders of school failure. In H.T. Trueba, G.P. Guthrie and K.H. Au (eds), *Culture and the Bilingual Classroom*. Rowley, MA: Newbury House.

McDermott, R.L., Gospodinoff, K. and Aron, J. (1978) Criteria for an ethnographically adequate description of concerted activities and their contexts. *Semiotica*, 24(3/4), 245–275.

MEXT (2002) *Developing a Strategic Plan to Cultivate 'Japanese with English Abilities'*. At http://www.mext.go.jp/english/news/2002/07/020901.htm (accessed 4 March 2008; English-language document since removed from website).

MEXT (2003) *Regarding the Establishment of an Action Plan to Cultivate 'Japanese with English Abilities'*. At http://www.mext.go.jp/english/topics/03072801.htm (accessed 4 March 2008; English-language document since removed from website).

Miles, M.B. and Huberman, M.A. (1994) *Qualitative Data Analysis: An Expanded Sourcebook* (2nd edition). Thousand Oaks, CA: Sage.

Minamimura, T., Asai, M., Ishihara, Y., Itoh, T., Iwamoto, K., Goi, C., *et al.* (2006) *Vivid English Course* (new edition). Tokyo: Daiichi Gakushusha.

Nam, K. (2011a) A critical look at interaction in a Korean middle school classroom: Its role in development of students' communicative abilities. PhD thesis, Pusan National University.

Nam, K. (2011b) A critical look at interaction in a Korean middle school classroom: Its role in development of students' communicative abilities. *English Language Teaching*, 23(1), 1–25.

O'Donnell, K. (2005) Japanese secondary English teachers: Negotiation of educational roles in the face of curricular reform. *Language, Culture and Curriculum*, 18(3), 300–315.

Richards, K. (1997) Teachers for specific purposes. In R. Howard and G. Brown (eds), *Teacher Education for LSP* (pp. 115–126). Clevedon: Multilingual Matters.

Richards, K. (2003) *Qualitative Inquiry in TESOL*. New York: Palgrave Macmillan.

Sakui, K. (2004) Wearing two pairs of shoes: Language teaching in Japan. *ELT Journal*, 58(2), 155–163.

Sato, K. and Kleinsasser, R. (1999) Communicative language teaching (CLT): Practical understandings. *Modern Language Journal*, 83(4), 494–517.

Sato, K. and Kleinsasser, R. (2004) Beliefs, practices and interactions of teachers in a Japanese high school English department. *Teaching and Teacher Education*, 20, 797–816.

Stake, R.E. (2003) Case studies. In N.K. Denzin and Y.S. Lincoln (eds), *Strategies of Qualitative Inquiry* (2nd edition) (pp. 134–164). Thousand Oaks, CA: Sage.

Thamraksa, C. (1997) A Descriptive Study of Teachers' Questioning Behaviors in Thai ESL Classrooms. PhD dissertation, Indiana University of Pennsylvania.

Watanabe, Y. (2004) Teacher factors mediating washback. In L. Cheng, Y. Watanabe and A. Curtis (eds), *Washback in Language Testing: Research Contexts and Models* (pp. 129–146). Mahwah, NJ: Erlbaum.

Whyte, W.F. (1984) *Learning from the Field*. Beverly Hill, CA: Sage.

Wolcott, H.F. (1994) *Transforming Qualitative Data: Description, Analysis, and Interpretation*. London: Sage.

Woods, D. (1996) *Teacher Cognition in Language Teaching*. Cambridge: Cambridge University Press.

6 Think Aloud

Case Study: Jinrui Li
Commentary: Thomas S.C. Farrell

CASE STUDY

Introduction

This chapter reports part of a wider case study, conducted at a New Zealand university, on the beliefs and practices of a group of 16 university tutors relating to the provision of assessment feedback to undergraduates on their written assignments. Specifically, it discusses the methodological implications of using think aloud (TA) procedures to capture their cognitive processing while they marked assignments.

Assessment of undergraduates' written work is an important pedagogical activity in tertiary education and has long been a focus of debate in the areas of applied linguistics, composition studies and studies on educational assessment. There is increasing agreement in the literature that assessment is usually both formative and summative in most disciplines (Lea & Street, 2000), although in principle the intention to assist students to improve future writing – the formative role – should prevail over simply providing summative judgements (Hounsell *et al.*, 2008; Lilly *et al.*, 2010).

However, it seems difficult for teachers to use assessment as a tool to facilitate the improvement of learning. Recent studies have demonstrated that teachers are often confused about how their assessment feedback can help students improve their writing skills (Bailey & Garner, 2010). This may be due to a number of factors. For example, the modular pattern of many academic courses, in which students' work is submitted according to a strict timetable, leaves little space for improvement after assessment (Price *et al.*, 2011). Across different courses, there is a wide range of expectations about writing (Lea & Street, 2000; Lilly *et al.*, 2010) and different assessment criteria are applied (Barkaoui, 2007; Becker, 1991). Also important is the general lack of assessment education among teachers (DeLuca & Klinger, 2010).

Assignments for large classes are often marked by subject tutors who, compared with lecturers and professors, have lower academic and professional status. The limited number of studies on such tutors' beliefs and practices in relation to assessment have revealed that tutors could not describe explicitly 'what a well-developed argument looks like in a written assignment' (Lea & Street, 2000: 39) and their feedback was used to justify an awarded grade rather than to inform students for improvement (Ivanic et al., 2000). It has been found that the assessment practices of individual tutors are based on different constructs: their personal 'implicit criteria' (Rust et al., 2005: 232); their divergent understandings of the 'explicit criteria' (Rust et al., 2005: 232); and their 'intuition in action' (Anson, 2006: 104).

However, current studies are mainly based on data collected by survey and/or interview (e.g. Ivanic et al., 2000; Lea & Street, 2000) or interview and/or document analysis (e.g. Lilly et al., 2010; Orsmond & Merry, 2011). These data-collection methods are unable to catch cognitive processes during the actual practice of assessment.

To sum up, assessment practice has rarely been observed in natural working contexts and not among subject tutors. There is a need for in-depth exploration of tutor cognition and practices of assessment.

Methodological Focus

Compared with surveys (see Chapter 1) and interviews (see Chapter 4), TA is a more appropriate method for collecting data on cognitive processing. TA was originally used in psychological studies on participants carrying out tasks in controlled experimental environments. Based on information processing theory, Ericsson and Simon (1984) provided a set of procedures for data collection and analysis using the TA method in experimental conditions. The three basic principles of collecting TA data are that: TA tasks should be carefully selected; training should be provided; and the researcher should have minimal interaction with the participants because only the direct verbalisation of thought could be regarded as valid data. However, Ericsson and Simon's (1984) model is applied to quantitative research that intends to explore cognitive processes of context-free tasks. More recently, TA methods have been applied to qualitative research in various studies (Swain, 2006). Sociocultural researchers such as Smagorinsky (1998) trace the theoretical origins of a qualitative approach to TA back to Vygotsky's (1986) theory of inner speech and socially constructed cognition, arguing that 'verbal protocols are socially situated constructs rather than mere representations of individual cognitive processes' (Sasaki, 2008: 349–350). Issues such as addressivity (Sarantakos, 1998) and reactivity (Stratman &

Hamp-Lyons, 1994) in relation to TA have been raised in various studies as challenges to Ericsson and Simon's (1984) assumption that language accurately reflects thought. However, the specific procedures for conducting qualitative TA research in natural settings have not been systematically developed, perhaps due to 'serious logistical difficulties' (Borg, 2006: 224). Consequently, most studies applying TA have followed the quantitative tradition (Bowles, 2010). Some studies have mixed different elements of quantitative and qualitative approaches; according to Grotjahn (1987), introspective approaches could be categorised into eight types, ranging from pure quantitative to pure qualitative.

In relation to the assessment of written work, TA has been used in a limited number of studies on the cognitive process of raters, mainly following the quantitative tradition. Participants have included university language teachers (Barkaoui, 2007; Vaughan, 1991), raters of a large-scale language tests (Lumley, 2005) and examiners within a specific discipline (Crisp, 2008). These studies have been conducted in controlled experimental environments in which the participants marked written work for the primary purpose of data collection. To my knowledge, only one study has used TA in natural assessment contexts: Jeffery and Selting (1999) explored how 10 non-composition university teachers in 10 departments, including natural and social sciences, identified themselves predominantly as 'assignment judges' when reading students' writing, and how these teachers were influenced by their perceived identifications in their responses to student writing. TA instructions were given to the teachers in advance and they were then asked to talk to an audio-cassette when marking any one piece of their students' writing. Seven of the teachers returned the recorded TA and six of them also included a copy of the marked paper. The researchers found that these teachers' major concern in assessment was to measure writing products rather than to facilitate the improvement of writing. However, this study did not reveal the interactive cognitive process of assessment, nor did it explore the role of contextual factors in the process of assessment.

The Study

The study aimed to investigate tutor beliefs and practices in relation to the provision of assessment feedback, and the various factors that influence those beliefs and practices. The research questions were:

• What are tutors' beliefs about assessment feedback on students' assignments?

- What are their actual practices of giving assessment feedback?
- What are the factors that influence their beliefs and practices?
- How can these issues be investigated?

To address these questions, five data-collection methods were used: survey, individual interview, TA, stimulated recall and focus group interview. Survey data were collected from 52 tutors from nine university departments, and interview data from 16 tutors, among whom nine volunteered to participate in the TA and stimulated recall sessions. Seven of the 16 tutors participated in two focus group discussions.

While the tutors' beliefs and general attitudes were elicited by survey and interviews, their actual practices were explored by TA and stimulated recall. The focus group sessions enabled the participants to share their ideas and experiences.

The setting was a faculty of a New Zealand university within which the individual departments offered various courses and provided assessment feedback on undergraduate students' assignments. Due to the large enrolment on some courses, tutors and sessional assistants were recruited each term by the department to help the lecturers mark assignments. The number of tutors varied in different departments in different semesters according to the number of students and the department's financial circumstances.

As in Jeffery and Selting's (1999) study, my participants were not composition specialists; a major difference was that my participants were tutors and most of them were novices. They were asked to think aloud when they were marking one or two of their students' assignments in their normal working context. The purpose of using TA in my study was to find the interaction between tutors' cognition and other factors that influence their cognitive processing while assessing assignments. A purely qualitative approach was taken for the following reasons. Firstly, my study was based on Vygotsky's (1978) sociocultural theoretical perspective and aimed to provide an in-depth understanding of factors that interacted with tutors' cognition and which influenced their assessment feedback in practice. Secondly, research intervention into participants' work was minimised not only for the quality of data but also for ethical reasons. Thirdly, feedback itself is dialogic, even though tutors usually do not verbalise it at work when others are not around. Besides, tutors may on request subsequently need to explain the written feedback and grades orally to students or to supervisors of their work. Therefore, the use of TA in my study is not purely for the benefit of data collection, but also fits the nature of the tutors' work.

Procedural steps of TA

The TA sessions with individual participants were conducted at least three weeks after the interview, to diminish the possible influence of the points raised during that interview on participants' actual practices. Training was not given to tutors for the three reasons given in the above section. Instead, the following written instructions were emailed to participants in advance:

> You are expected to talk aloud whatever is going through your mind while you are marking one or two of your students' assignment. I will be present but will keep quiet, taking some notes. It will last about half an hour and will then be followed up with another half an hour discussion.

The participants were asked whether they thought they could think aloud while marking assignments. All tutors expressed their confidence to do so and agreed that I could be present during the session, and that the TA could be audio-taped with a small digital recorder. The time and place of data collection were negotiated with participants beforehand.

I started each TA session with greetings and some small talk. The participant would then introduce the assignment to me and I briefly explained the TA process, making it clear that I wished them to do a monologue and ignore my presence (as far as possible). I assured them I would try not to interrupt their marking process.

Then I sat on one side of the participant and kept silent for most of the time except when occasionally showing my attentiveness by quiet back-channelling. My main activity during the TA session was to keep field notes. These included: the venue, time, type and length of the assignments; operations of giving feedback, including sounds (laughter or other vocalisations) made by participants; expressions and gestures which could not be audio-recorded; symbols they used as feedback; details of in-text and overall feedback they gave (if I could see or hear); and the special features of the feedback or impressions I had at certain points. While keeping field notes, I also marked the points that I would explore in the stimulated recall sessions that immediately followed the TA sessions. The points I selected for the stimulated recall included issues or difficulties participants met in the process of assessment, which were expressed verbally or by body language such as erasing a comment or keeping silent for a while, or intangible murmuring while making decisions. These points were made for the purpose of compensating for and confirming the TA data.

All but one of the nine participants started to read and mark from the beginning of the assignment. Some read aloud most of the assignment while marking, while others read silently. All but two of the participants referred to marking guidelines or sample answers; the other two said they did not bring the marking guidelines with them as they had the criteria clearly in mind. All participants thought silently before they verbalised their feedback and most spoke very quietly. Some error corrections, like spelling mistakes and routine feedback comments such as 'Good' and 'Well done', were spoken aloud while the tutor was writing. However, there were relatively longer periods of silence when a participant was thinking about the sentence structure or giving longer feedback – especially as regards negative aspects. Subsequent analysis of the data showed that no participant kept silent for more than three minutes.

After the TA session, I started the stimulated recall conversation by thanking my participants and then enquiring whether I could ask him or her questions about the TA process. When asked whether they found it difficult to think aloud, answers ranged from 'A little bit, but it was okay' to 'Not at all'. Most participants said that it was 'a bit weird' for them to talk aloud by themselves and my presence was necessary to motivate them to talk.

Ninety percent of the TA and stimulated data were transcribed with NVivo8 software (Bazeley, 2007). Then, I compared the transcripts with my field notes and inserted the participants' observed performances and the significant points I noted in the field notes into NVivo8 as the memos of the TA transcripts. The transcripts were member checked. Data were analysed using a grounded theory approach (Glaser & Strauss, 1999). Content analysis of transcripts was carried out with NVivo8 for initial open coding. I firstly open coded each piece of the transcript by highlighting any words or parts of a sentence that represented a piece of information. I used the original words or a summative phrase as descriptive codes. I then categorised the codes into a hierarchical level of codes or tree nodes in NVivo8. Constant comparison was made between TA transcripts. Then, thematic categories were established and the categories were compared with those of other sources of data. These categories were then manually checked. Themes emerged by axial coding.

Table 6.1 shows examples of the TA data from one of the participants (Simon) and the categories that were developed inductively.

Methodological Implications

A number of limitations were found in the TA data-collection process. Firstly, some of the recorded speech was inaudible or unintelligible (see also the discussion in Chapter 5), especially when the addressees of the TA were

Table 6.1 Examples of coding the TA data

TA data	Initial codes	Categories
Phew! What!	Negative emotional reaction	Emotion
Erm, maybe Hollywood tends to be////	Constructing corrective feedback	Feedback
I cannot understand what they're saying.	Difficulties caused by students' expression	Good/bad written work
But how do I reword it to actually make sense?	Difficulties in providing corrective feedback	Feedback
And here I am not very sure. I am thinking what the ESOL teachers or my Japanese teachers about what is the useful way of correcting people's sentences. Do you need to write the whole sentence out again, or can you just scribble a line and people actually learn that way for second-language learners. I'm not sure	Difficulties in providing corrective feedback/ Historically distributed cognition applied to current action	Feedback

the participants themselves. Secondly, TA added an extra cognitive load for the participants and this, at least to some extent, detracted from their ability to focus on the feedback task at hand. Thirdly, it was challenging for me, as the researcher, to play multiple roles during the TA procedure, such as observing, note-taking, back-channelling and identifying issues for the stimulated recall interviews held immediately afterwards. Another problem was the inevitable variability of researching tutors in their normal practices, rather than my attempting to control key variables. There were important differences among the tutors, such as the different types of assignment they reviewed, their ability to verbalise their thinking and the time available for them to undertake a TA session. In such aspects, the participants' choices of how to undertake the TA were fully respected.

It is difficult to establish the extent to which my (minimally verbal) presence in the room seriously affected the participants' normal work routine. However, I felt that my presence was justified on the following grounds: firstly, it was a stimulus to think aloud because it is unusual for an adult to talk aloud without an obvious interlocutor; secondly, it allowed me to keep field notes of the participants' assessing processes for use in the following stimulated recall session; and thirdly, my cognitive experience of observing the TA facilitated my interpretation and eventual triangulation of all the data collected in the project.

Finally, because assessment was an activity relating not only to the tutors but also to the students and lecturers, there were ethical implications relating to the social context of the study. It would have been helpful for me to have seen the students' assignments before the TA session, but to have done so would have been to breach the privacy of the students concerned. In addition to the ethical dilemma in getting students' permission before tutors assessed their written work, there were practical constraints: on the one hand, the researcher could not reach students without the permission of the tutors, nor would the researcher know what and whose assignment the tutors would assess; on the other hand, the tutors themselves were not sure what and when the lecturers would ask them to assess, and therefore when they would be able to assess writing on campus in my presence. The first tutor who agreed to participate withdrew from the project when asked whether he could help me get the permission of the student whose written work he was to assess in my presence. To resolve this issue, I asked the tutors to remove all identification of the students whose work I would oversee during the TA session, and I made no copy of these assignments. Moreover, the criteria used by most of the tutors were devised by their supervising lecturers, who may have had objections to their work being viewed and possibly critiqued by an outsider. In the event, I contacted the chairperson of each department to inform lecturers of my research procedures, and to enquire whether there were objections to my presence while the tutors assessed students' written work according to their criteria or model answers. No objections were made.

Reflection

The strength of this study, in my view, lies in the combination of multiple methods of data collection which reveal not only beliefs but also practices of assessment feedback, at both the individual and the collective level. In particular, the TA data revealed emotional reactions to students' work and the difficulties the tutors experienced in their assessment. In summary, the TA sessions provided me with the opportunity to reveal the interactions between tutors' cognition, emotion and action in the actual context of assessing writing.

My experience of using TA leads me to suggest that the appropriateness of data-collection procedures is constrained and shaped by the context of studies. It is inappropriate to copy procedures and standards established in the laboratory settings of quantitative studies and to apply them rigidly to qualitative studies. This suggestion is based on two perspectives. On the one hand, different research questions require different data-collection procedures. If the purpose of using TA is to understand people's thought in the process of carrying out actual social activities, then TA data are best collected in normal working contexts, without any experimental controls. In my study, the time, place and type of task for TA needed to depend on participants' natural flow of work, to avoid leading participants in directions other than those they would normally take. The tactful presence of the researcher as a virtually silent interlocutor was more likely to assist than to hinder the participants in thinking aloud.

On the other hand, researchers in different data-collection contexts may not encounter the same problems as other researchers, regarding the nature of the TA activity, the identity and relationship between the participants and the researcher, and the ethical issues in the specific context. Researchers need to seek the best possible solutions to serve the purpose of TA data collection in their particular context. For example, unlike in conventional TA approaches, I did not train participants, for the following reasons. In the first place, the TA sessions were a combination of my observation and participants' verbalisations on how the assessment was done, what decisions were made and what contextual factors interacted with the decision-making process. The purpose was to collect data on the actual practice of assessment. It was not, as in conventional studies, to explore thinking patterns of private speech. Secondly, the task to be thought aloud was participants' work, rather than something separately designed or provided by the researcher. In addition, it was possible that participants had developed some understanding of my project and familiarity with me as a researcher before the TA sessions, because of their responses to an online survey and interviews. Thirdly, my participants received my brief instructions on TA in advance and expressed their willingness and confidence to think aloud without training. Therefore, no more training was provided than brief written instructions in advance and further oral clarification just before the start of the TA session.

COMMENTARY

In most of the university settings I have taught in over the years (Korea, Singapore and Canada as well as guest teaching in Japan and the USA) I have found myself leading or assisting a group of part-time instructors, tutors and/or teaching assistants as they grade written assignments. I have tried almost everything to make sure that they all use the same criteria when grading these written assignments, so that the grading is fair for the students. I have also tried to ensure that they provide valid feedback that not only reflects the grade given but can lead to development of that student as a writer. Invariably what occurs, however, is that some markers will assess assignments based on their own internal and tacitly held criteria of what good writing is. So when I see a study such as Jinrui Li's in this chapter that tries to capture the thought processing of tutors while marking the written assignments of undergraduates, I am immediately attracted to it. Knowing more about the beliefs and practices of markers/graders of undergraduate students is of great importance to many people who teach in university settings, because most of them must assess written work. Therefore, I was interested to read how Jinrui captured these cognitions.

Most studies on this particular topic have used surveys or interviews to gauge teachers' marking methods, usually after they had finished the marking. Jinrui has taken this approach one step further by employing a TA protocol to explore the beliefs and practices of markers while they occur. She also employed other data-collection methods to triangulate her information and answer the four research questions (although the fourth question is really a question about an approach to methodology): survey, individual interview, TA and stimulated recall sessions, and focus group interview. Jinrui maintains that 'while tutors' beliefs and general attitudes were elicited by survey and interviews, their actual practices were explored by TA and stimulated recall'. I would suggest that beliefs, too, could be explored by TA because what teachers say they do continuously shifts even as they speak (see Senior, 2006, for research on changing teacher beliefs). So although her research focus was on the type of feedback that teachers provide while marking assignments for undergraduate students, which in itself is worthy of comment, it is the research methods, and especially the use of TA protocols to collect data, that will be the focus of my commentary.

The use of TA methods for this type of study is very interesting and has to be commended. When used with other methods of data collection, it can only add to the reliability and validity of the data, regardless of whether the approach is qualitative or quantitative. Personally, though, I am not sure that we can call TA 'a more appropriate method for collecting data on cognitive processing'. Rather, perhaps we can say that TA can be an additional method for triangulation purposes, as I will explain further below. That said, it is the case that few studies have used TA in naturalistic settings to gauge the beliefs of markers. While acknowledging that Junrui's example is an excellent first use of such an approach, from which other researchers can learn when conducting similar research in the future, I have a few points of commentary regarding how TA was used in this particular study.

Firstly, I will comment on the exact method of collecting data using TA protocols. Jinrui asked the markers to think aloud when marking one or two of their students' assignments and was present but 'quiet, taking some notes' in the same room. Herein lies my first point about the use of TA as a data-collection instrument. My concern is that the presence of the researcher could have some effect (either positive or negative) on the result, because it not natural to have someone (1) say what they are thinking and (2) know that someone is present, listening to what is being said and taking notes. Indeed, Jinrui seemed also to be involved in the thought process by 'occasionally showing my attentiveness by quiet back-channelling'. I am not sure why she felt this need to show attentiveness, as the instructions to each participant included the statement that the researcher would remain 'quiet'. Such back-channelling may interrupt the thought processes and expressions of these processes through language. One way of avoiding this problem in future studies may be to video-record the sessions in order to minimise the presence of the researcher and any interruptions that may take place. Video-recording the marker as he or she speaks aloud provides non-verbal reactions and thus facilitates the matching (or mismatching) of the comments made to the non-verbal reactions, which can be discussed in more detail later with each participant. That said, I also agree with Jinrui that her presence (as the researcher) enabled her to obtain more information, such as expressions and gestures that could not be audio-recorded.

Secondly, rather than relying on participants' common sense, or intuitive ability to think aloud, it is preferable to let them first try out some activities in order not only to familiarise them with TA methods but also to give them some necessary practice before the actual data-collection sessions. Just as in classroom observations, where many teachers feel that they do not 'perform' their best teaching because they are being observed, or during interviews, when teachers may feel they cannot adequately verbalise their feelings about teaching, so too with TA methods. Some teachers may feel they cannot verbalise what is going on in their head while undertaking tasks such as marking assignments. At least one practice activity where participants can be trained and familiarised with TA procedures would help to ensure that the main TA activity will be more successfully undertaken. If possible, before the study they could also be provided with an example of a video-recording of a participant performing a TA activity successfully, so that they know more precisely what they are volunteering to do. Of course, I realise that no data-collection process is entirely without its drawbacks; the best we can do as researchers is to try to select the method that gives us the most information required.

Thirdly, a methodological issue of importance when using TA protocols is how we can analyse the data once we have collected them. Jinrui used NVivo8 software to help her with analysis and recounts that:

Constant comparison was made between TA transcripts. Then, thematic categories were established and the categories were compared with those of other sources of data. These categories were then manually checked. Themes emerged by axial coding.

The categories that Jinrui derived from the data (Table 6.1) all look very interesting but I am unsure about their validity or reliability, given the above comments, and I would suggest the need for another rater (I believe Jinrui was the only rater). Having another rater who could cross-check to verify the findings would give a better sense of the reliability of these categories. The idea of video-recording participants could also help to strengthen reliability, as different raters could compare categories and results. The passage 'While keeping field notes, I also marked the points that I would explore in the stimulated recall sessions ... issues or difficulties participants met in the process of assessment, which were expressed verbally or by body language such as erasing a comment' raised another question for me. Why were these considered important points to explore and what assumptions are they based on? It would be useful to see examples of verbal and body language expressions to help the reader and others who may want to replicate such research. An alternative approach would be to ask the marker to explore what he or she considers important rather than for the researcher to make his or her own selections.

My last comments pertain to the findings themselves and whether the use of TA can truly be said to represent actual cognitive processing in real time. In other words, can verbal reporting as represented through TA protocols provide a complete record of the individual's thought processes in synchronous reporting or does this procedure actually distort the thinking–speaking process? Some researchers suggest that producing TA protocols places a strain on recall and memory, as the participant not only has to recall but also has to analyse and justify what he or she is recalling at the same time (for more on the issue of reactivity in TA protocols, see Ericsson & Simon, 1993; Leow & Morgan-Short, 2004). The TA process is not just about reporting thoughts but also involves active, on-going analysis, so it is no wonder that Jinrui reported that 'All participants thought silently before they verbalised their feedback and most spoke very quietly'. Participants may not be used to such a process that requires them not only to verbalise their thoughts but at the same time to justify these thoughts. Bowles and Leow (2005) refer to the former form of verbalisation as 'non-metalinguistic' and the latter form as 'metalinguistic'. This point, taken together with the fact that a researcher is also present in the room listening and taking notes, may make a participant (re)consider carefully what he or she will actually reveal through spoken language.

That said, my overall reflection on Jinrui's important study is that its real strength lies not only in the use of TA protocols but also in the combined use of other data-collection methods, which can offer greater validity to the findings. For the most part, Jinrui's use of TA protocols is an excellent start to what I hope to see more of in similar studies of 'on-line' thinking. The study highlighted in this chapter makes a significant contribution to our understanding of the use of TA protocols in exploring how tutors make marking decisions in real time.

REFLECTIVE QUESTIONS

(1) What do you think are the differences between collecting TA data in controlled research settings and natural work settings?

(2) Do you agree with Thomas Farrell that participants will probably need some practice before undergoing a TA session? If so, what sort of practice do you think would be appropriate?

(3) An alternative to asking individuals to think aloud individually is to ask them to engage in a conversation in pairs, for example in planning a lesson, devising a test, evaluating a unit in a course book. Can you think of other examples? In what way would the data collected through this method be different from that gathered in individual TA sessions?

(4) What are the advantages and disadvantages of the researcher being present during a TA session? What factors would influence your decision on whether or not to be present? (You might want to reflect on what Andrew Gladman says about this in Chapter 3, in relation to focus groups.)

(5) To what extent do you think it is valid for TA procedures to be undertaken in a second language? What are the advantages and disadvantages?

(6) Ask one or two colleagues to think aloud while doing a task such as marking a student's assignment while you record the process. How effective were your methods of collecting the data?

References

Anson, C.M. (2006) Assessing writing in cross-curricular programs: Determining the locus of activity. *Assessing Writing*, 11(2), 100–112.

Bailey, R. and Garner, M. (2010) Is the feedback in higher education assessment worth the paper it is written on? Teachers' reflections on their practices. *Teaching in Higher Education*, 15(2), 187–198.

Barkaoui, K. (2007) Rating scale impact on EFL essay marking: A mixed-method study. *Assessing Writing*, 12, 86–107.

Bazeley, P. (2007) *Qualitative Data Analysis with NVivo*. London: Sage.

Becker, H.J. (1991) When powerful tools meet conventional beliefs and institutional constraints. *Computing Teacher*, 18(8), 6–9.

Borg, S. (2006) *Teacher Cognition and Language Education: Research and Practice*. London: Continuum.

Bowles, M.A. (2010) *The Think-Aloud Controversy in Second Language Research*. New York: Routledge.

Bowles, M.A. and Leow, R.P. (2005) Reactivity and type of verbal report in SLA research methodology. *Studies in Second Language Acquisition*, 27, 415–440.

Crisp, V. (2008) Exploring the nature of examiner thinking during the process of examination marking. *Cambridge Journal of Education*, 38(2), 247–264.

DeLuca, C. and Klinger, D.A. (2010) Assessment literacy development: Identifying gaps in teacher candidates' learning. *Assessment in Education: Principles, Policy and Practice*, 17(4), 419–438.

Ericsson, K.A. and Simon, H.A. (1984) *Protocol Analysis: Verbal Reports as Data*. Cambridge, MA: MIT Press.

Ericsson, K.A. and Simon, H.A. (1993) *Protocol Analysis: Verbal Reports as Data* (2nd edition). Cambridge, MA: MIT Press.

Glaser, B.G. and Strauss, A.L. (1999) *The Discovery of Grounded Theory: Strategies for Qualitative Research*. New York: Aldine de Gruyter.

Grotjahn, R. (1987) On the methodological basis of introspective methods. In C. Faerch and G. Kasper (eds), *Introspection in Second Language Research* (pp. 54–81). Clevedon: Multilingual.

Hounsell, D., McCune, V., Hounsell, J. and Litjens, J. (2008) The quality of guidance and feedback to students. *Higher Education Research and Development*, 27(1), 55–67.

Ivanic, R., Clark, R. and Rimmershaw, R. (2000) What am I supposed to make of this? The messages conveyed to students by tutors' written comments. In I.M.R. Lea and B. Stierer (eds), *Student Writing in Higher Education: New Contexts* (pp. 47–65). Buckingham and Philadelphia: SRHE and Open University Press.

Jeffery, F. and Selting, B. (1999) Reading the invisible ink: Assessing the responses of non-composition faculty. *Assessing Writing*, 6(2), 179–197.

Lea, M.R. and Street, B.V. (2000) Student writing and staff feedback in higher education: An academic literacies approach. In M.R. Lea and B. Stierer (eds), *Student Writing in Higher Education: New Contexts* (pp. 31–46). Buckingham and Philadelphia: SRHE and Open University Press.

Leow, R.P. and Morgan-Short, K. (2004) To think aloud or not to think aloud: The issue of reactivity in SLA research methodology. *Studies in Second Language Acquisition*, 26, 35–57.

Lilly, J., Richter, U.M. and Rivera-Macias, B. (2010) Using feedback to promote learning: Student and tutor perspectives. *Practitioner Research in Higher Education*, 4(1), 30–40.

Lumley, T. (2005) *Assessing Second Language Writing: The Rater's Perspective*. Frankfurt: Peter Lang.

Orsmond, P. and Merry, S. (2011) Feedback alignment: Effective and ineffective links between tutors' and students' understanding of coursework feedback. *Assessment and Evaluation in Higher Education*, 36(2), 125–136.

Price, M., Carroll, J., O' Donovan, B. and Rust, C. (2011) If I was going there I wouldn't start from here: A critical commentary on current assessment practice. *Assessment and Evaluation in Higher Education*, 36(4), 479–492.

Rust, C., O' Donovan, B. and Price, M. (2005) A social constructivist assessment process model: How the research literature shows us this could be best practice. *Assessment and Evaluation in Higher Education*, 30(3), 231–240.

Sarantakos, S. (1998) *Social Research* (2nd edition). South Melbourne: Macmillan Education Australia.

Sasaki, T. (2008) Concurrent think-aloud protocol as a socially situated construct. *IRAL*, 46, 349–374.

Senior, R. (2006) *The Experience of Language Teaching*. New York: Cambridge University Press.

Smagorinsky, P. (1998) Thinking and speech and protocol analysis. *Mind, Culture, and Activity*, 5, 157–177.

Stratman, J. and Hamp-Lyons, L. (1994) Reactivity in concurrent think-aloud protocols. In P. Smagorinsky (ed.), *Speaking About Writing: Reflections on Research Methodology* (pp. 89–112). London: Sage.

Swain, M. (2006) Verbal protocols. In M. Chalhoub-Deville, C.A. Chapelle and P. Duff (eds), *Inference and Generalizability in Applied Linguistics: Multiple Perspectives* (pp. 97–114). Amsterdam: John Benjamins.

Vaughan, C. (1991) Holistic assessment: What goes on in the rater's mind? In L. Hamp-Lyons (ed.), *Assessing Second Language Writing in Academic Contexts* (pp. 111–125). Norwood, NJ: Ablex.

Vygotsky, L.S. (1978) *Mind in Society*, translated by M. Cole. Cambridge, MA: Harvard University Press.

Vygotsky, L.S. (1986) *Thought and Language*. Cambridge, MA: MIT Press.

7 Stimulated Recall

Case Study: Jonathon Ryan
Commentary: Susan Gass

CASE STUDY

Introduction

This chapter reports an investigation into areas of miscommunication in interactions between first- and second-language speakers of English at a New Zealand university. Specifically, it focuses on the way that problems may be triggered by the use of noun phrases that are referentially ambiguous or misleading in context. For example, from a referential perspective, the utterance 'I saw him yesterday' is communicatively successful only if the hearer correctly identifies which person (the *referent*) the speaker claims to have seen. Problems occur when the hearer either identifies the wrong referent (misidentification) or no referent (communication breakdown). The focus of the chapter is to report on how stimulated recall (SR) was used to identify such problems.

However, identifying miscommunication is inherently problematic. For example, many studies rely on the analysis of transcripts (e.g. Cook-Gumperz & Gumperz, 2002; Verdonik, 2010), but a serious methodological limitation of such approaches is that miscommunication often leaves no clear verbal trace, particularly when it goes unnoticed by both interlocutors. Unrecognised miscommunication is also an obvious limitation for studies involving self-reported data (e.g. Tzanne, 2000).

The approach of the present study was to access the hearer's mental representation of the discourse and compare this with the speaker's intended message. To achieve this aim, a film-retelling task was used to elicit linguistic data, providing strong grounds from which to identify the speaker's intended meaning. This procedure was followed by an SR interview in which the hearers described how their mental model of the discourse developed. This approach potentially offers much richer insights into the hearer's interpretation of learner speech than text-based approaches.

Methodological Focus

Stimulated recall is a type of introspective research methodology, differing from think aloud (see Chapter 6) in that it involves the verbalisation of cognition retrospectively rather than concurrently. It is a method used to elicit qualitative data relating to the thought processes associated with performing an action or participating in an event. To assist recall of these thought processes, a stimulus is used, such as a video-recording of the activity. It is argued that such stimuli may enable a participant 'to relive an original situation with vividness and accuracy' (Bloom, 1953: 161).

For much of the 20th century such introspective methods were treated with suspicion (Ericsson, 2003). More recently, such methods have gained respectability through the theoretical basis provided by researchers such as Ericsson and Simon (1984) and the contribution of multiple researchers in developing best-practice guidelines. Nevertheless, even supporters of SR express caution. There are, for instance, multiple pitfalls in implementing SR procedures (see Gass & Mackey, 2000: 84–99) and it is of some concern to Lyle (2003: 861) that few studies 'treat the procedures involved as unproblematic and few studies report the SR protocol in critical detail'. In particular, Lyle warns that care is required to minimise the risk of SR data not accurately representing cognitive processes from the time of the original event, particularly in relation to processes such as reordering, reasoning and 'sanitisation'.

Stimulated recall has most often been used to explore aspects of cognition that lie behind the participants' decisions and actions. For example, it has been used to explore teacher cognition (Polio et al., 2006), learner cognition (Lam, 2008), language processing in translation (Dechert, 1987) and learner reflection and self-evaluation (Murray, 2010). Less frequently, SR procedures have been used to explore hearer responses to speech, as in Tyler's (1995) study of the perceptions of conversational interactants, and Bloom's (1953) study of learners' thoughts during lectures and tutorials. The present study employed this methodology in an area that had not been explored in the studies cited: how interlocutors' mental models of a narrative developed during discourse. In particular, it attempted to identify mismatches between the intended referential meaning of speakers and the interpretations of addressees.

The Study

The main research questions of the study concerned the extent to which second-language learners (SLL) are pragmatically competent in communicating referential speech acts in English and the conditions under which referential miscommunication occurs.

I collected data from 60 participants, arranged in 30 dyads, in which each partner was assigned a role as either a speaker or a hearer. Some speakers were native English-speaking students and others were students for whom English was a second language; all the hearers were first-language speakers (L1) and among these were teachers of English as a second language.

Linguistic data were elicited through a film-retelling task adapted from Perdue (1984, 1993), in which an edited version of the silent Charlie Chaplin film *Modern Times* is used. The participants in each pair watched the first five minutes of the film together; the 'hearer' was then called away while his or her partner continued watching the movie. A few minutes later, the hearer returned and asked to be told what had happened in the film during his or her absence. This retelling task was video- and audio-recorded and was immediately followed by a two-part SR interview with the hearer, using the video-recording as the recall stimulus. These interviews are the focus of the present chapter.

Procedural steps

Prior to the interview, the hearers were informed that the main focus was on their thoughts at the time of the original interaction. They were asked to cast their minds back to when the narrative was being delivered and to comment on what they recalled of their understanding at that time. In the first part of the SR interview, the hearers were shown a video-recording of the narrative interaction. The video-recording was then periodically paused by either myself or the participant, and the participant reported his or her (original) understanding of the narrative or made other (often evaluative) comments. At this point, I was often, but not always, able to identify miscommunications that had occurred. Interestingly, I missed some miscommunications because my knowledge of the film influenced how I interpreted the hearers' comments (completing a circle of miscommunication).

In the second part of the interview, the hearers were shown Part Two of *Modern Times* and were asked to comment on anything that was different in the film to what they had pictured. At this stage I was able to confidently confirm or disconfirm earlier evidence of miscommunication, and also to identify further instances that had gone unnoticed.

The research protocols were adapted from those outlined in the literature, particularly those discussed by Gass and Mackey (2000). Prior to settling on specific protocols, I conducted 16 pilot sessions over six months and spent considerable time reflecting on the efficacy of specific procedures. It became clear that substantial practice is required in conducting SR interviews: the techniques are subtle and the data are easily compromised by inadequate technique. I found it particularly valuable to have 'critical friends' observe or participate in interviews and comment on the procedures. Many of the most useful comments came from critical friends with no direct connection to applied linguistics or the education setting but who brought skills from an unrelated field (e.g. a licensed professional counsellor). Even so, I noted further issues during formal data collection, forcing minor procedural modifications. Finally, I also commissioned a colleague to prepare and conduct a similar task with myself as the participant. This happened too late in the data-collection process to influence the procedures I used, but it did strengthen my thinking in relation to best-practice procedures and in relation to certain theoretical issues relating to the research topic. For future studies, I recommend that researchers adopt the role of a participant in the final stages of piloting their data-collection method.

Data samples

Examples of the data are presented in Tables 7.1 and 7.2, in which the extracts presented are from an L1–L1 and an SLL–L1 interaction respectively (in each case the teller is labelled A, the hearer B and the researcher Res). The left-hand column presents data from the narrative retelling task, while the right-hand column presents corresponding comments from the two-part SR interview. In Extract 1, the hearer reveals in the first part of the SR

Table 7.1 Extract 1, from an L1–L1 interaction

Narrative retelling	SR interview
A – Charlie falls on <u>the fat woman</u>, like two times and <u>she</u>'s all like like this (GESTURE) B – [LAUGHS] A – and then um <u>she</u> like gets up and looks real mad?, like <u>her</u> face?, and then suddenly like <u>she</u> pushes the policeman or something	*Part 1* Res – who got up and looked mad? B – the fat woman *Part 2* B – ah, it WAS her [[*the banana girl*]], [LAUGHS] I thought the fat angry woman got angry

Table 7.2 Extract 2, from an SLL–L1 interaction

Narrative retelling	SR interview
A – so, you know at the last part, we see together, when they bringed the machine?	B – when she said the machine, I thought of two machines obviously*
	B – there was the conveyor belt, Res – ah, and that other one B – and the other big machine where the guy talked to him and he changed the speeds

Note: Some intervening comments have been omitted

interview that she interpreted all of the underlined pronouns to be referring to 'the fat woman'. However, as the hearer discovers while viewing the film in the second part of the SR interview, this had been a miscommunication.

In Extract 2, the hearer reveals that she had identified two possible candidates (both forms of machinery) as the relevant referent, but was uncertain which one was intended. However, knowledge of the *Modern Times* narrative confirms that the speaker was referring to neither of these, but a third machine, which had been only briefly sighted by the hearer.

Methodological Implications

A number of methodological issues arose during piloting and this section focuses on how these were addressed. These relate to time lapse, memory or reinterpretation, use of a video stimulus, timing of recall prompts and the formulation of recall questions.

A critical issue when using SR is how much time elapses between the activity and the interview, as the greater the delay, the greater is the potential for memory decay (Gass & Mackey, 2000). One of the decisions I faced was whether to closely examine the video-recording prior to the SR. However, it seemed that the potential benefits of doing so might be outweighed by issues of reliability stemming from memory loss. In addition, because I was present in the room during the retelling task, I was able to mentally note salient issues at that time. I therefore decided to conduct the interviews immediately after the retelling task, with perhaps two or three minutes of transition time in setting up the video playback. On reflection, this approach appears to have been the right choice, although I became aware during transcription of certain issues that I would like to have probed further. However, these missed opportunities appeared relatively few and were minimised by my training as a researcher through the piloting stage: I became much more aware of how to elicit full and appropriate information, and of potential ambiguity in the data and the hearers' responses.

Secondly, it is essential in SR that participants comment on memories rather than on a present interpretation. The interviewer can guide interviewees by using questions with past tense verbs (Gass & Mackey, 2000: 92–93) and adverbial time markers. However, past tense verbs appear sometimes to be overlooked by hearers (and are, after all, not always indicators of past time) and a subtle yet important issue may be the placement of adverbial time markers at the beginning of an utterance rather than at the end. For example, the placement of the adverbial phrase at the end of the question in sentence 1 below may prompt hearers to begin formulating an answer relating to their present interpretation before they realise that the question relates to a memory. This could compromise the accuracy of the recall. In contrast, the second sentence seems to clearly establish prior to any further mental processing that a memory is being sought.

(1) What did you think she meant when she first said it?
(2) When she said first said that, what did you think she meant?

A third procedural issue relates to the effective use of the video stimulus. Although it is usually argued that video is the most powerful prompt of memory recall, it has also been argued that video may 'produce a much more foreign stimulus than audiotapes' (Yinger, 1986: 271). One consideration is that observing themselves on video may reposition interviewees in relation to the event. For example, studies of teacher cognition employing SR techniques face a problem in that participants view themselves from a perspective that is very different from their original experience of the actual event. Initially, I filmed both the speaker and the hearer, assuming that the hearer's physical responses would provide an important recall stimulus. However, I found that hearers often became distracted by seeing themselves on video, sometimes focusing more on their appearance than on recalling their understanding of the narrative. In response, I altered the direction of the camera to capture only the speaker. This modification appeared more effective in recreating the experience of the original interaction.

A fourth procedural issue is the timing of recall prompts. During piloting, I frequently paused the video immediately after the use of a referring expression (RE), to discover which referent the hearer had identified. Underlying this decision was an (erroneous) assumption that hearers immediately identify the referents of REs. However, even before recognising this error, I found these pauses to be unnatural, as they interrupted the flow of discourse. Furthermore, the hearers often seemed unsure and would ask to view the clip again, even when they felt there had been no miscommunication during the original interaction. It soon became clear that some REs are resolved not immediately, but at the end of a clause or tone unit (see Kehler, 2002). In response, I began pausing only at natural discourse boundaries, such as complete syntactic units, tone units and episode boundaries.

This issue of timing of recall prompts relates to a fifth procedural issue: the focus of recall questions. Initially, after the use of a RE, I would directly ask hearers which referent they had identified. This type of question is illustrated in sentence 3 below. However, I found it more effective to ask the participant to describe a more general picture of their understanding of the narrative at that point. This approach enabled the discourse to be segmented into larger units that did not disrupt the discourse flow and often also clarified in one utterance how the hearer resolved a number of REs. Further, it appeared unnatural to frequently ask questions about the identity of referents and seemed to slightly unnerve the participants, perhaps feeling more like an interrogation than a discussion. I therefore preferred to use question types such as those illustrated in sentences 4 and 5 below. Single questions like these were able to elicit the hearer's understanding of a larger stretch of discourse and, in so doing, reasonable inferences could be made of how the hearer interpreted multiple REs.

(3) When she said 'that big guy', who did you think she meant?
(4) What was your understanding of the film at this point?
(5) What was your mental picture of the film at this point?

A crucial question raised in the literature (e.g. Gass & Mackey, 2000: 20–24) relates to the type of cognitive experience that can be researched using SR techniques. It is widely assumed, for example, that declarative knowledge is available for recall, while procedural knowledge is not. The assumption of mainstream approaches to literacy is that narrative comprehension does result in declarative knowledge: from very early stages of learning to read, learners are asked to declare aspects of their understanding of narratives. The evidence for this assumption appears strong and, in this respect, miscommunication appears to be a suitable topic for investigation with SR. It is important to note, however, that the processes involved in comprehending narratives are mostly procedural and other types of analysis are required to identify what triggers miscommunication.

This simple declarative view of comprehension outcomes aligns with traditional approaches to reference, which hold that in fully successful communication hearers resolve all references. Yoshioka, for example, states that '[i]n order to construct intelligible discourse, it is essential that the identities of referents are *made clear at all times*' (Yoshioka, 2008: 236, emphasis added). With this in mind, in the initial stages of the data collection I assumed that the hearers should be able to identify the referents of every RE. I further assumed that any doubt or ambiguity represented at least communicative strain, if not communicative breakdown. I persisted with this view through the piloting stage, and it undoubtedly influenced the types of questions I asked, as well as the significance I placed on certain unresolved references. However, the comment reported in Table 7.3 changed my thinking.

Table 7.3 Extract 3: Referential ambiguity

Narrative retelling	SR interview
A – and in the next part it shows Charlie and that other guy still doing … whatever's [LAUGHS] happening on the conveyor belt	Res – when she said Charlie and that other guy, did you know who she meant?* B – oh nah yeah, I was thinking it was this guy, or that guy, but I didn't really care, I was like 'anyway, next part of the story'

*Note: Some intervening comments have been omitted.

In this extract, the hearer indicates that she had not, in fact, attempted to precisely resolve the reference, despite her obvious cooperation in interpreting the overall narrative. What appears to happen is that, under some circumstances, the speaker will signal, and the hearer will tolerate, some referential ambiguity (see Ryan, 2012, for discussion of degrees of referentiality). An important methodological implication is that a direct question from the researcher (as in Extract 3 and sentence 3 above) may actually prompt the hearer to settle on an interpretation of the reference *during* the SR interview. That is, the researcher's question may prompt a resolution when no such resolution actually occurred at the time of the original interaction. To counter this problem in subsequent interviews, direct questions about reference resolution were used more sparingly and with greater caution.

The issue illustrated in Extract 3 also highlights the importance of minimising participant anxiety. It was only after re-evaluating my theoretical stance on reference (and introducing the concept of degrees of referentiality) that I was able to recognise that my question in Extract 3 was a leading one. However, this insight may have gone unnoticed if the hearer had not been sufficiently confident, relaxed and perhaps strong-willed: these factors may have enabled her to assert what she recalled of the interaction, rather than be led by the question.

The importance of avoiding leading questions is well known and is one of the key recommendations made by Gass and Mackey (2000). However, when checking my understanding of the participants' utterances, I sometimes found an inherent tension between not leading the participant and needing to present myself as a cooperative listener. To confirm or disconfirm miscommunication, I often needed to check my understanding of what the interviewee had said. Ideally, checking would be done with an open question (e.g. *who stole the bread?*), but to repeatedly do this may have appeared either uncooperative or perhaps have signalled problems with the interviewee's recount. I therefore settled on a balance between open and confirming questions (e.g. *so the girl stole the bread?*), reserving the latter for cases where I was reasonably confident in my interpretation. This use of leading questions for confirmation checking is supported by Kvale (1996: 158).

In studies involving SR, attention must also be given to the concept of face and, in particular, threats to it. This issue becomes relevant in many applied linguistics studies where participants may feel that they need to justify their actions or use of language, particularly where they perceive a threat to their status as teaching professionals or competent language users. The risk is that participants report not on their recall, but provide a rationalisation of or justification for their behaviour, especially if they feel defensive. In the present study, the most salient face threats were those created by miscommunication. As Tzanne (2000) argues, miscommunication poses a face threat to the speaker's need to be viewed as a competent communicator, and also to the hearer's need to be viewed as an intelligent, cooperative listener. Although I did not interview the speakers (where face appears most at risk), there were three interviews in which I felt that the hearers became slightly defensive over some questions relating to miscommunication, and on some occasions appeared reluctant to acknowledge some of the problems. In one such case the participant was a teacher working at a school where I had previously been the academic manager, and she may have felt (despite the pre-interview assurances) that there was an evaluative aspect to the interview (see also the discussion in Chapter 4). Although I developed procedures to minimise anxiety, Bloom (1953: 162) notes that the rapport established during the interview is critical to eliciting the interviewees' more private thoughts. In hindsight, it may have been better to spend longer developing rapport between myself and the participants.

Reflection

In this study, I used SR to address a fundamental problem in miscommunication research: how to confidently identify miscommunications that go unnoticed by the interactants. While there can be no certainty that all miscommunications were identified, it is clear that a large proportion of those that I identified would have remained undetected in a text analysis approach, or any other approach which did not seek to compare directly the addressee's interpretation with the original narrative (see also Ryan & Barnard, 2009).

As I have argued, there appear to be strong reasons to believe that the interpretation of oral narratives results in declarative knowledge that can reside in long-term memory and be available for accurate recall. There are also, however, fundamental limitations in the use of introspective methodologies, including SR. In the present study, for example, despite doing the SR immediately after the narrative task, the delay between a participant's initial experience of the narrative and the recall means that some memories were lost. This problem appears inevitable when information is transferred from short- to long-term memory (Ericsson & Simon, 1984). There are also a number of other issues of validity, such as whether participants are recalling memories or responding directly to the stimulus, and whether introduction of the stimulus alters the original memory. In addition, there are validity issues specific to this study, such as the effect of face concerns on participants' willingness to identify miscommunication. These concerns cannot be dismissed but, rather, need to be managed through maintaining best-practice procedures, such as those summarised by Lyle (2003: 865–866).

Turning now to issues of teacher cognition, I initially intended to include an exploration of how miscommunications involving teachers (as hearers) compared witih those involving non-teachers. As Gass and Varonis (1984) demonstrate, familiarity with the learners' language assists in making sense of SLL discourse, and James (1998: 211) has noted that if a particular type of error occurs frequently, then interlocutors have 'to learn to accommodate it, and to make adjustments in one's readings'. A consequence could be that teachers become oblivious to the potential for certain persistent learner errors to trigger miscommunications with less experienced interlocutors. Ultimately, due to time and space constraints, such issues were not pursued in this study, but SR techniques are likely to prove useful in exploring them in future research.

In conclusion, when used with due caution, SR seems an appropriate method to elicit data in miscommunication research and, more generally, in research concerning the interpretation of discourse. It could also be used to research learner success in comprehending L1 oral and written language, and to explore aspects of teacher cognition in relation to the interpretation of interlanguage. However, it is important to remember that SR provides access only to the conscious outcomes of comprehension, not to the cognitive processes involved. The actual triggers of miscommunication must be inferred within a relevant linguistic, sociocultural or cognitive framework.

COMMENTARY

Stimulated recall is a tool that is part of a broader set of methodologies known as verbal reports (Bowles, 2010). Verbal reports themselves cover a range of elicitation types, including those which occur concurrently with an event (think aloud) as well as those which occur after an event. SR falls into the latter category and in the past decade has become a frequent way of understanding second-language learners' cognitive processes while carrying out a task, most frequently an oral interactive task.

An early discussion of verbal reports can be found in works by Ericsson and Simon (1984, 1996). In their work, they categorise reports according to two key characteristics: temporal characteristics (concurrent or retrospective) and whether actual thoughts are tapped or whether additional information is being provided by a participant. Following these two parameters, SR is retrospective and requires thoughts about a prior task.

Stimulated recall is, by definition, a complement to other data, since other data are used as a stimulus for the recall. Simply put, a stimulus from a task is used as the basis for asking participants about their thoughts during that task. Production (and even receptive) data (e.g. reading) are not sufficiently rich to allow researchers to understand learners' concurrent thought processes. SR fills this gap.

With some production data, for example, writing data, one can more easily obtain data on what learners are doing during production. These are known as 'think aloud' reports. With oral production or interaction data, this is clearly not possible, since one cannot simultaneously participate in an oral task and verbally provide thoughts about it. In other words, it is virtually impossible to gather concurrent reports during oral interaction (but see Chapter 6 in this volume, where Jinrui Li reports on the use of think aloud during the marking of assignments).

The most common scenario for the use of SR as a methodological tool in second-language research (see Gass & Mackey, 2000, for a fuller description) is for learners to complete an oral interactive task. The stimulus for the SR is the audio- or video-recording of the task itself. The researcher and the learner meet following the interaction and watch or listen to the recording of the task. The playback is stopped at strategic points (e.g. when there is a communication breakdown) and the learner is asked to comment on what she or he was thinking at the time of the task. The stimulus, thus, serves as a reminder of the event.

As with any research tool, SR must be done carefully or, as described more fully in Gass and Mackey (2000), one can easily find oneself with contaminated data. In other words, if we are aiming to understand what learners are thinking as they are producing language, we must be certain, as far as possible, that the thought processes that are being verbalised truly reflect the thought processes at the time of the original task. The purpose of having a stimulus is to trigger actual memories of what someone was thinking about. This minimises the well known problem of veridicality (see Bowles, 2010, for further discussion of this issue). All too often, recall comments slide into comments about what learners are thinking about when seeing the video or are listening to the audio, rather than what they were thinking about during the original task production. Another way of maximising validity of the tool is through timing. The closer the recall is to the event, the more likely it is that the recall itself will not be influenced by memory decay. A final issue related to the validity of data has to do with how questions are asked. A question such as 'What were you thinking about when you said/wrote X?' is appropriate because it asks about thoughts at the time of doing. A question such as 'What are you thinking?' or even 'What were you thinking?' is not appropriate because it can often lead learners to produce their thoughts at the time of the recall, even when those thoughts may be about the original event. In such cases, one might get a response like 'I was thinking that I wish I had said Y'. A researcher is then left not knowing whether that is what the learner was thinking after the fact or whether that is what the learner was thinking at the time he or she was involved in the interaction.

Comments on Ryan's Case Study

With this discussion as a backdrop, I turn to Jonathon Ryan's report, which is a thoughtful commentary on the use of SR. And it breaks new ground in the area of oral production data, as he investigates specific referential information. His approach departs from data that I and others have collected in attempts to delve into thought processes involving learners' specific use of language and reactions to corrective feedback (e.g. Mackey *et al.*, 2000) or reactions to the benefits of captions (Winke *et al.*, 2010) or thoughts about rating oral speech samples, as is common in testing research (e.g. Winke *et al.*, 2011), or even with teacher data (Polio *et al.*, 2006).

Jonathon brings into the mix of research questions addressed by SR questions of miscommunication, or lack of understanding during listening. This is clearly not an area that has been explored using this methodology. In his report, the issues discussed relate to the methodology without much discussion of non-native/native interaction, so it was difficult for me to see in this short reflective piece how second-language issues played a role, although it should be noted that the reader is referred to his dissertation. This difficulty was further compounded because, as far as I could tell, the SR was done with native-speakers as the participants. Notwithstanding, Jonathon's case study confirms difficulties already known to be a problem with SR and brings in others that are not as commonly dealt with. He is to be commended for the careful and thoughtful modifications made along the way in response to difficulties encountered as he was conducting his research. Important also is his commentary on the role of SR in the study of teacher cognition. One final comment relates to his methodology, although not related to SR directly: the telling of the end of a story to someone who had seen only the first part of a video is an innovative and realistic twist on the story-telling methodology used by many to elicit data. It sets the scene for a more natural data-collection methodology.

Problems Revealed: Old Problems and New Problems

I have dealt with the problems of validity of SR and Jonathon acknowledges many of them as well. In Ericsson and Simon's model, the authors refer to different types of verbalisation. Verbalisations with the least amount of reactivity are those that do not have metacognitive information. They also discuss verbalisations that have additional (metacognitive) information. These they claim may slow processing and cause changes in cognitive processing (see Bowles, 2010). It is not clear whether Jonathon differentiated between these two types of verbalisation. For example, he says, 'The video-recording was then periodically paused by either myself or the participant, and the participant reported his or her (original) under-standing of the narrative or made other *(often evaluative)* comments' (emphasis mine). If Ericsson and Simon are correct, these latter comments would not be accurate reflections of cognitive processes. Further, we do not know whether these responses were or were not included in the final analysis.

Decay, as noted above, and as recognised by Jonathon, is of critical importance when dealing with the veridicality of SR. He used this concept as a guide to set up the recalls to occur within two or three minutes of the actual event. From his description, however, it was not clear how long the original interactive session was. If the sessions were long in duration, then the recall was itself quite a distance from the original event, despite the two- to three-minute lapse in time between the end of the original interaction event and the beginning of the recall session. This, however, cannot be helped, other than by making the interaction event short.

In describing his thought processes as he was setting up his experiment, Jonathon noted that some participants were bothered by seeing themselves on the video (personally, this has never been the case in my research or, at least, I was not aware of it). As a result, he faced the camera away from the hearers to avoid this discomfort. As with all research, choices have to be made and this one solved one of the problems, but it results in the inability to question just those moments of lack of understanding by being able to say, for example, 'You look confused here. What were you thinking?'

His careful thinking about the questions to be asked was excellent. For example, sentences 1 and 2 are impressively thought out. Contextualising the question by putting the adverbial phrase first shows the care that was put into this research and is an indication of how subtle differences may influence one's research tool.

There were other issues raised that can be characterised as new issues, in that they are not often discussed in studies that use SR. One such issue is that of face. While this is not a new issue in the pragmatics literature or the wider applied linguistics literature, it is not often discussed in the context of SR. Jonathon's sensitivity to this issue comes from the fact that some of his participants were teachers who may have felt that their professional credibility was at stake. As he points out, 'participants may feel that they need to justify their actions or use of language, particularly where they perceive a threat to their status as teaching professionals...'. It is not clear how this aspect affected their recall, but it is a reminder that recalls are influenced by more than just a recollection of what a participant was thinking at the time of the event.

Yet another outcome of his detailed and thoughtful examination of his procedures, of previous literature and of his data was the recognition that referring expressions may not be resolved until 'the end of a clause or tone unit'. This knowledge led him to not stop the tape until there was a 'natural discourse' boundary. Doing so earlier would have been tantamount to asking participants to reveal incomplete cognitive processes. This is an interesting and novel contribution.

In conclusion, Jonathon Ryan has added yet another dimension to the use of SR. He has taken the reader on a well reasoned journey and shown that meticulous piloting and constant thinking about a research tool can lead to beneficial and important changes. Finally, he shows how a research tool, in this case SR, can be made to do what it is intended to do.

REFLECTIVE QUESTIONS

(1) Susan refers to the two types of verbalisation identified by Ericsson and Simon. How clearly can these be differentiated in an SR session?

(2) What linguistic and other difficulties are likely to occur when conducting SR sessions with participants in their second language?

(3) Reducing the length of time between the event and the subsequent SR session is critical, as Susan says, to reduce memory decay. However, a delay of a few minutes reduces the amount of time that the researcher has available for pre-SR reflection or preliminary analysis of the recently received data. How do you think this dilemma might be resolved?

(4) Video-recordings are commonly used to stimulate a participant's recall of events. What other means can be used to stimulate recall?

(5) For what sort of activities do you think SR procedures are desirable, or even necessary?

(6) Jonathon makes the point that, despite extensive piloting, he made changes to his procedure once his field work was under way. To what extent do you think this reduces the reliability of his study?

(7) Make a note of the technological (e.g. recording) and logistical (e.g. time and place) issues required to carry out a SR session.

(8) Replicate Jonathon's narrative task with one or two colleagues. What issues of miscommunication arise? You can download excerpts from the *Modern Times* film on YouTube.

(9) Draft a letter of information to potential participants about a hypothetical research project you intend to carry out. Include a paragraph explaining why and how you want them to take part in an SR session.

References

Bloom, B. (1953) Thought processes in lectures and discussions. *Journal of General Education*, 7, 160–169.

Bowles, M. (2010) *The Think-Aloud Controversy in Second Language Research*. New York: Routledge.

Cook-Gumperz, J. and Gumperz, J. J. (2002) Narrative accounts in gatekeeping interviews: Intercultural differences of common misunderstandings? *Language and Intercultural Communication*, 2(1), 25–36.

Dechert, H.W. (1987) Analysing language processing through verbal protocols. In C. Færch and G. Kasper (eds), *Introspection in Second Language Research* (pp. 96–112). Clevedon: Multilingual Matters.

Ericsson, K.A. (2003) Valid and non-reactive verbalization of thought during performance of tasks: Towards a solution to the central problems of introspection as a source of scientific data. In A. Jack and A. Roepstorff (eds), *Trusting the Subject? The Use of Introspective Evidence in Cognitive Science* (vol. 1, pp. 1–18). Exeter: Imprint Academic.

Ericsson, K.A. and Simon, H.A. (1984) *Protocol Analysis: Verbal Reports as Data*. Cambridge, MA: MIT Press.

Ericsson, K.A. and Simon, H.A. (1996) *Protocol Analysis: Verbal Reports as Data* (3rd edition). Cambridge, MA: MIT Press.

Gass, S.M. and Mackey, A. (2000) *Stimulated Recall Methodology in Second Language Research*. Mahwah, NJ: Lawrence Erlbaum Associates.

Gass, S. and Varonis, E.M. (1984) The effect of familiarity on the comprehensibility of nonnative speech. *Language Learning*, 34(1), 65–87.

James, C. (1998) *Errors in Language Learning and Use: Exploring Error Analysis*. London: Longman.

Kehler, A. (2002) *Coherence, Reference, and the Theory of Grammar*. Stanford, CA: CSLI Publications.

Kvale, S. (1996) *InterViews: An Introduction to Qualitative Research Interviewing*. Thousand Oaks, CA: Sage.

Lam, W.Y.K. (2008) Metacognitive strategy use: Accessing ESL learner's inner voices via stimulated recall. *Innovation in Language Learning and Teaching*, 2(3), 207–217.

Lyle, J. (2003) Stimulated recall: A report on its use in naturalistic research. *British Educational Research Journal*, 29(6), 861–878.

Mackey, A., Gass, S. and McDonough, K. (2000) How do learners perceive interactional feedback? *Studies in Second Language Acquisition*, 22(4), 471–497.

Murray, J. (2010) Politeness and face in professional speaking tests. Paper presented at the 18th International Conference on Pragmatics and Language Learning, Kobe University, Japan.

Perdue, C. (ed.) (1984) *Second Language Acquisition by Adult Immigrants: A Field Manual*. Rowley, MA: Newbury House.

Perdue, C. (ed.) (1993) *Adult Language Acquisition: Cross-linguistic Perspectives. Vol. 1: Field Methods*. Cambridge: Cambridge University Press.

Polio, C., Gass, S. and Chapin, L. (2006) Using stimulated recall to investigate native speaker perceptions in native-nonnative speaker interactions. *Studies in Second Language Acquisition*, 28(2), 237–267.

Ryan, J. (2012) Acts of reference and the miscommunication of referents by first and second language speakers of English. PhD thesis, University of Waikato.

Ryan, J. and Barnard, R. (2009) 'Who do you mean?' Investigating miscommunication in paired interactions. *TESOLANZ Journal*, 17, 44–62.

Tyler, A. (1995) The coconstruction of cross-cultural miscommunication: Conflicts in perception, negotiation, and enactment of participant role and status. *Studies in Second Language Acquisition*, 17(2), 129–152.

Tzanne, A. (2000) *Talking at Cross-purposes: The Dynamics of Miscommunication*. Amsterdam: John Benjamins.

Verdonik, D. (2010) Between understanding and misunderstanding. *Journal of Pragmatics*, 42(5), 1364–1379.

Winke, P., Gass, S. and Myford, C. (2011) *The Relationship Between Raters Prior Language Study and the Evaluation of Foreign Language Speech Samples*. TOEFL iBT Research Report. Princeton, NJ: Educational Testing Service.

Winke, P., Gass, S. and Sydorenko, T. (2010) The effects of captioning videos used for foreign language listening activities. *Language Learning and Technology*, 14(1), 65–86.

Yinger, R.J. (1986) Examining thought in action: A theoretical and methodological critique of research on interactive teaching. *Teaching and Teacher Education*, 3(2), 263–282.

Yoshioka, K. (2008) Gesture and information structure in first and second language. *Gesture*, 8(2), 236–255.

8 Oral Reflective Journals

Case Study: Jenny Field
Commentary: Jill Burton

CASE STUDY

Introduction

This chapter reports one aspect of a long-term collaborative research project at the National University of Timor-Leste (UNTL). The project is being carried out by teachers there and by applied linguists at the University of Waikato, New Zealand. I was a member of the team, having spent one year on a voluntary assignment at UNTL in 2005. One of the aims of this project is to introduce and then 'normalise' (Bax, 2003) computer-mediated language teaching/learning strategies among the students at UNTL who were training to become teachers of English in the national high schools. Other aims are broad support for curriculum development in the English department, which has resulted in three action research projects being currently undertaken within the department (Amaral *et al.*, 2009).

In a resource-poor nation such as Timor-Leste, books and other print material, and even photocopied worksheets, are both scarce and expensive. Thus, the idea of using computer-based technology was an attractive proposition, not least since the students, perhaps more than the lecturers, are 'computer natives' and well-accustomed to using electronic communication for social, if not for pedagogic purposes, through the use of mobile phones and social networks. The University of Waikato team introduced a collection of specially written digitalised texts using the Greenstone library system (Wu & Witten, 2007) to the English department at UNTL, which provided the basis for a set of flexible language-acquisition (FLAX) tasks. The FLAX tasks are part of the wider Greenstone system created in the University of Waikato, which deploys digital library software to access free print and multimedia resources from around the world to build collections of contextually appropriate texts (see http://flax.nzdl.org/greenstone3/flax?page=home).

Greenstone provides a cost-effective way to organise information and thereby assists users, particularly in universities, libraries and other public service institutions, to build their own digital libraries. According to Amaral *et al.* (2010: 289) electronic storage of texts in digital library collections can overcome the lack of printed resource materials for language instruction, especially where financial resources are scarce. The FLAX software enables teaching staff to develop their own texts and tasks, using any computer which can run a CD-ROM. During 2007 and 2008, several UNTL staff visited Waikato and were introduced to Greenstone and FLAX and helped to create a digitalised collection of contextually appropriate texts and pedagogically suitable computer-mediated FLAX tasks. My part in the project was to visit UNTL in 2009 to lead professional development workshops (especially for staff who had not yet visited Waikato), to give them opportunities to implement the new application and then to investigate the teachers' perceptions of the impact of FLAX on teaching and learning at UNTL. My research questions aimed to investigate the teachers' initial perceptions and apprehensions relating to the introduction of digital software and to note any changes of attitudes after the familiarisation period. The study also investigated adoption of digital facilities within the curriculum, and also the extent to which FLAX contributed to the eventual normalisation of digital facilities in the setting.

This chapter outlines the rationale for deciding on oral reflective journals as an appropriate way to collect the teachers' perceptions of the FLAX tasks, to report their initial experience of applying them and to discuss the methodological implications of collecting data in this way.

Methodological Focus

It is recognised by educationalists that curricular innovations such as computer-mediated strategies need to take into account the perceptions of the key stakeholders in order to avoid a gap between the 'intended' and the 'realised' versions of the curriculum (Markee, 1997; Sakui, 2004; Wang, 2008). Of these stakeholders, teachers play a crucial role because they are the executive decision-makers in the classroom settings in which the innovation is implemented. The task of gathering teachers' thoughts and ideas lends itself to qualitative methods of investigation and enquiry. Watson-Gegeo (1988: 580) states that the rationale for using a qualitative perspective rather than a quantitative one is that it involves understanding the inside, or emic, context rather than being viewed from an outside, or etic, perspective. Burns states that 'this viewpoint holds that social facts cannot ultimately be seen as fixed, and that quantification glosses over the diversity of multiple and socially constructed meanings' (Burns, 1999: 22).

Heigham and Croker (2009: 17) note that 'in most qualitative studies, researchers use a variety of research methods to collect data, in order to obtain as many perspectives as possible on the phenomenon being researched'. After considering a range of data-collection methods to access teachers' perceptions, I initially thought of asking the UNTL teachers to write a narrative journal that would yield useful information about their reflections on the new application. Richards and Lockhart (1994) suggest that teachers' journals serve two purposes: firstly, the recording of events and ideas facilitates later reflection; and secondly, the process of writing itself helps trigger insights about teaching. In this sense, writing serves as a discovery process.

Burton (2009: 1) considers that reflective journals are a positive, meaningful and socially oriented way of 'getting to the heart of teaching'. She states that 'many teachers are not sure what they think before they write, but find that writing about their practice brings new insights and understanding, a sense of personal and professional accomplishment, and a readiness to share insights with others'. She also suggests that teachers use writing every day as a key tool to write notes or get 'something down on paper' (Burton, 2009: 2), with the potential to be a readily accessible source of professional learning. She further acknowledges that writing which consciously involves reflection, such as critiquing course texts, composing reports or reflecting on a student's progress, may create anxiety. 'As a result', she states (Burton, 2009: 2), 'formal writing often feels hard to do. Teachers are probably much more aware at these times of the interplay of thinking, writing, and meaning.'

However, other researchers commenting on their experiences of using reflective journals with teachers have reported that the use of written journals has a number of limitations. For example, Richards and Ho (1998) introduced journal writing as part of their in-service course for second-language teachers; the teachers made journal entries once or twice a week and posed reflective questions at the end of the entry, and some of this process was incorporated into class time. The results of this study suggested that although journal writing can provide an opportunity for teachers to write reflectively about their teaching, in itself it does not necessarily promote critical reflection, as teachers differ in the extent to which they can write reflectively.

Similarly, Nayan (2003: 2), when trialling reflective journals with pre-service teachers in Malaysia, found that there was limited value in the written reflections, as 'most of their writings were general or specific layer comments made without looking at the consequences or implications'. Dwyer (1994: 10), who taught English for specific purposes (ESP), found that 'feedback obtained from students' writing journals came in the form of fragmented sentences'. In this action research project, he went on to collect their views about a new course in an oral journal and found that 'substantial information was derived and that the method is useful for tapping students' perceptions which might not otherwise be revealed' (Dwyer, 1994: 19).

Barkhuizen (1995: 25), cited in Nayan (2003: 2), suggests that 'not all students enjoy journal writing' and Nayan, when writing about the impact of reflective journals on pre-service teacher training, found that her participants were 'unable to go beyond the narrative and descriptive level to analysis and evaluation in their written reflections'. Barkhuizen (1995) reconsidered the use of reflective journals and found that some students in the pre-service English-language teaching (ELT) course he was teaching had some quite negative feelings towards the activity. More recently, Barkhuizen and Wette (2008) have used 'narrative frames' (see Chapter 2) as an alternative to reflective journals, to ease the burden of writing lengthy journal entries, especially in contexts where journal writing is an unfamiliar practice. Moreover, many of the studies which have requested participants to write – especially in a language other than their own – seem to yield rather limited data. As an alternative, Richards and Lockhart (1994: 7) suggest that 'some teachers prefer to audiotape their responses to teaching, keeping an "audio journal" rather than a written journal'.

As a result of analysis of the literature, and taking into consideration the situation for the teachers at UNTL, I finally decided to utilise *oral* rather than written journals. One reason for this was that almost all teachers and students at the university communicate effortlessly in at least three languages. Another reason arose from the strong oral tradition that forms the background of the participants. The ritual poetic songs associated with traditional culture in Timor-Leste are passed on to the next generation through verbal means. Speech-making and seminar-giving were familiar to the participants as they are incorporated into the curriculum in both high school and at university. My observation was that participants found engaging with these spoken media both familiar and enjoyable.

In order to make the oral reflections a more natural spoken process, I decided to ask participants to talk in pairs rather than to speak alone into a cassette-recorder. In self-selected pairs, they could choose to converse either in English or in the national language, Tetum. Three of the pairs elected to use English and the other pair used Tetum. On my return to New Zealand, I asked Timorese students at Waikato to translate the latter into English.

This dialogic approach seemed conducive to the co-construction of ideas as each participant gives his or her input within a community of practice (Lave & Wenger, 1998). One of the other reasons for these paired discussions was to encourage the teachers to express and share their ideas without my physical presence. Having previously interacted with the participants as a volunteer, I did not want my presence or their perceptions of my perspectives to shape their views. Returning to the site as a researcher placed me in the role of a partial insider, due to my collegial relationship with the participants. I considered that removing myself physically from the data-collection process may enhance the validity and reliability of the data, as the participants would be freer to express their views.

The Study

The primary data collection consisted of three audio-recordings of oral reflections by six teachers in the English department over eight weeks. The participants met every two weeks at a time and location suitable to them. As mentioned above, one of the four pairs chose to speak in Tetum and the three other journals were recorded in English. Each journal session was held after I had led a workshop session which was intended to develop the participants' understanding of the FLAX application and the range of activities that could be supported by the tasks.

Each journal entry followed approximately the same format, as I provided them with the following rubric to consider when they met to have a discussion.

In pairs ask and answer these questions together. You could answer them one by one or have a discussion together about each one.

Describe what you have done with the FLAX application this week.
What was interesting for you?
What was difficult for you?
What do you plan to do next week with FLAX?
Are there any further comments you would like to make?

In addition I held two focus groups, one in week 1 and one in week 6, with the same participants, in which I presented the same questions for group discussion (focus groups are discussed in Chapter 3). There were five or six participants at each focus group. I also kept a daily reflective journal during the six-week visit to record my impressions. At the end of the six weeks, I adjusted the design of my study because it became evident that further participant reflections were needed after a period of implementation of the FLAX application. As a result, one further collection was made after four months, by another member of the Waikato team.

Audio reflective journal data samples

Unless specified otherwise, the following points were made in English and the names are pseudonyms.

First journal entry

> **Felix:** If me, I haven't done too much about FLAX because the reason is sometimes I'm very busy, so I don't have time to do much with FLAX.
>
> **Felix:** Everything for me was interesting … and about the difficulties because one I need the difficulties are, try to explore many things … the difficulties … we are not ready for it yet this FLAX maybe we need to get more training … get more explanations … and also some instructions … try to learn more from instructions.
>
> **Joao:** … means that this technology will help or give a lot of advantages for the teachers to make easy and not to waste a lot of time but only keep few minutes and it will out automatically. So I think this is very helpful and I like it very much.
>
> **Francisca:** So it will help us improve our vocabulary.

These entries revealed that although the participants were excited about the application and could see the potential benefits of such an application pedagogically, they felt they needed further training in the application itself before they could realise its full potential.

Second journal entry

> **Felix:** All right … so far I have done about twice with FLAX technology because I got twice training from Mrs Jenny regarding to this technology. It seems that it is quite helpful for us especially teachers and also it is possible to introduce to students.
>
> **Francisca:** Me too, I also have done exercises with FLAX which was helped by Jenny. I did word guessing and also read a story and then do the exercise how to fill the blanks by retell the story … retell the story.
>
> **Alberto** *(in Tetum)*: I have obtained a new knowledge and methodology that reinforce my capacity. Moreover, it also strengthen my current experience.

Alberto *(in Tetum):* It is difficult for us to facilitate it to our students as we do not have enough computers in English department. I thought it is a slight difficulty for us to its implement this program. We need computers to implement this program. So, slight difficulty but I suppose that university can help us.

In the second entry, the participants felt more confident about the application and could see the benefits both for their own teaching capacity as well as for their students. However, they expressed concerns about whether the department had the technical capacity to fully implement the benefits of the application.

Third journal entry

Francisca: Yeah I think what they explained is maybe we need to create our own stories and then make the exercises.

Felix: I do hope that if it is possible we can create our own stories inside especially the real things that related to our environment or our country… this will be great.

Francisca: And the students maybe. We can guide the students to make their own stories.

Felix: Actually nothing was difficult with them. The FLAX can be said it is easy for us if we want to practise it frequently it might be easy for us.

Felix: I think so. Finally FLAX is useful for us especially for the teachers.

Francisca: Yes for the teachers … to guide the students to learn English through the FLAX.

Felix: FLAX is great technology, it is helpful.

Francisca: Technology for us to access. Yeah, it will be useful.

Francisca: Yeah, I think what they explained is maybe we need to create our own stories and then make the exercises.

Felix: Yeah yeah, I do hope that if it is possible we can create our own stories inside especially the real things that related to our environment or our country… this will be great.

Francisca: And the students maybe. We can guide the students to make their own stories.

Alberto *(in Tetum):* Technically, we are ready; we can use it to teach the students. Even though there is the difficulty, we have to afford ourselves to find the way in order to realise this method.

Manuel *(in Tetum):* … encourage student to keep practice, to be independent, self-learning. If student do not understand, I can help student by giving the clue. We are like the guider.

Alberto *(in Tetum)*: … perhaps it can be extended to other people who want to know English, not only for us. I think not only in university but also in secondary school and intermediate school. So, they can attend this program because this program can quickly help us learn English.

In this third collection of comments the participants felt both confident about using the application and had ideas about how to implement it within the curriculum in a number of ways – for example, students creating stories for the library. They also could envisage possible changes in their role, as more of a 'guide', and they also thought there were possibilities of sharing the program with colleagues in other schools and institutes. This final dataset revealed a greater degree of co-construction of ideas than in the previous collections.

Summary of early findings

Early findings showed that the participants considered the FLAX program had potential benefit for the English department, both for their own language development as well as for that of their students. They had some concerns early in the process that related to their own capacity to use it and asked for further training. By the third collection of reflections, they felt confident about using the application as a teaching tool. They were pleased that the digital libraries reflected the Timor-Leste context, and could see possibilities for both teachers and students to extend the collections and tasks in the future. They were pleased to have been offered training and had confidence they could use the application with students after creating their own tasks. Their major concern was that the electricity supply and the physical resources such as computers may not always be available to support the application.

Methodological Implications

After considering other options, I decided to use oral journals as a con-textually sensitive method of gathering data. Given oral traditions of communication in Timor-Leste, engaging in a focused spoken discussion seemed to be a culturally appropriate way to assist participants to feel at ease and to express their views. The reiterative nature of the questions from one interaction to the next provided a framework for participants to shape their contributions. Later discussions showed that they increasingly revealed their personal ideas about the application and its impact. Oral reflection seemed to enable a freedom of expression that may not have occurred through a written medium. These perspectives align with earlier studies undertaken by Nayan (2003) and Dwyer (1994).

Although this method appeared to be effective overall, there were limitations that impaired the data collection. These included the limited numbers of participants and recording sessions, the novelty effect of the method, which might have drawn attention from the content, an aspect that was especially noticeable in the first entries, and the possibility that reflections were restricted by the circumscribed nature of the questions. My own reflective journal showed that, at the time, I was concerned that the participants may lose motivation to sustain the same form of dialogues over the six-week time frame. I decided to maintain interest by incorporating regular workshops about FLAX and its uses. Combining a training element into the data-collection process seemed to provide an approach that supported the teachers as they learned more about the application.

Offering a choice of using English or Tetum meant that participants could choose to express their views in the language in which they were more comfortable. For those considering using oral reflective journals, I would suggest that this method, which contains opportunities for reflection yet excludes the technological and linguistic burden of writing, has merit. If questions are used to frame the discussion, they need to be well constructed and open-ended. In my study, I made the decision not to be present during the recording sessions. Such a decision depends on contextual factors and the researcher's evaluation of whether his or her presence would inhibit or encourage the co-construction of the participants' perceptions (see also the discussions in Chapter 3 and Chapter 6).

The data collected from these oral reflective journals were triangulated with information from other sources, particularly the subsequent focus group sessions. Also, my own reflective journal provided background information about the participants' take-up of ideas and suggestions during the workshop sessions. Journals, whether oral or written, can constitute one element of a multi-method research design, with other means of eliciting teachers' experiences also being considered before final decisions are made. For example, a researcher could consider whether questions asked at strategic points in one or more semi-structured interviews would yield the same or less rich data. Decisions about which data-collection methods are preferable might also be empirically investigated during a pilot phase, as in Li and Barnard's (2009) study of the different effects of eliciting information in interviews versus focus groups.

Reflection

This research, investigating teachers' perceptions of a new innovation called FLAX, was an initial stage in the process of 'normalising' computer-mediated learning in the UNTL. The use of oral reflective journals as a method of gaining participants' insights seems to have merit, especially in a setting where sharing ideas through oral means is a more natural way of communicating than is a written form. Although there were a number of difficulties associated with the data collection, I would argue that the approach adopted was ethically sound and contextually sensitive, with audio journals providing valuable insights into the participants' thoughts and perceptions about the FLAX application.

COMMENTARY

Jenny is to be truly thanked for sharing the processes of her research. I have found much that is of interest in her account. In the following commentary, I have tried to show what one reader, at least, looks for and reads into a paper written about research involving spoken interaction of the kind Jenny was studying. Written research papers are typical end-products or requirements of research, so I hope the following discussion is useful on what I, as just one researcher reader, look for. It is worth adding that mediated by editors Anne and Roger, Jenny and I have interacted and the final case study and commentary read quite differently in places from our original versions. Jenny has added and refined information to suit Anne, Roger and me as her initial readers, and I have adjusted my comments in response.

Although much research is published, not many published accounts exist of participants using oral reflective journals in teacher research (but see Ho, 2003, on language learners recording spoken journal entries for the teacher researcher) compared with the numbers published on written dialogue journal research. There are at least a couple of reasons for this lack. One is that there are already a number of widely used methods that elicit spoken data (such as interviews), which yield very similar kinds of reflective data (e.g. Ferris *et al.*, 2011; Wyatt, 2011). Second, although spoken journals are easy to record, they lend themselves less readily to analysis than written journals. So it is interesting to read Jenny's rationale for her research methodology.

Jenny thought long and hard about the merits of different methods and their potential impact on her participants in the research environment, and with good reason. Ethically, researchers have a duty of care not to compromise the work, reputation or privacy of their research participants in any way. So, thinking about the ease and comfort of participants in the research process is important. Thinking also about what they might gain from the process is similarly important. The immediate educational potential of research is quite often ignored but, sensitively handled as it was in this case, the research process can be educational for all participants. In this research, what participants were asked to respond to invited them to think about how they were teaching and their teaching resources. In fact, many qualitative research processes involving journals, focus group discussions (see Chapter 3), interviews (see Chapter 4), spoken protocols and so forth have the potential to help solve teaching dilemmas or open up new possibilities for participants.

For researchers, the interactive element of such research methods affords them opportunities to gather additional insights and revise their expectations. A research design which is also cyclical or one that is implemented in several stages, as this research was, allows them even more reflection time. Piloting research processes is important as well, especially for researchers working in cross-cultural settings. It is often not until researchers try out reflective questions or prompts that they can identify ambiguities or insensitivities or, on the other hand, identify which questions or prompts might prove really generative with sensitive probing. So the educational possibilities of research have practical benefits for all participants, researcher and researched.

Having stated the research goals and described the research context, Jenny carefully considered the potential impact of research on her participants, including which sort of research situation they would prefer and whether they would rather participate alone or interact with a colleague whom they knew and could relax with (e.g. speak in their first language if they chose). Her research processes were culturally sensitive and educationally sound. But did they help her to collect adequate data to address her research questions? Would other methods have served her needs better out of the wide range which a case methodology enables?

Take written dialogue journals and interviews as examples. Although they have limitations, as Jenny discusses, both methods allow researchers to probe, pull back, change tack, such strategies potentially making all the difference between getting limited data and getting rich data. For instance, one of the most widely recognised strengths of written dialogue journals – see for example Davies (2001), who reports language learners writing regularly about spoken interaction to their teacher researcher, who responded each time by providing systematic feedback on their language use and concerns, as well as Peyton (1990), Quirke (2001) and Reichmann (2009) – is that they facilitate continuing personalised feedback and learning, and not just to the person being researched. Also, there are occasions when they can stimulate feedback without the researcher having to be physically present – a condition Jenny found important in designing the oral journals procedure.

In addition to paired oral journals, Jenny recorded focus groups, delivered information workshops on the teaching materials being investigated and kept her own reflective journal, though the methodology was primarily dependent on spoken oral data. Were spoken reflection journals any more effective than other interactive, spoken qualitative research procedures, such as interviews, might have been? Further, does the term 'oral reflective journal' accurately capture the research process used? The process described could also be called 'self-conducted, semi-structured interview pairs'. The defining feature, and benefit, of journals in my view is that they offer continuing, systematic opportunities for reflection, rather than a few timed glimpses.

Jenny's procedures are certainly context-responsive but, in prioritising the comfort of her research participants, did Jenny sufficiently consider her own requirements as a researcher? There's no commentary or evidence in the case study that she believed she had obtained sufficient research input (although this impression may be a feature of the writing about the research method, not the research itself, and I comment on research writing later), a problem common to new researchers.

For example, early-career researchers often find it hard to present themselves as researchers, especially in settings where they may previously have fulfilled different roles; instances of this are teachers who decide to research their teaching settings and circumstances for doctoral study. It can be very hard to shift roles. First of all, new researchers may not feel confident as a researcher; secondly, the colleagues where they are researching may not like their adopting that role. In combination or alone, such factors can jeopardise the process and outcomes of research. What can a new researcher do? I think it is vital to remember the primary goals of research, which are to gather and analyse data that can provide useful information. There is no point in undertaking research unless these aims are conscientiously followed. A researcher's prime responsibility is to the research.

The responsibilities are slightly different for a teacher researcher, but there is still a research responsibility. In the case of teacher researchers, the responsibilities are twofold: a researching role which explicitly serves teaching outcomes but which is as important as the teaching role. Clearly, Jenny is a researcher who identifies with the needs of the teachers who participated in her research. However, her primary role here would seem to be that of a researcher in a large study which goes beyond the classroom, so it is the goals of that overarching study and her own research that one would expect to be the primary motivations here.

Qualitative research acknowledges the multiple, often delicate roles researchers may find themselves in with procedures designed to embrace complexity and encourage researchers to be interested rather than neutral about their studies and their contexts. Qualitative researchers can question their own positions in the research setting, as Jenny did, and make such analysis part of their research, with the aim of producing rich, nuanced analyses. Jenny covers this aspect well in providing a rationale for her research.

A primary concern in this study, however, is whether Jenny obtained sufficient data to respond to the research aims. For the purposes of the research, I believe primary written data would have strengthened her study and helped the analysis considerably. Written dialogue journals, for example, are a flexible research tool that have two big advantages over spoken reflective journals and, indeed, over interviews as well: firstly, reading journal entries is quicker than listening to oral recordings; and secondly, the data readily lend themselves to qualitative analysis.

In contrast, spoken data have first to be transcribed. While technology is rapidly providing voice recognition tools which convert speech to written form, they are not yet universally available and, so far at least, the written product is not wholly reliable. So transcripts still need to be checked against original oral texts. Anyone who has transcribed spoken data can tell you that it is a time-consuming process. Also, there are decisions to be made about how to transcribe spoken discourse in accordance with the research focus: for example, whether to capture the linguistic features of spoken discourse or only its content, as in this case. In Jenny's case, as she documents in her study, there was also a decision to make about the language to use for transcription. Finally, even when researchers do have access to others to transcribe oral recordings for them, as is quite common in large research projects, they always need to check the transcripts against the original recordings in real time. So a researcher working with oral reflective journal data has a lot to do before beginning data analysis.

But the problem of transcription does not exist, of course, unless and until researchers have first collected interesting, relevant data. The research description in the case study does not fully explain what and how much data were collected and how they were analysed. This may be a limitation of the research process, or it may be due to the writing, and this is the final major point I want to comment on.

Writing about research is important for two main reasons. It can be another level of data analysis (I will come back to this) and it is the only information readers get about the research. Readers need to understand exactly what was done, why, how and when, and be able to assess for themselves what the research achieved. So research writers have to convince readers from the outset that their research processes and outcomes are trustworthy. In short, because the written account, such as a journal article or a book chapter, is all readers have, research writing is crucial.

A research paper should provide a rationale for the research and its methodology, explain clearly how data were generated, report findings and evaluate research outcomes against that information and the research goals. These details enable readers to assess the value of the research. Ho (2003), for example, provides a clearly argued and supported account of researching the use of audio-taped journals with language learners. Davies (2001) is equally clear; she spells out the research rationale for her study of language learners' spoken English via written dialogue journals, describes how the research was conducted and analysed, and considers its implications.

Although this case study provides a clear rationale for the research methodology and data collection, clear reporting of the findings and the conduct of the analysis is missing. What does the data corpus look like as a whole? How many themes did the researcher find, discard as outliers and so on? (See Freeman, 1998, for helpful strategies for analysing qualitative research thematically.) Small amounts of data are included in the case study, with linking commentary drawing readers' attention to what is evident in the quotations. How and why were these quotations chosen: are they, for example, representative, unusual, or opportunistic? Was the analysis grounded or a priori? And so on. Research writers usually first report or summarise findings as a whole as context for a discussion of specific research outcomes. Tables are often helpful to supply this overall survey and to contextualise and support the key outcomes, which are then elaborated and illustrated with quotations in the ensuing argument. The momentum of a research paper actually forms a sequential story, enabling readers to understand and evaluate the research. For example, quotations from the data cannot alone tell the research story; they merely confirm or highlight findings or stages of argument. And research does not have to be successful – that is, meet all its original aims – to generate an interesting and useful story.

As this discussion might suggest, research writing actually stimulates further levels of data analysis, each of which gives researchers a text or partial text to work with. Working with them, they might ask, 'Is that what really happened? Is that what I really think?', or 'Why did this happen this way?', or 'If I analysed these data a different way (e.g. foregrounding different themes), what would happen?' Additionally, written drafts of the whole or parts of the paper can be shown to others for comments. Writing is always provisional, even when it is in black and white! Ultimately this is an advantage because, as I have said, each draft and reading offers opportunities for analysis and reflection.

In sum, all stages of research are opportunities for learning, and reflective research processes are potentially very effective research aids, as Jenny realised. It pays to plan carefully, as Jenny shows us, by examining the practical, educational and ethical aspects of the research methodology but, I would argue, design decisions do not end there. The research processes must primarily address the research objectives and the data as well as the circumstances of their conception. Jenny's research processes were responsive to context and participants, and she is to be congratulated on that, but to my mind the data processes were either not fully realised or the research writing has not accurately reflected them (or both). Nonetheless, her research processes will have generated interesting ripples in the research setting and these are definitely worth continuing to examine.

REFLECTIVE QUESTIONS

(1) Journals are frequently used to elicit teachers' or learners' reflections. Do you think it is useful to distinguish terms like 'journals', 'accounts', 'logs' and 'diaries'?

(2) There are advantages to using oral, rather than written, journals to elicit participants' reflections. In relation to your research context, which would you prefer to use?

(3) How practicable do you think it would have been for Jenny to pilot both oral and written reflective journals, and then decide which to use?

(4) Do you think that narrative frames (see Nguyen Gia Viet's case study in Chapter 3) could have been used in Jenny's setting?

(5) Jill draws attention to the balance that needs to be drawn between the participants' comfort and the researcher's agenda. What are the dangers of overbalancing on one side or the other?

(6) Jenny offered her participants the choice of which language to use for their journals. What would you have done?

(7) Jenny considered herself to be both an insider and an outsider in her research setting. What ambiguities do you think might have arisen in her participants' minds? (You might want to reflect on what Judy Ng says about this in Chapter 1.)

(8) Draft a letter of information to potential participants about a hypothetical research project you intend to carry out, which includes a paragraph explaining why and how you want them to engage in (oral) reflective journals. Add a consent form for participants to complete.

References

Amaral, M.A., Field, J., McClellan, J. and Barnard, R. (2009) Timor-Leste collaborative project: A short report. *New Zealand Studies in Applied Linguistics*, 1(1), 47–55.

Amaral, M.A., Barnard, R., Field, J. and McLellan, J. (2010) Collaborative evaluation of the English language curriculum at Universidade Nacional Timor Lorosa'e (UNTL). In M. Leach, N. Canas Mendes, A.B. da Silva, A. da Costa Ximenes and B. Boughton (eds), *Hatene kona ba/Compreender/Understanding/Mengerti Timor Leste* (pp. 284–290). Dili, East Timor: Swinburne Press.

Barkhuizen, G. (1995) Dialog journal in teacher education revisited. *College ESL*, 5(1), 22–35.

Barkhuizen, G. and Wette, R. (2008) Narrative frames for investigating the experiences of language teachers. *System*, 36 (2008), 372–387.

Bax, S. (2003) CALL – past, present and future. *System*, 31, 13–28.

Burns, A. (1999) *Collaborative Action Research for English Language Teachers*. Cambridge: Cambridge University Press.

Burton, J. (2009) Reflective writing – Getting to the heart of teaching and learning. In J. Burton, P. Quirke, C.L. Reichmann and J.K. Peyton (eds), *Reflective Writing: A Way to Lifelong Teacher Learning* (pp. 1–11). Available at TESL-EJ Publications. Available at http://tesl-ej.org/books/reflective_writing.pdf.

Davies, A.C. (2001) The highs and lows of learning to speak English: Journals on speaking experiences from university EAP students. In J. Burton and M. Carroll (eds), *Journal Writing* (pp. 37–46). Alexandria, VA: TESOL.

Dwyer, R. (1994) *Augmenting ESL Class Evaluations Through Oral Journals*. Educational Resources Information Center. Available at http://www.eric.ed.gov.

Ferris, D., Brown, J., Liu, H. and Stine, M.E.A. (2011) Responding to L2 students in college writing classes: Teacher perspectives. *TESOL Quarterly*, 45(2), 207–234.

Freeman, D. (1998) *Doing Teacher-Research: From Inquiry to Understanding*. Boston, MA: Heinle and Heinle.

Heigham, J. and Croker, R.A. (2009) *Qualitative Research in Applied Linguistics: A Practical Introduction*. Basingstoke: Macmillan Palgrave.

Ho, Y-K. (2003) Audio-taped dialogue journals: An alternative form of speaking practice. *ELT Journal*, 57(3), 269–277.

Lave, J. and Wenger, E. (1998) *Communities of Practice: Learning, Meaning and Identity.* Cambridge: Cambridge University Press.

Li, J. and Barnard, R. (2009) Differences of opinion: Methodological considerations regarding addressivity in individual interviews and focus groups. *New Zealand Studies in Applied Linguistics*, 15(2), 15–29.

Markee, N. (1997) *Managing Curricular Innovation.* Cambridge: Cambridge University Press.

Nayan, N.F.M. (2003) *Reflective Journals: The Role of Reflection in ESL Preservice Teacher Education.* Kuala Lumpur: University of Malaysia.

Peyton, J.K. (ed.) (1990) *Students and Teachers Writing Together: Perspectives on Journal Writing.* Alexandria, VA: TESOL.

Quirke, P. (2001) Maximizing student writing and minimizing teacher correction. In J. Burton and M. Carroll (eds), *Journal Writing* (pp. 11–22). Alexandria, VA: TESOL.

Reichmann, C.L. (2009) Constructing communities of practice through memoirs and journals. In J. Burton, P. Quirke, C.L. Reichmann and J.K. Peyton (eds), *Reflective Writing: A Way to Lifelong Teacher Learning* (pp. 49–62). Available at TESL-EJ Publications. Available at http://tesl-ej.org/books/reflective_writing.pdf.

Richards, J.C. and Ho, B. (1998) Reflective thinking through journal writing. In J.C. Richards (ed.), *Beyond Training: Perspectives on Language Teacher Education* (pp. 153–170). Cambridge: Cambridge University Press.

Richards, J.C. and Lockhart, C. (1994) *Reflective Teaching in Second Language Classrooms.* Cambridge: Cambridge University Press.

Sakui, K. (2004) Wearing two pairs of shoes: Language teaching in Japan. *ELT Journal*, 58(2), 155–163.

Wang, H. (2008) Language policy implementation: A look at teachers' perceptions. *Asian EFL Journal*. Available at http://www.asian-efl-journal.com/pta_August_08.pdf (accessed 30 March 2009).

Watson-Gegeo, K. (1988) Ethnography in ESL: Defining the essentials. *TESOL Quarterly*, 22(4), 575–592.

Wu, S. and Witten, I. (2007) Content-based language learning in a digital library. Paper presented at the International Conference on Asian Digital Libraries, Hanoi, Vietnam. Available at http://www.cs.waikato.ac.nz/~shaoqun/publications/07-SW-IHW-Contentbased%20LL.pdf (accessed 30 March 2009).

Wyatt, M. (2011) Teachers researching their own practice. *ELT Journal*, 65(4), 417–425.

Final Thoughts
Anne Burns and Roger Barnard

In our introduction to this volume, we pointed out that many academic journals do not have enough space to enable the authors of empirical studies to discuss important methodological details of their projects. Simon Borg, in his methodological analysis, commented that 'judgements about research rigour cannot be made if readers are not provided with adequate detail of how a study was conducted'. That is why each of the eight case study authors in this volume was asked to focus on only one of the several data-gathering methods that he or she employed. Even so, it was inevitable that the authors discussed some matters in more depth than others. It is very useful, therefore, that the commentators for each of the case studies drew attention to some of these lacunae, in addition to evaluating the approach and techniques adopted by the authors. In doing so, they have each made useful recommendations for the conduct of research within that particular approach, many of which apply to qualitative research methods more generally. In this brief conclusion to the book, we would like to draw together some of the key points made by our commentators that we believe should be taken into account by qualitative researchers.

Flexibility

Qualitative researchers need to be flexible as well as rigorous. As Susan Gass said about Jonathon Ryan's use of stimulated recall techniques (Chapter 7), 'meticulous piloting and constant thinking about a research tool can lead to beneficial and important changes'. A readiness to be flexible once they are in the field will enable researchers not only to achieve their intended goals but also to take advantage of sheer serendipity when things may appear to be, or actually are, going awry. In his commentary on Judy Ng's use of questionnaires (Chapter 1), J.D. Brown said 'it is the anomalies in my own research over the years that I have found to be the most interesting and productive results – often leading to other research ideas that would never otherwise have occurred to me'. Likewise, Jerry Gebhard considered that it is the unexpected issues that arise which make research 'an adventure in exploration' (Chapter 5). All the case study authors knew that their initial research designs had to be carefully thought through in advance, data-gathering skills extensively practised and the selected tools and procedures carefully piloted. However, once they were in the field they came to realise that they had to be ready to fine-tune their instruments to meet the challenges imposed by unanticipated obstacles.

The Right Tool for the Job

Researchers need to use the most appropriate means to collect data. Martin Bygate put it this way in his commentary on Nguyen Gia Viet's use of narrative frames (Chapter 2): 'A fishing net is a useful piece of equipment if you go fishing, but we would use a different net for different-size fish'. Thus, new researchers would be well advised to use well tried methods to collect their data, building their own expertise on the validated experience of others. On the other hand, as Susan Gass pointed out, it is also important that the data-collection tool 'can be made to do what it is intended to do' and therefore researchers sometimes need to make changes to conventional tools to meet local factors. It is sometimes necessary, in other words, for innovatory approaches to be considered and adopted, especially alongside more conventional ones in multi-method projects. Thus Viet's utilisation of narrative frames, Jenny's use of oral reflective journals and Jonathon's application of stimulated recall procedures not only extended their own repertoire of research skills but also pushed methodological boundaries of qualitative research in a more general sense. Inevitably, any new approach will have teething problems; yet there are often productive results. As Thomas Farrell said of Jinrui Li's use of think aloud (TA) techniques, 'it is the case that few studies have used TA in naturalistic settings to gauge the beliefs of markers'.

Precision of Terms and Constructs

Because of academic imperatives to work with abstract concepts, researchers frequently bring to their empirical studies knowledge of theoretical terms or constructs that may be unfamiliar to their research participants. For example, in the case of Viet's interest in teachers' views of using task-based language teaching, his research was underpinned by assumptions of teachers' knowledge of current discussions about newer teaching approaches. As Martin Bygate stresses, if 'TBLT is an innovation for teachers, they may not know much about it'. It is very valuable, therefore, for novice researchers to critically evaluate the terms – and the assumptions underpinning them – that they employ in their research from the perspectives of the participants they work with and to consider how these participants may interpret them. In a similar vein, researchers need to be clear about how they operationalise key terms and ensure they are consistent in their usage of such terms in constructing accounts of their research. At the beginning of this volume, Simon Borg's careful scoping of the terms he intends to employ in his scene-setting review of teacher cognition research offers a useful illustration for novice researchers aiming to define the key constructs of their analyses.

Talking and Thinking

Donald Freeman prefaced his commentary on Andrew Gladman's use of focus groups by asking 'What does talking together reveal about thinking?' (Chapter 3). In this case, he was thinking specifically about the different ways in which people use language in group situations, pointing out that 'what participants say – or more importantly may not say – is influenced by the attributes of that particular group: who is in it, when and where it is happening and so on'. However, as he says, the relationship between speech and thought extends to all elicitation research. One way or another, all of the case studies relied on participants verbalising their thoughts, attitudes or beliefs – whether explicitly to the researcher, for example in interviews, or more subtly, by thinking aloud. But to what extent does what people say, or not say, reveal what they are thinking? For example, Thomas Farrell asks 'can verbal reporting as represented through TA protocols provide a complete record of the individual's thought processes in synchronous reporting or does this procedure actually distort the thinking–speaking process?' Donald Freeman bluntly put it in this way: 'As a researcher, I think it borders on the naïve to simply say that people are telling you what they think' and therefore researchers need to consider carefully the issue of veridicality, mentioned by Susan Gass, at all stages of their project.

Choice of Language

Connected with the issue of talking and thinking is the choice of which language is to be used by both the researcher and the researched. As Judy Ng said, it is usually more efficient and courteous to use participants' first language, but this may create problems in a multilingual society like

Malaysia. Of course, where the researcher does not speak the language(s) of the study participants, a common option is to elicit information in a second language, such as English. However, if one assumes that there is inevitably a filter between thought and language in one's mother tongue (thus raising issues of veridicality) one must ask how much thicker and stronger this filter might be when participants are asked to express complex thoughts or deep-seated beliefs in another language. For this reason, researchers may consider using narrative frames or perhaps email interviews, so that participants can express themselves in their written language, which could then be translated and interpreted by reliable bilingual research assistants – although this in itself can set up another filter that obstructs meaning. Perhaps researchers should constantly ask themselves, as did Nguyen Gia Viet in relation to his narrative frames, 'why should this person be telling me the truth?', and indeed question what they mean by 'truth'; statements that are not literally factual may reveal important 'truths' about a participant's beliefs and values.

Researcher Positioning

Commenting on Le Van Canh's discussion of interviews (Chapter 4), Alan Maley remarked that it 'is important to note how critical it was for the success of the project that Canh was an "insider" … also he was a native-speaker of the teachers' language and a person who shared their culture and society'. In this case, it is difficult to imagine how a cultural and linguistic outsider could have obtained the quality of data collected by Canh. Like him, the other case study authors relied on their 'insider' status to gain and sustain access to their research settings and to cultivate interpersonal relationships with their participants, and they used their insider knowledge to interpret what they were told and what they observed. However, there may also be disadvantages to being an insider. For example, an insider's local knowledge may lead him or her to overlook contextual or cultural peculiarities that might immediately strike an outsider, thus preventing him or her from taking the ethnographic stance of 'making the familiar strange and the strange familiar'. Moreover, as Judy Ng noted in Chapter 1, because she was an institutional insider, 'A number of lecturers admitted to me that some viewed me as a threat to their professional face', a point also considered by Jonathon Ryan in Chapter 7. Such threats to face may be even more acute in studies involving classroom observation. Many teachers are nervous about their teaching being observed, and even more so audio- or video-recorded. This tension often results from previous observations used to evaluate (often negatively) the teacher's per-formance. If the observing researcher is a colleague, she or he will become aware of the inevitable shortcomings in the observed teacher's practice, and this may lead to an uncomfortable professional and personal relationship between the two, especially if – wittingly or unwittingly – the observer reveals some of the uncomfortable truths to other people. Therefore it is incumbent on researchers, whether insiders or outsiders, to convince their participants of their honesty, impartiality and non-judgemental intentions, perhaps by taking what Jerry Gebhard referred to as a 'one down' position. If such sensitivity is manifested, then, as Jill Burton says in Chapter 8, 'the research process can be educational for all participants'.

Ethical Considerations and the Researcher's Agenda

Most researchers affiliated to 'western' universities are obliged to adhere to principles and procedures regulated by their university's human research ethics committee. However, they also have to be sensitive to local cultural conventions and regulations, especially in what Alan Maley (Chapter 4) referred to as hierarchically organised societies where school principals may regard research 'as a disruptive and potentially threatening intrusion into their domain'. Even when gatekeepers grant formal access, there may be problems in actually gaining consent from participants. One of the teachers in Simon Humphries' observational study (Chapter 5), for example, felt like he was about to 'donate a kidney' after signing a consent form. This is because in many countries, such as Japan where Simon's research took place, it is more culturally appropriate to give oral than written consent. But the issue of informed consent itself may be tricky: consent to what, exactly? In his commentary on Simon's case study, Jerry Gebhard suggested that 'each classroom observer carefully consider what and how much to disclose to the teacher and students, while at the same time trying sincerely to build trust and acceptance as an observer within the classroom culture'. In other words, a researcher must tell the truth, but not necessarily the whole truth – as he goes on to say: 'too much disclosure about the goals of the research can cause observed people to behave in unnatural ways'. Such courtesy and ethical consideration is, of course, vital in all qualitative studies but, as Jill Burton remarks about Jenny Field's project in Timor-Leste (Chapter 8), the 'research processes must primarily address the research objectives and the data as well as the circumstances of their conception'.

Multi-Methods

In his commentary in Chapter 2, Martin Bygate made a point similar to that made by Jill Burton: 'research involves someone seeking answers to questions or responses to puzzles.... This is just as important as the agency and ownership of the teachers in providing the data.' In other words, there is little point in the researcher being so sensitive to issues of face or interpersonal relationship that he or she fails to obtain the appropriate quantity and quality of information to address the aims of the project. But this merely underlines the importance of using a variety of methods to collect data: any single method of data collection, however thoroughly conducted, can provide only a partial view of the complex reality of educational contexts and especially, as Simon Borg makes clear in his preliminary chapter on methodological analysis, when studying language teacher cognition. Obtaining data from different sources provides a variety of perspectives: for example, issues raised in interviews may be confirmed, clarified, refined or rejected in subsequent observations, stimulated recall sessions and so on. As Jill Burton stated in her commentary on Jenny Field's case study, 'For researchers, the interactive element of such research methods affords them opportunities to gather additional insights and revise their expectations. A research design which is also cyclical or one that is implemented in several stages, as this research was, allows them even more reflection time.'

Triangulation

In connection to the point about methods, in Chapter 1 J.D. Brown asks, rhetorically, 'is it sufficient to just use multiple data sources, or should researchers carefully triangulate two or three aspects of their research…?' and, indeed, most of the case study authors refer to 'triangulation' of data. The key word here, perhaps, is 'carefully', because, as Simon Borg pointed out, 'strategies such as triangulation and respondent validation may enhance, but not ensure, validity or trustworthiness'. It is worth exploring the construct of this term, now widely seen in discussions of qualitative research. The metaphor derives from the use by land surveyors of at least three points of reference in order to pinpoint a precise location; such triangulation is applied in quantitative research to permit the studies to be 'objectively' considered valid, reliable and generalisable. However, as J.D. Brown points out, 'in the qualitative research tradition researchers attend to analogous concepts like dependability, credibility, confirmability and transferability', and these concepts are inherently subjective. Thus the interpretations derived from qualitative case studies, however the data are triangulated, cannot be considered 'objective' and so Jerry Gebhard suggests that 'observers be careful about their interpretations of what the data mean'.

Grounded Analysis

Most of the commentators have drawn attention to the importance of a careful analysis of the data collected. Some considered the case study authors' accounts of their approaches to their data analysis to be inadequate, if they are to allow other researchers to examine and perhaps replicate the study (although it needs to be suggested that qualitative research cannot be truly replicated). This point was also made by Simon Borg in relation to most of the studies he reviewed, although he also notes that 'Word constraints often contribute to such brevity'. It is reasonable to point out such lack of detail, but the emphasis in this book is on the collection, rather than the analysis, of data. Had fuller attention been paid to the latter, the book would have been twice as long and would most likely still have left major questions unanswered. Qualitative data, and especially data collected from several sources, need to be subjected to thorough processes of 'grounded' analysis. This means constantly interrogating the data to find comparisons and contrasts among them, and the consequent identification from this process of categories and themes which will enable plausible interpretations to be made. These interpretations, in turn, will enable the researcher to seek explanations, more or less tentatively, of relationships within the context or setting of the project – in other words a *grounded* theory. The process involved in moving from the collection, collation and management of data, through grounded analysis to grounded theory is controversial as well as extremely complex and time-consuming. Readers wishing to explore these issues in depth are advised to seek advice from works devoted both to the theoretical basis and to the appropriate analytical software.

Last Words

As we anticipated in our introduction to the volume, we hope readers will have joined in these discussions, by using the reflective questions in the third part of each chapter as a way of thinking about and trying out their previous, on-going or future data-collection procedures. As the editors of this book, we have worked over time with the researchers and commentators who contributed most generously their time and energy to making this collection interesting and relevant to its readers. Ultimately, our hope is that these accounts will, above all, provide helpful insights at whatever stage you might be in conducting your research.

Index

Lightning Source UK Ltd.
Milton Keynes UK
UKHW020329031019
350886UK00005B/56/P